CROOKS 2
MORE STORIES BEHIND
THE HEADLINES

ALSO BY PAUL WILLIAMS

Crooks
Gilligan
The Monk
Almost the Perfect Murder
Murder Inc.
Badfellas
Crime Wars
The Untouchables
Crimelords
Evil Empire
Gangland
Secret Love (ghostwriter)
The General

Paul Williams is Ireland's leading crime writer and one of its most respected journalists. For over three decades his courageous and ground-breaking investigative work has won him multiple awards. He is the author of thirteen previous bestselling books and has also researched, written and presented a number of major TV crime series. His first book, *The General*, was adapted for the award-winning movie of the same name by John Boorman. He is a former presenter on Newstalk Breakfast and currently writes for the *Irish Independent*. Williams holds an MA in Criminology and is a registered member of the International Consortium of Investigative Journalists based in Washington, DC.

CROOKS 2
MORE STORIES BEHIND THE HEADLINES

PAUL WILLIAMS

First published in Great Britain in 2025 by Allen & Unwin, an imprint of Atlantic Books Ltd.

Copyright © 2025 by Paul Williams

The moral right of Paul Williams to be identified as the author of this work has been asserted by him in accordance with the Copyright, Designs and Patents Act of 1988.

All rights reserved. No part of this book may be reproduced or transmitted in any form or by any means, electronic or mechanical, including photocopying, recording or by any information storage and retrieval system, without prior permission in writing from the publisher.

No part of this book may be used in any manner in the learning, training or development of generative artificial intelligence technologies (including but not limited to machine learning models and large language models (LLMs)), whether by data scraping, data mining or use in any way to create or form a part of data sets or in any other way.

Every effort has been made to trace or contact all copyright-holders. The publishers will be pleased to make good any omissions or rectify any mistakes brought to their attention at the earliest opportunity.

All photographs in the picture section have been supplied by the author.

A CIP catalogue record for this book is available from the British Library.

Trade paperback ISBN 978 1 80546 597 3
E-book ISBN 978 1 80546 598 0

Printed and bound by CPI (UK) Ltd, Croydon CR0 4YY

10 9 8 7 6 5 4 3 2 1

Allen & Unwin
An imprint of Atlantic Books Ltd
Ormond House
26–27 Boswell Street
London WC1N 3JZ

www.atlantic-books.co.uk

Product safety EU representative: Authorised Rep Compliance Ltd., Ground Floor, 71 Lower Baggot Street, Dublin, D02 P593, Ireland. www.arccompliance.com

*To the many extraordinary and inspiring people
who trusted me to tell their stories.*

*And to my dear friend Joe Duffy, the voice of the
people. The best president Ireland never had.*

CONTENTS

	Prologue: Grooming a New Generation 1
CHAPTER ONE:	Shooting the Messengers 7
CHAPTER TWO:	Exposing the Church's Dirty Secrets 27
CHAPTER THREE:	Tracking Down the Pimpernel of International Organized Crime 75
CHAPTER FOUR:	Revealing 'Mr Big' 107
CHAPTER FIVE:	Mikey Kelly – the Gangster Politician 151
CHAPTER SIX:	Exposing Gangland's Jimmy Savile 197
CHAPTER SEVEN:	The Accidental Hero and the Terror of Murder Inc. 239
CHAPTER EIGHT:	Murdering the Innocent, a Hero's Stand and the Mob's Downfall 271
CHAPTER NINE:	The Anglo Tapes and the Crime of the Century 335
CHAPTER TEN:	An Army Reservist, Training a Terrorist and Joining the Rangers 363
	Epilogue: Full Circle 395
	Acknowledgements 399

PROLOGUE

GROOMING A NEW GENERATION

The two detectives stopped and searched the thirteen-year-old boy as he walked through the desolate Limerick ghetto that the gangs had claimed as their territory. The mob had embarked on their version of social engineering, using intimidation and violence to force decent people out of their homes as they turned the area into an open lawless prison for the remaining inhabitants, especially the kids.

I stood in the background with a baseball cap pulled down tight around my head to prevent being spotted and causing all hell to break loose. Other members of the four-member squad, who were covering their colleagues with machine guns, also wore baseball caps so I didn't stand out. I was there to do a fly-on-the-wall feature as part of my coverage of the longest, most brutal gang war in Irish criminal history.

The heavily armed cops were members of a specialist team sent from Dublin to break the grip of Limerick's notorious Murder Inc. mob. It was a cold morning in February 2009 at the height of the madness that had engulfed the city.

The cops suspected the young lad was one of the gang's low level street dealers. He was wearing the uniform of a teenage foot soldier:

new designer tracksuit, hoodie and runners. There was no way that his parents could afford to buy the expensive gear for him. He was also supposed to be in school that morning. His parents probably didn't care about what he was up to.

The search proved negative. The kid had nothing on him.

I watched as the detectives tried to engage with the shifty teenager. Part of the unit's policing strategy was attempting to reach out to the small army of youngsters the gang groomed and then forced to do their dirty work. The kids were being used to distribute drugs, move guns, carry out arson attacks, throw bombs and even kill.

I was witnessing a microcosm of a sociological disaster, a new phenomenon in the world of organized crime – how throughout Ireland impressionable, vulnerable children, mainly boys, were being groomed and enslaved by dangerous gangsters in much the same way predatory paedophiles select their victims. Since the boom in the drug trade in the late 1990s gangs have realized the value of using kids, some as young as ten. Within the criminal hierarchy immature foot soldiers are at the bottom of the food chain and are exploitable, dispensable assets.

Children living in deprived estates across the country are routinely seduced into crime with the offer of riches and a hedonistic lifestyle. Many of them come from already chaotic, dysfunctional family situations that include drugs, petty crime and mental health issues. They are invariably allowed to run wild and have problems at school. Some suffer from undiagnosed disorders such as ADHD and autism making them particularly vulnerable. Others come from decent families but are lured away from their hard-pressed parents who cannot afford the luxuries on offer in the gangster's paradise. There is also the immature perception that being part of a gang means that ordinary people are afraid of them. These children are easily manipulated. Once they have been sucked into the vortex and it is too late, they find themselves trapped through drug debts and fear. Like boy soldiers in wars around the world they are indoctrinated by the gang cult.

Traditionally the pathway to crime begins when boys are in their early teens. Practically every criminal I have ever encountered began their career as a youngster. Some worked their way up to become household names. Many, like Daniel Kinahan, follow in their father's footsteps.

Over the years I have sat with innumerable heartbroken, helpless parents who lost their children to the mobs. The reminders were always there on the mantelpieces: smiling faces of the innocent who became hopeless junkies or died from drug overdoses. Others were beaten, shot or murdered. Some had been driven to suicide to escape the despair. More had ended up in prison serving long sentences after being given no choice but to commit serious crimes including murder.

Then there were the terrified families I met who were forced to borrow money they cannot afford to pay off their children's drug debts rather than see them maimed or killed. So many lives are destroyed by the virus of the criminal drug culture.

A major academic project conducted over several years by the University of Limerick revealed that up to 1000 children across the State are involved with criminal networks, some of whom are as young as eight years old. Based on my own experiences and from talking to police and social workers I believe that figure to be very conservative.

The most grotesque example of how children can fall prey occurred in Drogheda in 2020 when two local mobs began feuding. In January seventeen-year-old Keane Mulready-Woods was abducted and murdered by a notorious Dublin killer called Robbie Lawlor. The thirty-five-year-old, who already had four murders to his name, was determined to send a chilling message to his enemies.

Together with his cronies Lawlor deliberately dismembered the teenager's body. Some of the severed limbs were stuffed into a sports bag which was then dumped on a street in Darndale, north Dublin, for young kids to find. Other body parts were discovered in a burnt out car the following day in nearby Drumcondra. A few months later the boy's torso was found in Drogheda, Co. Louth.

The unconscionable act of mindless barbarism, reminiscent of the Colombian and Mexican narcos, was one of the most shocking incidents ever recorded in the fifty-year history of organized crime in Ireland. Lawlor wanted to send a clear message out with no fear of the consequences, to demonstrate that there were no longer any boundaries beyond which the monsters would not cross.

Like the thirteen-year-old wannabe gangster in Limerick, Keane Mulready-Woods was lured to the dark side when he was in his early teens. He thrived on the prestige of being part of the gang and the money he earned from selling drugs in the Drogheda estates. Keane also splashed the cash on designer tracksuits and matching runners. When the feud kicked off he was a willing soldier and had been involved in many of the seventy plus incidents of arson and serious assaults connected to it before his demise.

Keane wanted to make a name for himself. Instead his name will be forever remembered as the victim of a murder that horrified an entire nation. Lawlor was later assassinated on a street in Belfast. No one shed any tears for the monster. But by then he had left his grisly bloodstained mark on history.

One youngster who found himself in the clutches of the drug gangs bluntly described the type of people who turned teenagers like Keane into victims and killers:

> Scumbags to the highest degree – they're all junked up, they're all on steroids… They're all fucked up in the head, they're manic in the head. They're very dangerous people.

He added that he was living in fear of his life and the lives of his family because 'they threaten your mother's house'. He claimed that he had witnessed an 'awful lot of beatings' being dished out to customers and dealers who owed money or were being deliberately extorted for money they didn't owe.

In recent years the Government has introduced legislation and extended social services to curb the phenomenon of young people being groomed for a life of crime. The gardaí launched specialist units to specifically target gangs involved in drug debt intimidation against innocent families. The problem is that Ireland's administrative infrastructure and its agencies have not kept pace with an expanding population and the demands of an increasingly complex, troubled society. It means that the State will always have to play the game of catch up. Sometimes in my darkest moments I am tempted to think that it is all a bit too late.

In Limerick on that icy February day in 2009 the gardaí examined the teenager's expensive mobile phone. It was another status symbol for juvenile criminals seduced by the bling lifestyle offered by Murder Inc.

Just then a text popped up. It was from one of the senior figures in the mob, a brutal thug called Jimmy Collins who had already introduced his own children to crime. It read: 'Where in fuck are ya'… move yer arse if you wanna b a drug dealer.'

One of the cops showed me the text without speaking. The message said it all and confirmed their suspicions that the kid was indeed a courier for the mob.

The cop handed the kid back his precious phone and tried in vain to talk some sense into him. He told the aspiring drug peddler that the likes of Collins or his psychotic bosses, the Dundon/McCarthys, had no concern for him or his mates and that he was just being used and abused. 'You know if you keep down this road it will end in disaster; you'll end up in prison or be killed. . . or both,' said the garda, as if he was talking to his own child.

'We know lads like you are afraid of these boys. They'll ruin your life like they have a lot of other young lads around this city,' he continued, as the teenage gangster looked down, kicking stones with his expensive new runners.

Then he asked petulantly: 'Can I go now?' Without another word he shrugged his shoulders and laughed before moving his arse as the text demanded.

'That tells you everything you need to know about this place. . . the kids don't know any better,' one of the officers remarked as we went back to the police jeep.

'That lad is like a lot of them around here. . . he's beyond saving. . . it is depressing to watch.'

CHAPTER ONE

SHOOTING THE MESSENGERS

The taste of blood swirled around my mouth as one of the most dangerous terrorist crime lords in Ireland came barrelling towards me in a fearsome rage. The strange thing was that there was no blood. It was as if my unconscious brain was anticipating what seemed like the inevitable – a serious beating that might well require me being fed through a tube into the foreseeable future.

I have never experienced such a sensation either before or since. But after all the years of confronting nasty, violent people it seemed to be programmed into my mental hard drive. As the six-foot plus, muscle-bound thug drew within punching range my five-foot-eight frame tensed up and I braced for the impact.

I remember the incident as if it were yesterday. It was a sunny afternoon in April 2011 and the guy coming at me was one Alan Ryan, the Dublin leader of the dissident republican mob the Real IRA who I had been writing about for over two years. It was little wonder then that he got so angry when I tracked him down to his hideout.

The then thirty-year-old 'revolutionary' from Donaghmede in north Dublin was classified by gardaí as one of the top five most dangerous criminals in the country. The self-styled republican hero was an unlikely terrorist. He was only fourteen when the 1994 IRA ceasefire heralded the beginning of the peace process and the end of the Troubles which in any case had not affected him growing up in Dublin. But that hadn't stopped him getting involved with the Real IRA (RIRA), one of the hybrid republican groups that sprouted up to oppose the peace. The RIRA was formed by members opposed to the Good Friday Agreement when they split from the Provos. Its membership comprised the dregs of the republican movement and opportunistic criminals.

Ryan had been radicalized in his teens and claimed to be fighting for a united Ireland. His 'brave' comrades were responsible for the Omagh bombing in 1998 which killed twenty-nine people, including a pregnant woman and her unborn twins, and left hundreds seriously injured. The bombing was the second worst atrocity recorded in the thirty years of the Troubles. The RIRA would carry out over thirty murders and several bomb attacks in the UK as part of their 'war'.

Ryan was typical of the young thugs who were drawn into terrorism. He first came to the attention of the police around the same time as the Omagh outrage. He was eighteen when the Garda Special Branch caught him with a loaded firearm. A year later he and his older brother Anthony were arrested along with nine others when gardaí raided a RIRA training camp in an underground bunker at Stamullen, County Meath.

In 2001 the Special Criminal Court sentenced them to four years for being found in the terrorist training camp and he also got three years for possession of the firearm. Since his release from prison Ryan had worked his way up to become the leader of the Real IRA in Dublin and had been causing havoc for two years by the time I tasted blood in my mouth.

Ryan was a typical narcissist – an egotistical sociopath – who had more brawn than brains. Tall and handsome he was known as a womanizer who liked his lovers to refer to him as 'the model'. The non-drinker acted like a mafia boss, surrounding himself with sycophantic followers and admiring women as he held court in a north inner-city pub, the Players Lounge, which served as his base of operations. The pub was owned by fellow republican sympathizer John Stokes, the father of former Celtic F.C. star Anthony Stokes.

As a key figure of the 32 County Sovereignty Movement, the RIRA's political wing, Ryan's fight for freedom involved protest marches and several attempts to cause riots and disturbances in Dublin. On one occasion Ryan and his fellow 'patriots' hijacked a peaceful student protest against government cutbacks and turned it into a mini riot. They were also involved in the Shell 2 Sea campaign to prevent a gas pipeline being constructed in County Mayo. In 2009 I presented a documentary for TV3 – now Virgin Media – exposing the organization's sinister involvement in the protest. *The Battle for the Gasfield* led to several complaints to the Broadcasting Authority of Ireland (BAI) which found the programme to be fair, accurate and balanced.

Ryan once tried to impress an attractive female journalist by claiming that he could trace his republican heritage back to Wolfe Tone and insisted that he was trying to preserve the ideals of generations of dead 'freedom fighters' who had given their lives for Ireland. Amongst his heroes, he bragged, was Bobby Sands and the 'eight' other hunger strikers who died in 1981. The plucky reporter reminded him that there were in fact ten hunger strikers. She later reported that she had felt intimidated during the encounter.

Nevertheless the ill-informed 'model' portrayed himself as a brave patriot who was fighting to protect his community from the scourge of organized crime and a capitalist state. The truth was a lot less romantic. Ryan and his gang were parasites in the underworld eco system who thrived on the back of criminal activity. His mob was responsible for scores of incidents in which people were threatened, tortured, bombed and shot. He was connected to at least three gangland killings.

Ryan organized the murder of drug dealers on behalf of other drug dealers. Just like the Provisional IRA had done in Dublin back in the 1980s, Ryan and his hypocritical henchmen extorted money from drug dealers in return for allowing them to sell heroin and cocaine on the streets. A drug dealer could stay in business as long as they paid towards the republican fight for a united Ireland. If they didn't, they were murdered. Many of the city's gangsters were terrified of him.

Much to Ryan's annoyance I had reported how some of the money had been sent north to fund the 'war' while he and his acolytes trousered the rest. In the *Sunday World* and then the Irish edition of the *News of the World* I had written extensively about how he controlled a vast protection racket targeting businesspeople, using the cover of a legitimate security company. I had also exposed the embarrassing fact that despite their terrorist convictions he and his brother had obtained licenses from the Private Security Authority, a state agency.

A number of weeks before I found Ryan's hideout I interviewed two brothers who told how he forced them to shut down their new pub and flee for their lives to the UK. Shane and Stephen Simpson were threatened by the terror boss just days after they opened their business because it was competing with the Players Lounge down the street. The brothers closed the pub in less than a week of opening and then left the country after gardaí officially warned them that there was a threat against their lives.

After the story appeared on the front page of the Irish *News of the World* Ryan resorted to his lawyers in an attempt to silence us. They threatened us with legal action because we exposed their criminal and terror-related activities. As usual he played the victim card. His solicitor's letter claimed:

> In addition, the allegations made are reckless and dangerous to our client and have undoubtedly placed him and his family at grave risk... Our client denies also the accusation that is clearly to be inferred from the article, namely, that he is a member of an unlawful organization.

But that wasn't his only attempt to shut me up. Earlier in 2011 garda intelligence sources, who had several informants in the RIRA ranks, also discovered that Ryan had sent gang members to reconnoitre my home with a view to launching an attack. They aborted their plans when they saw that there was a permanent armed garda presence at the house: I had been receiving full time police protection since 2003. Other criminals had done the same thing over the years. As I pointed out in *Crooks* I probably would not be here today if it wasn't for the gardaí.

The garda intelligence revelation made me even more determined to inform the public of what he really was, especially to the people living in the neighbourhoods that he controlled. I wanted to confront him face to face because we had a lot to talk about. To do that I needed to get him somewhere that he was not surrounded by his thugs. Ryan was hard to find. But then in April a garda source tipped me off that he spent three days a week with his girlfriend and mother of his three-year-old daughter in rural County Carlow.

The couple had been living in a council house in Carlow Town until the council built her a comfortable bungalow just outside the village of Ballon where she grew up. Intelligence sources revealed that he was regularly visited there by members of the RIRA terrorist group from Belfast and well-known criminals. A local person had also called me about Ryan's menacing presence. He said the local authority house had been fitted with expensive security cameras.

On the afternoon of Friday 22 April I decided to have a look and travelled to Ballon with two photographers from the Irish *News of the World*. The initial plan was that when we had located the house we would watch it in the hope of photographing Ryan in his hideout. Once we had the pictures in the bag I was going to knock on the door. At least that was the plan. To quote the Prussian military general Helmuth von Moltke, 'no battle plan survives contact with the enemy'. The same applies to journalists staking out terrorist thugs.

We located the house on a narrow country road. It wasn't hard to identify as it was the only one with CCTV cameras. We drove past it for an initial look. The photographers were in a second car driving behind mine. But there was no vantage point where we could watch it without being seen. As we drove past a second time Ryan spotted us. He was clearly on high alert. He jumped in his car and drove after our small convoy.

At a crossroads we stopped to turn around. Ryan drew alongside my car. When I rolled the window down he flew into a temper when he recognized me. I told him I was there to talk to him and said I would follow him back to the house. As we did I phoned the other guys and told them to make sure and get the pictures because the situation was likely to get messy. If it got violent I wanted them to get the pictures first and then call the ambulance and the cops. I told them to stay in their car so he didn't see that they were snapping him.

Back at the house I parked on the roadside about sixty feet from where Ryan parked his BMW and stepped out to face him. That was when he came barrelling towards me with clenched fists and I mentally prepared myself for a spell in hospital. I was in fight or flight mode but had no intention of showing fear or making a run for it. It was one of those unplanned situations where you just stand your ground and hope for the best. As he came towards me I said, 'I'm only here to talk to you.' But just as he got close enough to justify my instinctive apprehension the photographer's car also pulled up on the road.

Ryan looked over at the car and suddenly stopped. The photographer's car had blacked out windows and in that fleeting moment I realized that he thought it contained armed garda bodyguards. It was well known in the underworld that I had police protection. The fact that he couldn't see the lads and they remained in the car saved my bacon that day. They told me later that they had been shitting themselves and had no intention of getting out.

The underworld hardman was in an extremely hostile and angry mood. He ranted about me and the fucking guards turning up at his house to harass him. I shouted over him that I was only there to get a comment about his activities: I wanted to tell his side of the story. Just like every other criminal I had ever confronted Ryan portrayed himself as a victim from the start. He fumed as he looked between me and the 'police' car:

> What's your problem? Why are you doing coming to my home... what to fuck do you want with me? All the stuff that has been written about me is all lies made up by the guards and drug dealers, I am not goin' to give you any statement so you can turn your tape off. You are putting my life and the safety of my partner and children in danger.

I told him I wanted to know about his involvement with the 32 County Sovereignty Committee Real IRA and the allegations swirling around him. When I took out my notebook to write down what he said I had to control the shake in my hand.

> I am in the Sovereignty Movement, so what? I am a republican. Youse are saying that I have loads of money, but I can't even pay for the NCT on my fucking car [04 BMW]. I have a passport for ten years and have only gone abroad once and that was to a wedding. I haven't got a fucking penny.

I asked Ryan about his gang's involvement in protection rackets and his involvement in forcing the Simpson brothers to shut their pub down. He ranted, as he continued swapping his view between me and the other car:

> There is no truth that I have been involved in extortion. I am a republican who has stood up to drug dealers. I get hassle [from the police] because I stand up and am anti-drugs. I get harassed by the police because a bunch of drug dealers are sitting around a table and getting the cops to do their dirty work for them.

I asked Ryan about his arrest in connection with the murder of a drug dealer called Sean Winters a year earlier. 'I was arrested because I happened to be in the area at the time. There were nine other people lifted why don't you talk to them as well?' he shouted.

Ryan then made a series of bizarre allegations about incidents between the gardaí and a number of notorious drug dealers in Dublin.

'I have nothing to do with drugs. When members of the Provos got involved with drug dealers like Marlo Hyland I stood up and said it was wrong,' Ryan claimed.

His girlfriend then interrupted and ordered us to leave the area. 'You're putting our lives at risk,' she shouted at me.

When I pointed out that the only person putting anyone's life at risk was Alan Ryan she did not want to know. Her parents also arrived at the house and then ordered me not to write anything about Ryan or their daughter.

'You shouldn't be calling to my house,' Ryan continued. 'I never went to your house.' I responded: 'But you did send your boys to my house, didn't you Alan. . . what to fuck was that about?' He denied it and claimed that it was just 'shite talk' from the guards.

The confrontation lasted for about twenty very tense minutes before Ryan and his entourage returned to the house. I told Ryan he could contact me any time if he wanted to talk. Then I got in my car and left – with the bogus cop car behind me. I had survived without a scratch and got more than I could have anticipated.

On 24 April we put Ryan on the front page and spread the story over three pages inside. It was a great scoop. As I have mentioned in the past the life stories of major criminals tend to have a common, predictable theme – the protagonists either end up in prison or are killed, or both. Alan Ryan was gunned down in the street near his home in Donaghamede in September 2012. The hitman was paid for by a major crime boss in north Dublin.

My sources revealed at the time that a number of gangsters had pooled their resources to get rid of Ryan. I also discovered after his death that they could have saved their money. The leadership of the RIRA in Belfast had come to the same conclusion, that Ryan would 'have to go'. His erratic behaviour was attracting too much attention from the media and the police, who had riddled Ryan's organization with informants. On top of that the volatile terrorist had fallen out with other members of the terror gang. He had become a liability.

The RIRA and their political wing tried to turn Ryan into a martyr who died while fighting back against the scourge of the drug dealers. In an astonishing lapse on the part of garda management at the time, the dissident republicans took over the neighbourhood where he lived. A volley of shots was fired over his coffin as part of a paramilitary-style funeral. But the propaganda stunt made no difference. The public, especially the long-suffering people in his community, were glad to see the back of him, and he was quickly forgotten.

Eventually the RIRA also faded away into the back pages of history. They had to disband when the Garda Special Branch and the UK authorities broke the back of the mob.

The weekend following the funeral I wrote Ryan's requiem for the *Irish Independent*. It was the first major feature piece I wrote for my new employer after the closure of the *News of the World* and then leaving *The Irish Sun*. In December 2012 I also wrote about the life and times of veteran criminal godfather Eamon Kelly who had been one of the most powerful figures in Irish organized crime since it first emerged four decades earlier. As a man of 'respect' Kelly had dealings with all the gangs and mentored the likes of Gerry Hutch, the Monk and Eamon Dunne, the Don. When Dunne became a liability Kelly gave the go-ahead for his assassination in 2010.

Kelly had locked horns with Alan Ryan when they attempted to extort money from him. In 2010 Kelly escaped a botched assassination attempt organized by Ryan when the attacker's gun jammed. Kelly had been suspected of being involved in having Ryan executed. Ryan's comrades, who were now calling themselves the 'New IRA', were successful the second time around. But they made a mess of it and left so much evidence behind that the killers were quickly caught and later convicted.

Over the years I have upset my fair share of individuals, like Ryan and Dunne, who I have exposed to the world. Mostly it was the crime lords who resorted to death threats and other nefarious means to silence me. But the exposés also included the Church, dodgy bankers and so-called respectable citizens, involved in crimes such as fraud or sexual abuse. These days the job of reporting news has never been more crucial or difficult.

One of the high-minded adages of our profession, which we learned in journalism school, states that media should 'afflict the comfortable and comfort the afflicted'. I stopped repeating that line when I heard it being used by a racist, homophobic, ultra conservative 'journalist' who targeted me and others with lies that were later proven to be untrue. That individual was once lauded by the Irish media before everyone realized how toxic and basically insane that person actually was.

I prefer to quote one of the greatest journalists and writers of all time, George Orwell, who once said that journalism is about 'printing something that someone does not want to be printed. All the rest is public relations.' In nearly every story that is produced for public consumption the people who are written about can be broken into two broad categories: those who benefit from the publicity; and those who are utterly pissed off by it.

But in the era of declining revenues, fake news, artificial intelligence and the wholesale production of lies on social media traditional journalism faces an existential threat like never before. My journalistic colleagues, and by that I mean, professional, trained journalists and editors who work in newspapers, TV and radio, are under threat. I am not talking of the occupational hazard that crime reporters often endure – it is still the most dangerous end of the media profession in Ireland. Two of my colleagues and friends paid the ultimate price with their lives. Up to more recent times crime reporters were the only ones to suffer intimidation. But one of the most disturbing changes that has taken place since the murders of Veronica Guerin and Marty O'Hagan is that the intimidation of the media in general has intensified. Since it migrated to the sewers of social media keyboard warriors attempt to undermine and denigrate traditional journalism. The digital age has given a platform for every type of crank, extremist and criminal to vent what they like. They have no regard for facts and can say what they like while the mainstream media cannot.

The new threats come from all sides. Criminals, the far right and far left, including the woke brigade – the noisy minority – all act like bullies to censor and toxify legitimate public debate on a whole range of issues. They go on the attack and seek to cancel the proponents of free speech if they feel 'offended' or find what is said does not correspond with their own fundamentalist beliefs. Their concept of 'free speech' is that they alone have the exclusive right to speak freely and no one else. (Full disclosure here: I am a huge fan of Ricky Gervais.)

Appalling abuse is now routinely metedced out to politicians, celebrities, journalists or anyone who dares put their head above the parapet and express a view. In 2025 the Tánaiste Simon Harris and his family were subjected to a shocking campaign of intimidation that included threats to attack his children. Several other politicians have suffered the same sordid abuse and intimidation which is unacceptable in a democratic society.

I recall a particularly appropriate remark Ireland's respected and insightful broadcaster Joe Duffy once made about the anonymous ranting rabble. He said on air: 'I think the best advice to them is that they should pull up their trousers, turn off the computer and go out for a walk in the fresh air.' When Joe retired in 2025 it was a huge loss to the Irish broadcasting media.

Broadcasters and journalists are becoming more concerned about how to avoid inciting the cancel brigade than speaking the unvarnished truth. But they are not alone.

Also in the mix are some highly paid lawyers who perform a similar function on behalf of powerful individuals in the corporate and political spheres to scare off the media by launching expensive libel suits. Such actions are referred to as SLAPPs – Strategic Lawsuit Against Public Participation – which are filed to shut down negative publicity. While it might be a different kind of threatened 'slap' to the one I nearly got from Alan Ryan, they are both designed to shut down media inquiries. Traditional media are hobbled by draconian libel laws while social media, the biggest purveyor of defamation, largely goes untouched. The digital age is the new lawless frontier.

The charlatan-in-chief of the democratic world, Donald Trump, invented the term fake news to denigrate and demonize the legitimate press. His aim is to distract from his lies and deceit as he goes about dismantling freedom and human decency while pushing the world into a state of chaos before our very eyes. The histrionic Greek chorus on X and other platforms, including his most ardent critics in the woke brigade, regularly adopt Trumpian tactics.

As a result a free press has never been as important to society as it is today. Despite the fact that just like everything else in life it is not by any means perfect, a free press is an essential pillar of democratic liberal society. That is why it is the first victim of demagogues, dictators, terrorists and wrong doers. The term 'mainstream media' is now used pejoratively to undermine traditional journalism by claiming it represents vested interests and of toeing the government line. Gerry Hutch, the Monk, articulated that view after the 2024 general election when he was confronted with legitimate questions by RTÉ crime reporter Paul Reynolds. In a temper Hutch told Reynolds: 'You get paid from the State and RTÉ, that's what you do. The State is paying you to say this.' (See Chapter 5.)

Legitimate professional media has also paid a huge price in human blood. When Veronica Guerin and Marty O'Hagan were murdered it shocked the world. Back then it was a rarity to see journalists killed for what they reported. Since their deaths, it is estimated over 1600 journalists have been killed as a result of their work. Some were murdered for investigating crime and corruption. Others have been killed in wars or, like Lyra McKee in Derry in 2019, found themselves caught in the crossfire of violence. For instance, in Mexico the drug cartels have murdered or disappeared over 160 media workers since 2000. And then there is the world's most dangerous killing field – Gaza. As Israel continues to unleash genocide and famine on the Palestinian people the journalists reporting on the outrage have also been targeted. It is estimated that 270 journalists have been killed by Israeli forces since 2022.

The various methods of shooting the messengers are creating a chilling effect on journalism which is bad for everyone in society.

I have not been a stranger to abuse by the faceless digital trolls over the years. But after experiencing so many threats over the decades you become inured to abuse. The social media nuts don't bother me. But it is something which I try to advise younger journalists about: don't let the bastards get you down. Nor do I ever take any pleasure seeing awful things being written about people I don't like. I am aware that some journalists also hide behind anonymous accounts to spew their own venom. I don't use social media apart from LinkedIn and have long since stopped looking at what is said about me. But it can be quite satisfying at times to know that you have pissed off certain groups. It means that I must have been doing something right.

In *Crooks* I told the story of how I locked horns with fraudster Giovanni Di Stefano. He came to Ireland posing as a high-powered lawyer who claimed he would win the freedom of some of the country's most notorious gangsters. He was dubbed the 'Devil's Advocate' having gained international notoriety as he claimed to represent the likes of Osama bin Laden, Saddam Hussein, and UK serial killers Harold Shipman and Ian Brady.

Before Twitter/X, he used a website to launch ferocious attacks designed to discredit and intimidate journalists who crossed him in the UK. In 2006 he turned his full focus onto me after I exposed him as a fraud who had no legal qualifications and was in fact a convicted criminal. He then embarked on a full-on assault on my character. He accused me of being a cocaine addict, an extortionist, a paedophile, a user of prostitutes, a serial philanderer and a perjurer. He even claimed that I was responsible for murder.

He also posted pictures of my home on his website which gained huge traction in Ireland. The pictures had been taken by members of Marlo Hyland's gang when they staked out my home for possible attack. As in Ryan's case, they backed off when they spotted the garda presence there. Di Stefano eventually ended up where he belonged – behind bars.

Back in the early days, before Twitter/X, Ryan and other dissident republican groups used similar means to attack me. In recent years the Monk's acolytes lambasted me for months on end with every kind of rubbish. I took it as a compliment.

Ignoring it has been one of the many learning curves I experienced during my career. That is why I understand why so many journalists and editors are fearful of a social media backlash. Some outlets censor their own content just to avoid pissing off the digital warriors. As some of my great mentors over the years often reminded me: you are writing for the man in the street, not other journalists. That now includes the faceless social media brigade. There is no point in entering a combat zone if you're not prepared for a fight. I treat the online attackers the same way I did the ones making physical threats: show the bastards that they won't beat you down. In many ways I can thank Di Stefano for hardening me up for the many social media assaults I've experienced. There have been so many that I've lost count.

Shortly after the Kinahan/Hutch feud erupted in 2016 I was a guest on the *Late Late Show* with Ryan Tubridy and posited a history of the two mobs involved. As part of the appraisal I correctly predicted that the non-jury Special Criminal Court was going to be a vital weapon in taking on the powerful gangs, especially the

Kinahan cartel. The mob would do everything in their power to undermine the rule of law with the money and means to corrupt and intimidate juries in other Irish courts. The SCC is our anti-mafia court. Then I exposed the inherent hypocrisy of Sinn Féin's stance on organized crime, specifically the party's determination to abolish the Special Criminal Court. There was a general election campaign going on at the time and getting rid of the court was in their manifesto for government.

Sinn Féin's shadowy bosses in Belfast, who dictate what its elected representatives say and think, hate the SCC because it convicted so many IRA terrorists. I pointed out that the only people who would vote for that part of their manifesto were the crime bosses, the killers, the drug dealers and the kidnappers. As a result I trended on Twitter for days and was subjected to a torrent of vituperative abuse from the supporters of the supposedly democratic party, some of which included physical threats.

RTÉ received 128 formal complaints about the comments mostly from party supporters but only two proceeded to the Broadcasting Authority of Ireland (BAI), the media regulator – now called Coimisiún na Meán. The BAI later rejected them by a majority vote.

Sinn Féin quietly dropped their demands to abolish the SCC after the election because the public did not agree with their stance. Coincidentally Sinn Féin representatives are responsible for a disproportionate number of SLAPPS or threatened libel suits against the media in recent years – many more than the rest of the political establishment combined.

Another social media attack happened in July 2024, after I appeared with Pat Kenny on Newstalk to discuss anti-immigrant riots in Coolock, west Dublin. Similar riots had erupted in Dublin city centre in November 2023. I made the point that the opening of a migrant centre had provided an opportunity for some recreational mayhem by a group of anti-social thugs, many of whom were involved in crime. Like Alan Ryan they hitched their wagons to a cause – in this case the so-called far right – so that they could attack gardaí and burn things down in the ludicrous claim of defending their communities.

It is not a coincidence that dissident republicans are heavily involved with the far-right mob. The involvement in such causes benefits the participants in their criminal pursuits and gives them more power to intimidate the communities where they live. I suggested that garda chiefs were wrong to order their officers to stand back when they should have used their legitimate powers and baton charged the thugs off the streets.

I pointed out that while this country has a major problem with unregulated immigration that needs to be addressed, it was interesting that the far right never used their power to confront the scourge of home-grown gangs who are terrorizing working-class estates. For a few hours I became the focus of the mob's ire. Some of them pointed out where I lived and suggested I get a visit which clearly meant that those who did come would not be popping in for tea and a chat.

Proving that the vast majority of it is nothing more than hot air, the herd quickly moved onto its next target. But it illustrates how venomous keyboard warriors try to intimidate journalists and create a chilling effect on the media. I am well experienced in dealing with threats and intimidation, but it takes a huge toll on younger journalists who are simply reporting what is going on. I will continue to remind colleagues that coming under digital attack from these morons gives their work credibility.

In 2024 I marked forty years in journalism. During that time I have chronicled the evolution of organized crime in Ireland as a front seat observer in what was often a white-knuckle ride. Back then it was suggested by my publishing editors and some trusted friends that I should write a sort of semi-autobiographical book covering my personal experiences over that period. Basically they suggested taking my loyal readers on a ride-along behind the scenes of some of more notorious stories I worked on. The end product was the first volume of *Crooks*. I am deeply grateful to the readers who made it a bestseller.

I wrote about the first major godfathers I encountered, starting with the General and how he fuelled my interest in crime and criminology. It gave me a chance to tell how I witnessed gangland morph into a vast, multi-billion industry built on narcotics. Exhuming old ghosts by revisiting the dark corners of my career was at times an emotional experience. It brought back memories, both good and bad, of triumphs and loss. I relived many of the times that I came close to meeting the grim reaper and found myself admitting publicly for the first time that I suffered a bout of post-traumatic stress disorder (PTSD).

Writing *Crooks* was cathartic. It also gave me an opportunity to acknowledge the many brilliant people I had the honour to work with and who helped me in my career. *Crooks 2* is a continuation of the story of my personal journey.

Journalists everywhere have covered stories that they never forget the same way cops have cases that always live with them. Some stories have a tendency to pop up many years after they were first told. I have had many stories that I cannot forget as the experience is burnt into my memory banks. My first-hand experiences over a fourteen-year period exposing the mind-boggling violence of Limerick's Dundon/McCarthy clan, Murder Inc., in the longest, most brutal gang war in Irish criminal history is one of them.

As a journalist I have been nothing more than a conduit of information to the public. I have reported on the evil things bad people do to good people. In *Crooks 2* I concentrate on some of the extraordinary people who trusted me to tell their stories: individuals who have encountered adversity in its most extreme form and survived. To me they are all heroes. I am honoured to say that many of them became dear friends.

The memories from my career in journalism are filled with an awesome cast of characters. But not all of them were criminals in the traditional sense. One of the biggest stories I worked on was exposing a different type of scandal, a moral crime if you will, which fascinated the Irish public three decades ago. It involved exposing the secret life of one of Ireland's most famous and admired priests – Fr Michael Cleary.

CHAPTER TWO

EXPOSING THE CHURCH'S DIRTY SECRETS

On New Year's Eve 1993 Father Michael Cleary, the celebrity priest and the Catholic Church's most outspoken moral fundamentalist, died from lung cancer at the relatively young age of sixty. Coverage of the death of one of Ireland's most famous clerics dominated the news bulletins. A succession of church leaders, former parishioners and famous friends fondly remembered the charismatic man of the cloth in a blizzard of valedictory sound bites and comments.

The TV news showed iconic footage of Cleary and his by then disgraced best friend, Bishop Eamonn Casey, as they entertained 300,000 young people prior to Pope John Paul II's historic Youth Mass in Galway in 1979. It marked the high point of Cleary's fame.

All I knew about Michael Cleary on New Year's Day 1994 was what I had seen, heard or read of him in the media. Little did I know then that I would be the one who would reveal the secrets he had hoped to take with him to the grave.

Cleary's image was that of a much-loved man of the people and hardline stalwart of Catholic doctrine. He came from a wealthy family and enjoyed a privileged upbringing. Ordained in 1958, he never conformed to the traditional image of the austere, aloof clergyman. In appearance Cleary was unmistakable in a crowd. A tall thin man six feet four inches in height, he wore glasses, a bushy red beard and had wiry thinning hair. The chain-smoking padre always had a cigarette dangling from his mouth.

As a curate in the 1960s he worked in Dublin's most deprived parishes where he initiated some of the first outreach youth programmes at a time when the State provided little or no support to the disadvantaged in society. His image was that of a priest whose social work extended to supporting unmarried mothers in a less enlightened, cruel era when such women were incarcerated in notorious mother and baby homes. He also worked for a time in London where he was assigned to the Irish emigrant chaplaincy.

An accomplished raconteur who would sing, tell jokes and yarns for his adoring audiences Cleary was best known as the 'singing priest'. He co-founded the *All Priests Show* which staged charity concerts across Ireland over many years. Through his showbiz connections he was a religious mentor to celebrities in the entertainment and media industries.

He enjoyed considerable fame as a TV celebrity and newspaper columnist writing for the *Sunday Independent* and the *Irish Star* so that he could reach people at all levels in society. Over the decades he was a regular guest on the country's most watched TV programme, Gay Byrne's *Late Late Show*.

When it was launched by RTÉ in the early 1960s, the *Late Late Show* was castigated as being dangerous to the nation's moral well-being by the all-powerful Catholic establishment. Byrne was accused of corrupting the young by confronting issues of morality and sex that had never been discussed in public before. RTÉ came under intense pressure to ban the show. Cleary broke that taboo when he became the first priest ever to appear on it. He counted Ireland's chat show king as one of his close friends.

From the 1980s Cleary hosted a popular nightly local radio show on Dublin's 98FM where he freely expressed his conservative opinions and dispensed advice to listeners. The show was particularly popular amongst the inmates of Mountjoy Prison for whom he acted as a broadcast minister answering letters and music requests from his captive audience. He had a reputation for being a friend to both the poor and downtrodden as well as the rich and powerful.

That position made Cleary the poster boy of a church that had dominated every aspect of Irish life since the foundation of the State. Like Bishop Casey, he used his fame and affability to push Catholic doctrine on the Irish public. By appearing to be more down to earth than the average cleric he was one of the first Irish priests to present a more human face of the Church for a still largely devout, deferential population In reality Michael Cleary was one of the frontmen at the time when Ireland was still in the pedagogic, domineering grip of a hegemonic church. He used a blend of humour and jokes to deliver bombastic utterances on sin and morals.

My perception of Cleary was that of a moral boot boy who used his huge media profile to propagate the Church's strict precepts on divorce, abortion, contraception and homosexuality. He influenced public debate during constitutional referenda on issues such as divorce or abortion, or when topical legislation perceived to conflict with church doctrine on issues of morality and sexuality was brought before parliament.

In 1990 he publicly returned his BA to University College Dublin (UCD), It was a protest against the university's conferral of an honorary degree on a judge who had been instrumental in ruling abortion legal in the USA.

Cleary was particularly vocal in the run up to the country's first referendum on abortion in 1992 in the wake of the X case. The amendment had been proposed after the High Court, working from the existing legislation regarding the right to travel for abortion, initially stopped the Health and Safety Executive (HSE) from taking a 14-year-old rape victim to the UK for a termination. The ruling was later overturned by the Supreme Court and the child had the abortion. In the referendum a majority of the electorate voted along church lines in supporting an unequivocal constitutional ban on abortion.

Two other amendments, which permitted people access to information about abortion in other countries and the freedom to travel abroad for terminations were passed despite church opposition. The referendum results epitomized the nation's moral ambivalence: abortion was illegal but everyone knew countless thousands of Irish women were forced to travel in secret to the UK for terminations like they were criminals. It was kept out of sight and was like a parallel universe. It would take another twenty-six years before the country matured enough to eventually legalize abortion in a referendum in 2018.

I was in my twenties at the time of the first referendum and part of Generation X which was the first generation to begin the slow process of secularization by questioning the relevance and power of the Church. We began to call out the lack of empathy and understanding demonstrated by Cleary and his ilk. It was one of the reasons I wasn't overwhelmed by the news of his demise.

In *Crooks* I told how my wife Anne incurred the wrath of the Catholic Church when, as a trainee reporter with the *Longford*

Leader, she wrote a feminist column supporting a woman's right to choose if she wanted an abortion.

Just over a decade earlier one of Ireland's greatest writers John McGahern, who lived near my hometown of Ballinamore in County Leitrim, was sacked from his job as a teacher after his second novel, *The Dark*, was banned by a domineering church, led by the notorious Archbishop John Charles McQuaid. McGahern's books were among the first I ever read.

Like most of my peers, I rebelled against the Church and was a confirmed agnostic by the time I hit my teens. I remember once being beaten by a teacher in Ballinamore secondary school because I could not recite the 'Our Father' in Irish. He succeeded in beating religion and an interest in the Irish language out of me. When I was doing my Leaving Cert in Carrigallen Vocational school in Leitrim in 1983 – after being expelled from two previous secondary schools – I refused to attend religion classes. When the priest running the class ordered me to attend I told him it was a waste of my time and I would be more constructively employed actually studying the subjects for the exams. I'd deal with God in my own way.

The priest, a Father Collins, complained bitterly to the principal Mick Duignan and suggested that I was a bad influence on the other kids. My recalcitrance, he suggested, should be countered with the threat of expulsion which would mean the end of my education. I was delighted when Duignan stood by me which was unusual at the time. Vocational schools were the first second-level State run institutions that were independent of religious orders which was why they played an important and understated role in our social evolution. I also received the backing of his deputy, Eamon Daly, who taught me English and the value of questioning the status quo. Although practising Catholics, my parents also agreed that I was right to stand up for myself. I had won my first battle to break away from the clutches of mother church.

I learned the rudiments of my job in the Rathmines School of Journalism. It produced the generation of future reporters and editors who would go on to expose the moral corruption and hypocrisy which helped bring about the end of the Church's unquestioned role in Irish society. I remember reading an interview with a prominent priest in the 1980s who decried the educational revolution because better educated young people had begun to question the Church's teachings. In 1993 I had no love or devotion for the Irish Church or its vociferous disciples.

Cleary had assisted in alienating our more liberal generation. A few years before his death, he used an appearance on the *Late Late Show* to condemn as a harlot a female journalist with the *Sunday Independent*. Cleary was responding to an honest opinion piece in which the woman confessed that she carried condoms in her handbag to avoid getting pregnant or contracting HIV. In the final decade of the 20th century, his denouncement highlighted how women were still seen as second class citizens in the patriarchal Catholic world.

On another occasion he infamously argued that condoms were not a reliable device for controlling the spread of AIDS, making the ludicrous claim that the virus was smaller than the pores in the condom. All these years later it is hard to imagine that we lived in a time when prominent people could get away with such vacuous nonsense. It was also hard to take at the time. In his 2021 book, *We Don't Know Ourselves*, Fintan O'Toole wrote about how the younger generations staged a quiet revolution by navigating a path around the Church's interference and got on with their lives.

Cleary also took a hard line on priestly celibacy and the edict that breaching that preeminent tenet was considered a mortal sin. The law of chastity was introduced in the Middle Ages because the hierarchy in Rome feared that cleric's children would inherit church property – just like in the criminal underworld everything revolves around the money. But celibacy ultimately contributed in no small way to the eventual downfall of a hypocritical church – and Michael Cleary's exalted reputation.

The renowned psychiatrist, Professor Ivor Browne, who had intimate knowledge of Michael Cleary's hidden secrets, once described celibacy to me as the equivalent of blocking the natural course of a stream running down the side of a mountain. The water will inevitably find a path around the obstacle in search of alternative routes to continue on the journey that gravity intended for it. In the context of the Catholic Church the suppression of natural, instinctive God-given urges, coupled with the Church's disproportionately powerful status in Irish society, led to sexual perversion, hypocrisy and sordid secrets amongst its ranks.

In the early 1990s the trickle of information about child sexual abuse by priests and religious orders had begun. Criminals I interviewed at the time would talk about the horrific sexual, physical and psychological abuse they had suffered in Reform and Industrial schools run by church orders. From the time of our independence the Irish State abnegated its responsibilities by leaving orphans and young delinquents in the care of the Church-run gulags of suffering. As the years wore on the revelatory trickle grew into a raging torrent.

At the time scandals over celibacy were the first to emerge. The initial earthquake disclosure to rock Ireland and the Church to its foundations had occurred twenty months before Cleary's death.

In May 1992 his close friend Bishop Eamonn Casey was revealed by the *Irish Times* as a premier hypocrite after he was exposed for having secretly fathered a son, Peter, with his distant cousin, Annie Murphy, a twenty-five-year-old American divorcée. When the boy was born in a Dublin hospital in 1974 the then Bishop of Kerry was almost twice his lover's age.

The *Irish Times* revealed how Casey had fathered a child whom he had refused to acknowledge. It emerged he tried to convince Annie to put the child up for adoption. At a conference for an Irish Catholic charity established to support unmarried mothers, Casey once said: 'It is difficult to understand how the total rejection of their child. . . could be reconciled with Christian love and forgiveness.' In private the much-loved bishop had a different view. Annie Murphy later revealed that when the child was born he told her: 'He is not my son. He's entirely yours now.'

The scandal was compounded by the revelation that he had been secretly paying maintenance to Annie with money fraudulently siphoned from diocesan funds. In the hours before the story broke Casey was banished by his superiors in Rome. He was ordered to leave Ireland and sent into hiding as a missionary in Central America.

In January 1993 Annie Murphy's sensational book, *Forbidden Fruit: The True Story of My Secret Love Affair with Ireland's Most Powerful Bishop* became an international bestseller. It was the first time that such a book was published in Ireland. It revealed in lurid detail the sex and the lies of one of the country's most revered clergymen. The scandal sent shockwaves through Irish society and set in motion the process of undermining the moral authority and prestige of the Church. I remember reading the book and relishing the exposure of the hypocrisy.

But on New Year's Day 1994 Casey and the nation's mourning for Michael Cleary was all noise in the background and I really hadn't much interest. At home we were preoccupied by much more momentous news. On the same day that he passed away Anne discovered that she was pregnant with our second child, Irena.

By the time we celebrated Irena's first birthday I had exhumed the astonishing secrets that Michael Cleary had taken to the grave with him: the Church's outspoken moralist had fathered two sons with his housekeeper, Phyllis Hamilton. I was also in the process of ghostwriting her book, *Secret Love*, which became the second iconoclastic book exposing the secret proclivities of a famous clergyman. Getting to that point was a momentous period in my journalism career.

The funeral of Michael Cleary on 4 January 1994 was a huge affair. Ordinary punters rubbed shoulders with the great and the good of Irish society as over 1000 people crammed into a small church in Blanchardstown, west Dublin, where Cleary had grown up. The charismatic cleric received a fitting send off. But that was not the last we would hear of Father Michael Cleary. The first bombshell came eight days later.

On 12 January *The Phoenix* magazine published the earth-shattering claim that Cleary had secretly fathered two sons with an unnamed woman. The magazine revealed that it had been an open secret for several years in Michael Cleary's circle. It was all fascinating news to us younger reporters on the *Sunday World*. To say the story caused a sensation would be putting it mildly.

A succession of personalities and senior clerics launched a coordinated offensive of condemnation against *The Phoenix* and its editor Paddy Prendeville, along with vehement denials which were reported across the media. There was so much anger being expressed that it would not have surprised me at the time if the offices of the magazine were burned down.

The day that the magazine hit the shelves I quickly discovered how difficult it was taking on the powerful vested interests of the Catholic Church. Along with my colleague and fellow Leitrim man, Mick McNiffe, we decided to follow up the story and instantly found ourselves in trouble with our bosses. In 1994 the *Sunday World* was tired and jaded and had been haemorrhaging readers for years. The old formula that had made it the biggest selling newspaper in the country, as exemplified by the inclusion of scantily clad women on the front page and lurid 'tit-and-bum' stories, had become off-putting in a changing society. Its once impressive record of investigative journalism which had initially attracted me to join the paper in 1987 had long since vanished.

As I described in *Crooks*, there was an aversion to running anything controversial that upset the status quo or people in power. At the time I was banned by a senior executive from writing about the biggest gangster of the day, Martin Cahill, the General. But, in an ironic twist of fate, writing the General's posthumous biography was to play a role in me getting the scoop of a lifetime – exposing the full no-holds-barred story of Father Cleary's secret life.

I recall the morning after *The Phoenix* story appeared McNiffe and I told our news editor Sean Boyne that we were going to attempt to follow up on the Cleary story everyone was talking about. Sean Boyne was a great news editor, a superb journalist and mentor – he was like a father to us. The 'Sloop' as we called him, was frustrated and fed up with the ban on the General and so many other aborted stories. He apologetically told us that the word had come down from on high – as high as the board of directors – that we were to leave the Cleary story alone.

He was merely following orders. I knew where he was coming from. A few years earlier I had come into possession of a suitcase full of internal documents belonging to the Knights of Columbanus. At the time when the Church still held sway over the nation the fraternal group was a secretive, extremely powerful lay organisation that promoted conservative Catholic dogma from the shadows.

The Knights were the Irish equivalent of the Freemasons. Amongst the documents was a list of the group's influential and powerful membership. It included several well-known names in politics, business, the public service and media; a cabal who were secretly pulling the strings behind Irish society. The list included a senior director in Independent Newspapers, the company that owned the *Sunday World* at the time.

On that occasion, much to the annoyance of my news editor and myself, I had to give the documents back to the source because the explosive story would not even be considered for publication. I was told to say that the paper was concerned that it would be sued for libel; a catchall excuse that media organizations such as RTÉ still hide behind when they want to run away from a story. The source later gave the material to the more liberal left leaning *Hot Press* magazine who published it. So when Sean told us that we were to leave Cleary to rest in peace I knew where the dictate was coming from.

However, the publication of *The Phoenix* article happily coincided with the arrival of Michael Brophy as managing director of the *Sunday World* and a few weeks later Colm MacGinty as the new editor.

I knew Brophy from his previous job as the editor of the Irish version of *The Star* which he also revolutionized and turned into a circulation success. When I couldn't get crime stories into my own paper I passed them on to Brophy through his news editor, my long-time mentor, the legendary John Donlon. I decided to take full advantage of his arrival.

I still recall how a meeting had been called by the senior editorial executives to discuss the Michael Cleary story or, to be more precise, how they were going to avoid the story on behalf of the hidden hands controlling the newspaper's agenda. The *Sunday World*'s most famous columnist was, and still is, the much-loved Father Brian D'Arcy. Brian has been a key contributor since the newspaper first rolled off the printing presses in 1973. Since I first met him I always considered Father Brian to be a friend. He wasn't like any other priests I had ever met and wasn't dogmatic like Cleary. The complication was that Brian was also a close friend of Michael Cleary. It created an awkward conflict of interest for him and everyone else. Gay Byrne, Cleary's friend, was also a long-standing influential columnist with the *Sunday World*.

McNiffe and I decided, like every other reporter in Dublin, to head out and knock on some doors to see if we could get an angle on the story regardless of the instructions from on high. At the time we were like two Rottweiler news hounds that had been locked up in the yard and never let out for a run. We had some extraordinary stories in our notebooks that had never seen the light of day. In the months and years ahead that would all change.

Brophy was only in situ four days and hadn't yet made his presence or purpose felt. He was easing himself into the job and his mission – to reverse the terminal decline by redesigning and transforming the paper into a respectable investigative tabloid.

We bumped into Michael as we were leaving the newsroom on our illicit mission. He was looking to have a catch up with the editorial executives but we told him they were all in a meeting. A news man to his toes Brophy made small talk about the Cleary revelations which was the only story in town. We said we were going out to shake the trees and see what we could find out. He agreed that it was a good idea: after all that is what journalists do. *The Phoenix* would not have published the story if it wasn't true. We took his response as tacit approval that neatly overruled the earlier prohibition order. After all he was now the commander of the ship.

That morning we called to the Blanchardstown home of Michael Cleary's sister, Patricia Moynihan. We bluffed our way in the door for tea by implying, but not openly lying, that Father Brian knew we were there. It was cheeky and underhanded but necessary in the circumstances. Patricia was understandably deeply upset over the article and vehemently denied it was in any way true. She said Brian would understand why she didn't want to give an interview about the nefarious falsehood being circulated by *The Phoenix*.

Our next destination was to call to the Church-owned house in Harold's Cross, south Dublin, that Michael Cleary had shared with his housekeeper – and as yet unproven lover – Phyllis Hamilton. Cleary had been the diocesan promoter of missions and retreats from 1987 until his death. Minutes after leaving Patricia Moynihan's home my phone rang. It was Sean Boyne, and he was very irate. She had phoned Brian D'Arcy to report our temeritous intrusion and the fact that we had used his name. Brian in turn phoned the editor Colin McClelland. In the circumstances it was probably a natural human reaction that Brian was angered by what we did. The shock of *The Phoenix* revelations was still being absorbed.

Colin had only been following orders from higher up when he issued the dictate that the story was not to be followed up. He'd got on the phone to Sean Boyne and given him a bollocking about 'what to fuck are Williams and McNiffe up to calling on Michael Cleary's sister?' Shit always runs down the line and rarely up. What compounded our sin was the fact that we had inveigled our way into Moynihan's home using D'Arcy's name.

I expressed my surprise and confusion when I disingenuously told Sean that it was the new managing director who had instructed us to go after the story. I suggested that Sean tell the editor to take it up with his new boss. We were, like everyone else, just following orders. There were no more admonishments after that.

At Cleary's house we knocked on the door and a woman who was a friend of Michael and Phyllis answered. We went through the motions of asking if we could speak to her but the woman, who I later got to know quite well, politely said that Phyllis wasn't around. She referred us to Michael Cleary's family for comment. Then we left. There had been a long succession of journalists knocking on the door and photographers were watching the house.

We had no way of knowing that the media circus was taking a terrible toll on Phyllis and her son, Ross. Ironically I would later write about the media intrusions, including my own.

She later told me:

> The media were relentless. Like an army on the offensive, they came in their droves. Banging on the door, ringing the phone. The questions were aggressive. They demanded answers. As I

crouched in a room inside behind a locked door, I was pulverized with fear.

At the time she had been considering issuing a statement refuting the allegations but she had been advised against that by the Church. To compound the torment that she was enduring, Phyllis began getting nasty anonymous phone calls and letters. One male voice that repeatedly phoned at all hours called her a slut and a whore. On another occasion the voice screamed down the phone: 'You bitch, you bitch, I hope you are lonely, you slut you deserve to die.'

Phyllis was also threatened by anonymous callers that she'd be 'got at' by former prisoners in Mountjoy who were loyal to Michael if she didn't remain silent.

I knew none of this as I sat in the car with McNiffe watching the house for a while that day. I remember saying:

> The only way this story will ever be stood up is if the woman in there decides to speak out and I really don't think that's going to happen. Anyway, we'd never get that lucky.

There was no way to advance the story even if the newspaper wanted to.

Then we left and went in pursuit of more printable stories. I later hand delivered a letter to Phyllis asking if she would like to talk about the allegations. She sent the letter back to me.

She later said in her book:

> Although I hated Paul Williams the same as all the other journalists, the letter appeared to be sympathetic and understanding. But I could trust no one.

Over eighteen months later, when Phyllis did trust me enough to speak, she revealed that an assistant of the Archbishop of Dublin, Desmond Connell, had tipped her off about a rumour that one of her relatives had sold her story to the *Sunday World* that same week. She had phoned each of her siblings demanding to know if one of them had done so. It was completely untrue, just another part of the nasty mind games the Church played with the vulnerable woman.

She sought legal advice on whether she should seek a High Court injunction against us. That weekend we carried a short story, which had come through church channels to the news desk, that Cleary's alleged lover had attempted suicide. I would later discover that the story was a lie. It was part of the media counter-offensive being waged to discredit her.

That same weekend the *Sunday Tribune* which was part owned by the Independent group carried an astonishing front page. Under the heading "Fr Cleary's family 'to prove' innocence", Michael Cleary's nephew Tom claimed that his family had evidence that would completely disprove allegations his uncle had fathered a child. The story went on to claim that they had affidavits from two men stating that they were the fathers of Phyllis Hamilton's two sons.

It was further claimed that Cleary had taken a DNA test in London in 1992 to repudiate the allegations. The nephew promised that the documents would be released to the media 'soon'. The claims were designed to scare off nosey journalists and publishers from probing any further. In one mendacious fell swoop the Michael Cleary story died a death after that. I later exposed all the claims as a tissue of lies.

Behind the scenes it had left Phyllis Hamilton and her son in utter despair. I would subsequently reveal how shortly before

Michael's death his housekeeper got a visit from Patricia Moynihan. In a conversation witnessed by two others, she told Phyllis that she did not accept that Ross was her brother's son and demanded that she sign a sworn affidavit that someone else was the father. Fortunately, Phyllis had refused.

In the meantime I forgot about the Cleary story as life under the new regime had become exciting and busy. One of the first things Brophy and MacGinty did was to lift the censorship ban on the General. I wrote an extensive investigation of Ireland's infamous gang boss from the unpublished research I had compiled over a number of years. (See *Crooks*.)

My exposé led to the first death threats and consequent police protection which became a fact of life for my family and me over the next few decades. Then in August 1994 Martin Cahill was assassinated by the IRA. It was the biggest gangland story I had covered in the new world order of organized crime. Two days later our daughter was born.

When the excitement died down I decided to write Martin Cahill's biography, *The General – Godfather of Crime*, my first book. As the months rolled on I became completely immersed in my research for the book and the world of crime reporting.

The time was punctuated with security alerts at my home as members of his gang plotted to attack me. By January 1995 I was still working on the book when Veronica Guerin was shot in the leg by a lone gunman at her home. That incident illustrated that there were no longer any lines that gangsters were not prepared to cross including shooting a journalist. The furthest thing from my mind was Father Michael Cleary. All that changed a month later.

I still remember the evening I got the phone call which led to one of the biggest religious scandals yet to shock the country. It was February and I was in the throes of writing the final chapters of *The General*. It was John Burns, my old friend since college days. He wanted to talk about Michael Cleary and the story that I had assumed was buried and forgotten. John confided that he had been approached by a solicitor called Peter Lennon who was acting on behalf of Phyllis Hamilton with a view to telling her story.

The legal eagle had approached John because of his role as a senior reporter with the Irish edition of the *Sunday Times*. John later became deputy editor of the paper. Today he is the Deputy Group Business Editor of Mediahuis Ireland, the current owners of the old Independent News and Media (INM) group.

John had met Peter in his office where he was shown evidence that a relationship did indeed exist between Cleary and his housekeeper for twenty-six years. There was further evidence that he had fathered two sons with Phyllis, the first of whom had been adopted. He'd had to sign a strict non-disclosure agreement (NDA) before he was shown anything. The reason Lennon went to the *Sunday Times* was that he believed that the Irish media might be too afraid to touch the story.

The reason for the approach, John explained, was that Phyllis Hamilton felt she had been left with no other choice but to go public with her story. It would have to be dealt with sensitively and responsibly. Michael's friends, people who knew their secret, had publicly denounced the story of the affair and abandoned her and Ross fourteen months earlier. She had been left financially destitute.

After Michael's death the Church had provided Phyllis with a number of lawyers but she had discovered that their real purpose was to control what she said and to whom. A well-respected corporate lawyer, Lennon had taken on her case after a mutual friend, Hamilton's GP, had approached him to see could he help her and Ross. The doctor was concerned that the mother and son were going through a living hell due to the rejection and had nowhere else to turn. The doctor had no doubt that the story was true.

Lennon had much bigger and more lucrative corporate fish to fry but he was moved to help. He had taken a keen interest in getting justice and recognition for his new client. It was the best bit of luck Phyllis had experienced in a very long time. He was looking into aspects of Michael's will in which he had left her property but was being hobbled at every level by the Cleary family. That was when Lennon contacted John.

The lawyer had two main requirements for his client: firstly, to ease her financial burdens, he wanted Phyllis paid a sum of money in return for her story; secondly, to get her as much money as possible and give her story a wider spread, the journalist concerned would then have to be prepared to write her book about the affair. John said the *Sunday Times* wasn't interested at the time but, as a very honourable man, he still wanted to help in any way he could.

Then he recommended that I would be a suitable candidate because I was just completing a book and had the necessary experience to deal with such a story. He reckoned it would be a good fit with the new look *Sunday World* Brophy and MacGinty had created. John gave me Lennon's number and said it was up to me what I wanted to do. Thirty years later I am still incredibly grateful to John for that. The conversation had to be kept strictly secret.

I was stunned by the development. I immediately rang Colm MacGinty to relay the gist of the conversation. We both agreed that it was the biggest untold story of the time. The following day I phoned Peter Lennon and arranged to meet in his office. I signed the obligatory NDA and with the formalities out of the way he pointed me to a box of files and documents sitting on his varnished boardroom table.

Over the next few hours I perused letters, pictures and legal documents that confirmed what John had told me – on the basis of the documents alone the story stood up to scrutiny. I was stunned as I read love letters that had been exchanged between Cleary and his housekeeper, going back years. There were diaries and dozens of pictures of the unofficial secret family together. Lennon showed me a copy of Michael's will in which he had left property to Phyllis and Ross.

However, there was a complication which Lennon was worried would scupper a deal with the *Sunday World*. The executor of the will was Father Brian D'Arcy. In a letter written shortly before his death Cleary informed Phyllis: 'Brian D'Arcy, as you know, has his instructions, as we all discussed a few weeks ago in the kitchen.' Brian has always insisted that Cleary never confided his secret to him.

Peter then played a short recording of a conversation between Phyllis and Monsignor Gerry Sheehy from the office of then Archbishop of Dublin, Desmond Connell. Before his death Michael had given her Sheehy's number and told her to phone him if she ever needed help. Since Cleary's death her only income was her unmarried mother's allowance which he had insisted she continued collecting throughout their relationship. It was part of the cover. When the utilities bills piled up and she couldn't cope the diocese agreed to pay them. It was their way of maintaining control of the narrative.

Connell and his staff were obviously anxious to know whether she had talked to the media. Their sole concern was to keep the scandal under wraps just like they had done with serial paedophiles. In Ireland, and indeed across the world, the Catholic Church's modus operandi was to shift the perverts between parishes and countries which allowed them to continue abusing children. It would take another fifteen years before the government-appointed Ryan Report finally laid bare the full shocking extent of paedophilia in the Church.

On the recording Phyllis sounded confused and anxious about what she should do. It was clear from the tone of the conversation that the Archbishop's emissary had full knowledge of the secret relationship. She wondered out loud whether she had made a mistake by not clarifying the situation by issuing a media statement denying the allegations in *The Phoenix*.

Sheehy's voice came across as firm and adamant as he Jesuitically intoned:

> Not at all, not at all. All these people [the media] are looking for is to make money themselves... that is all there is to it. They are not in the slightest bit interested in you.

When Phyllis said she was prepared to take the secret to the grave with her the man of God agreed wholeheartedly: 'Oh, and that would be the place for it, Phyl.'

I was astonished by what I had just heard. Here was proof that the Church was aware of the situation and was actively trying to cover it up. We then discussed how the paper would handle the story and Lennon's conditions. I instantly agreed to the second part of the deal, to write her book. When the time came I would seek out a publisher and see what they were prepared to pay in terms of an advance. I said that I would go back to Michael Brophy and Colm MacGinty to discuss the next steps.

Back in the office I met my bosses in the MD's office away from prying ears. Given the explosive subject it went without saying that it would have to be dealt with in the strictest confidence. At the meeting I remember laying out the incredible bones of the story I had been shown and what it meant. I was in no doubt that the story was true.

The bottom line was we had evidence that at the height of Cleary's powers, when the bombastic cleric finished lecturing the world on all issues moral on his radio show or on the *Late Late Show*, he went home and got into bed with his housekeeper. It was a contradiction of everything the powerful priest had stood for.

Cleary had effectively lived for several years with his lover and son in full public view as a family unit in all but name. The cover was that Phyllis worked for Cleary as his housekeeper and personal secretary which, by all accounts, she was very good at. The public line was that she'd had a child out of wedlock and the kind-hearted priest was being charitable by giving them a home as part of the conditions of her employment.

The picture taking shape from the revelations disclosed Cleary as an intensely conflicted character. To some he would be seen as a hypocrite, a moral coward, a liar and a charlatan. But he was also a deeply flawed, dysfunctional and emotionally immature individual who was trapped between love, celibacy, ego and status.

Cleary's first son was adopted and he did not reject his second son, unlike his friend Bishop Casey. He seemed to genuinely love his illegitimate family although Phyllis would later tell me that she was never sure whether Michael stayed with her purely to ensure that their relationship remained a secret. If the story had ever come out it would have meant disgrace and the loss of the job that he clearly loved. He wanted it every way.

The story had everything. It exemplified the inherent contradictions and frailty of human life. But one thing was certain: it would be the Church and Cleary's relatives and friends who would ultimately take the blame for the story coming out. They had left Phyllis Hamilton with no option but to go public.

We knew that if we did eventually publish the story it would set off a firestorm on a par with the one that had blown up in the wake of the Casey affair. To my absolute delight, Brophy and MacGinty seemed to relish the challenge.

Brophy asked how much money Peter Lennon was asking for. I said he mentioned £30,000 (around €70,000 in today's values) which was, to my mind, an enormous amount at the time. Unlike the British tabloids there wasn't a culture of paying for stories in the Irish media. This was completely new territory for the three of us sitting around the table. But given all the circumstances of this case paying a sum of money was certainly justified. It was a perfect synergy of mutual interest.

We would inform the public of a terrible injustice by giving a voice to someone who had been trampled on, humiliated, lied about and left in penury by an all-powerful, mendacious church and its willing media acolytes. And all because of a woman's devotion and love for a high-profile priest who had broken his vow of celibacy. It would expose the infallibility and imperfection of a church which enforced a cruel moral code on its flock. And, most importantly for us, it would sell a lot of newspapers. It would be a win-win situation all round.

Michael Brophy said not to worry about the money. He would negotiate directly with Lennon himself. He was determined that we would get the story. When we talked about how we would go about presenting the story Brophy said that the facts would speak for themselves; there would be no need for editorializing or exaggeration. We would just tell it as it was. I remember expressing my concerns that despite their enthusiasm the investigation might never see the light of day because of the Church and Cleary's network of powerful friends which included people at the highest levels of our own newspaper group.

Brophy and MacGinty assured me that that would not be a problem either. That is what I admired most about my new bosses, their determination not to be intimidated by vested interests and their willingness to push out the boundaries. They were firm believers in the principal of print and be damned. That's what made them the best newspaper men I ever worked with.

There was no timeframe yet in play as we were still in the preliminary stages of a very complex process that none of us had experienced before. There was no guarantee that it would work out, especially if Phyllis changed her mind for some reason. We agreed that it would have to be kept a closely guarded secret not even to be shared with our colleagues.

I had a lot of work to do before I met with Phyllis. Every aspect of the story had to be corroborated because we knew we were taking on a powerful entity that would do everything to undermine her credibility and ours. We had to know every aspect of the story including any skeletons she had hidden.

A few days later Colm and I went back to Peter Lennon so that the editor could familiarize himself with the documentation that I had been shown. When the meeting was over Colm and I went for 'lunch' to celebrate and didn't leave the pub until closing time. The game was on.

In the weeks and months that followed I spent a lot of time compiling every piece of information I could find on Michael Cleary. At the same time my primary concern was putting the finishing touches to my book *The General* including editing the manuscript and having it screened by libel lawyers. It was a very busy time.

In early May Michael Brophy called me to his office with Colm. He announced that he had done a deal. He had agreed to pay £20,000 or the equivalent today of about €47,000. After that Peter Lennon organized the first meeting with Phyllis and Ross.

Peter, Colm and I met them in the lawyer's office. We wanted to firstly reassure Phyllis that we would handle her story sensitively and responsibly. We also had a mountain of questions to ask.

In the subsequent book Phyllis explained how nervous she was coming to meet us:

> The day we went to meet with them for the first time, Ross and I were terrified. They were the kind of people we had lived in fear of, the people Michael said never to trust... now we would find ourselves sitting across a table from them.

As they were leaving the house she described how Ross asked if they were doing the right thing. She replied:

> I don't know, Ross. We will never know that. All I know is that we have to do something because nothing is happening. It is the only way I can see us getting out of this hell.

She then described the meeting:

> I had expected two brash, obnoxious newsmen. Deep down I felt that I wouldn't like them, and we would decide not to go ahead. Instead, they were reassuring, courteous and friendly. Professionals with a human touch. I suddenly felt at ease with them and the knot in my stomach loosened somewhat. They had done their homework and put forward their proposals for how to deal with the story which they were totally happy with. There were a lot of questions and clarifications.

Our plan was to run two major interviews over consecutive weeks. The first instalment would be an in-depth interview with Phyllis, followed by a second interview with Ross. It was agreed that I would start the process of interviewing them both once *The General* was published and I had finished the publicity campaign around it. Looking back, it was one of the most rewarding and exciting times of my professional life.

I was also facing a daunting challenge. I was about to publish my first ever book and then, once the Cleary story had been published in the *Sunday World,* I would have to sit down and begin writing a second book immediately afterwards. I didn't know it at the time but I was about to make a tiny bit of publishing history by writing and publishing two books in less than eight months, as a provisional print date was set for 25 June 1996.

The General was published by The O'Brien Press on 19 May, the same day that I was scheduled to appear with Gay Byrne on the *Late Late Show.* Being invited onto the biggest TV show in Ireland was the kind of break that every journalist dreamt of. Colm MacGinty sent me down to Louis Copeland to get a smart new suit for the big night. I had been watching the show for as long as

I could remember. I was excited and extremely nervous. But I was also worried as the gardaí had increased patrols around our family home in case the General's men decided to mark the occasion with an attack of some kind.

It's funny the kind of things that stay in the memory banks. I still recall the moment I was led in to take the interviewee's seat behind the famous desk on the *Late Late* set in RTÉ's Studio One. I was the last guest that night. The lights were dimmed as the Dublin rock band, The Devlins, played their hit song 'Someone to Talk To'. My very first encounter with Gay Byrne, Ireland's chat show king, was the back of his chair as he sat watching the performance. I remember him offering his hand back to shake mine in welcome without turning his head.

The strange thing was that despite the nerves of appearing on TV for the first time to talk about my precious book, I couldn't get the Cleary story out of my head. In about a month's time I was about to traduce the memory of the host's dear friend and piss off a powerful elite. As I looked at the back of Gaybo's head I remember thinking that this would be the first and last time I would sit in the famous chair.

Just two years earlier Eamonn Casey's former lover, Annie Murphy, had sat in the same chair when Gaybo interviewed her about her groundbreaking book. It wasn't his finest hour, and he was later criticized for coming across as being hostile and sceptical about her story. Gaybo was one of the celebrities to pour scorn over the original story in *The Phoenix*. In any event my inaugural TV interview went well and *The General* quickly topped the book charts in the week that followed. It was a great experience and one of the highlights of my career.

Once the publicity tour for *The General* was out of the way I started interviewing Phyllis and Ross, going in and out of the house through the back door to avoid attracting attention. I found Phyllis Hamilton, who liked to be called Phyl, to be a kind and very generous woman who was extremely vulnerable. She had suffered with her mental health throughout her life which had been exacerbated by her dysfunctional secret relationship. There were a lot of tears, and it was obvious that she was still grieving for Father Michael. But her mind and her memory were razor sharp. She had an extraordinary story to tell.

In the first instalment Phyl chain smoked as she told me:

> Michael and I secretly shared marriage vows twenty-seven years ago and lived together as man and wife. I loved him with all my heart and when he died a part of me died with him. In fact I think I loved him from the moment I met him.
>
> If he came back and discovered what has happened to us he would raise absolute war... He would be outraged to see how his family and friends have rejected us and how deeply hurt and mixed-up Ross is.
>
> The past 18 months have been hell on earth for us. I find it so hard to believe that we have so many enemies simply because people consider our relationship to be an unmentionable scandal. We have been made to suffer because so many people made a virtual God out of a very human man and they refuse to accept that yes, he DID live a double life.
>
> They put him under tremendous pressure by placing him on a pedestal. He felt compelled to live up to their adulation.

> On one hand he was a very good priest who was caring and compassionate with a deep love of his people. On the other Michael was a lover, a father and a great friend.
>
> There were times when, like the rest of us, he was selfish, immature and irresponsible, as well as being kind, loving and considerate.
>
> The people who cannot face up to his secret life seem to forget that he was an ordinary man. Michael was three things - a priest, an entertainer and a man - he was the only man I have ever loved...
>
> And I will love him and cherish the memories of life with him until the day I die, and no one will take that from me. That is why I have decided to put the record straight for our son's sake so that when I am gone, he can hold his head high and not be afraid to say who his father was.
>
> We have suffered so much rejection and isolation that it is time we told our story so that the ordinary people of Ireland can judge for themselves.

Life had not dealt Cleary's unofficial 'wife' a fair hand. She had a tough upbringing in a home where she was beaten by her mother and sexually abused by an alcoholic father. Phyllis had also spent time in care in an appalling orphanage run by nuns. She revealed how she began a relationship with Cleary at the age of seventeen when he was twice her age.

It became clear that he had groomed and taken advantage of an innocent child. The 'marriage vows' they had exchanged are part of a classic grooming process. She described how he had then suggested that they consummate the 'marriage'. In his efforts to explain to his 'bride' how this worked she described how he masturbated in front of her. Many of the more lurid details of the story we kept out of the newspaper articles and I used them in her book.

Then two years later, when she was nineteen, she fell pregnant with the first of Michael's two sons. In March 1970 she gave birth to a boy she named Michael Ivor. They represented the first names of the two most important men in her life: Cleary and her long-standing psychiatrist Ivor Browne. Cleary arranged to have the child adopted. A year after Phyllis first went public that child was identified as Douglas Boyd Barrett, a brother of People Before Profit TD Richard Boyd Barrett, the adopted son of actress Sinéad Cusack. Douglas later appeared on the *Late Late Show* to tell his story.

Ross was born in 1976. She told me how Michael had pressurized her to put the child up for adoption. He could easily arrange it through his powerful contacts. However, she had held firm and insisted on keeping their son. After that they lived like a family. Phyl firmly believed that it was the intense stress of possibly being exposed in the wake of the former Bishop Casey scandal that had brought on Michael's cancer. Casey, she revealed, had been privy to their secret but the sharing of confidences hadn't been reciprocal.

As we waded slowly through the details of her troubled life there was an added tragic complication in the story which we would have to explain. Phyllis had a third child, a daughter Felicia, who had been born in January 1985. Felicia was later adopted by Phyll's friend and reared in Florida.

She told me how her daughter had been conceived when she was raped by a trainee priest. The deacon had been living with Michael, Phyl and Ross at the parochial house in Finglas when the attack took place. Cleary had moved to the sprawling suburb from Ballyfermot a year earlier when he was promoted to parish priest. The offender who subsequently dropped out before being ordained, had discovered the truth about Ross.

One night, when Cleary was out playing poker (he was a serious gambler), the deacon attacked Phyllis. She explained how she could not report the rape to the police for fear that her secret would be exposed. Her story was later corroborated by a number of sources who were aware of the secret, including Professor Ivor Browne, who had been treating Phyl for several years.

Browne later confirmed to me that Cleary had admitted everything to him about the relationship from the time it started. She believed that the deacon, who died several years ago, had also been blackmailing Cleary at the time. She always regretted the loss of her daughter but felt that if she was to stay with Michael, she would have to let the child go. It would not be acceptable for her to have two children living in the parochial house. Their secret dysfunctional love had created an appalling human tragedy.

I had to be careful how I wrote the story: she wanted it to reflect her enduring love for Michael throughout their twenty-seven years together. She didn't want him portrayed as the charlatan that was becoming more apparent with every interview.

Ross was a very articulate, intelligent eighteen-year-old kid. But it was hardly surprising that he was also angry and confused. He had a deep love for his father but growing up as a secret son had taken a terrible toll. His mother spoke of how Michael had spoilt Ross and even allowed him to start smoking when he was a young teenager. Ross lamented the fact that he had never been able to call Michael 'Dad'. The public denunciations and rejection after Cleary's death had also seriously harmed him. I had to deploy all the empathy and understanding I could muster to help them tell their stories.

As the print date grew closer it remained one of the best kept secrets in the Dublin media. In the *Sunday World* only a few people were kept in the loop to avoid a leak. There was always the possibility, however slight, that Cleary's family could come at us with an injunction. And then there was the fact that our top columnist, Fr Brian D'Arcy, had been a close friend of Michael Cleary. I felt that in some way I was betraying Brian for whom I had great affection. Brophy told me that he would deal with that awkward issue when the time came.

Colm MacGinty and the chief subeditor, JP Thompson, began mapping out the pages for the first week's instalment behind the locked door of the editor's office. The first week's coverage, including the exclusive family pictures, was to run over eight pages – all of which I had to fill.

On the Thursday of that week photographer Val Sheehan was dispatched to spend a day with Phyl and Ross taking portrait pictures of them to accompany the bombshell disclosures. At the same time the advertising department in the *Sunday World* was instructed to advise advertisers to ensure their ads were in the paper that weekend as there was a monster exclusive coming that everyone would be reading.

I had withdrawn to my home to write the biggest exclusive story yet in my career. I wrote it on the same old PC I had borrowed from our niece Sharon Donnelly to write *The General* on. With a young family, a mortgage and a modest wage, I couldn't afford a computer of my own at the time. When I had finally written the first instalment I put it on a floppy disc and brought it into the office for Brophy and MacGinty to read.

I remember how nervous I was when they sat down to read it. I heard a few grunts emanating from Brophy and then he remarked:

'Jesus Christ, I never thought I would be reading a story like this in all my years in journalism. . . this is unbelievable.' I was relieved. We had a winner on our hands.

We had arranged to take Phyl and Ross out of town in anticipation of the storm that was going to break that Sunday morning as they didn't want to be in Dublin for it. There would be a lot of journalists calling to the house in Harold's Cross after the exposé appeared.

On the Friday Colm and I drove in bright sunshine to the village of Donard in the Glen of Imaal where his friend owned an isolated holiday home. We wanted to check it out and hoped that they would feel safe there away from the madness. I took them to the house on Saturday morning. The hideaway had been stocked up with plenty of food and was equipped with all the creature comforts so they could enjoy the heatwave we were experiencing.

I went back to Dublin to wait for the first editions to roll off the presses. The whole front page was taken up with a monster picture of Michael Cleary with his arm around Phyl's shoulder. She looked tiny beside her lover. Superimposed on the picture was another picture of Phyl and Ross taken a few days earlier. The headline simply read: 'My life with Fr Michael Cleary – by the mother of his son and his wife of 27 years'. The strap across the bottom of the page declared: 'The love affair that could never be told until now'. It was understated, in keeping with Brophy's advice that the story would tell itself. I brought the copy of the newspaper back to the house in Donard and showed it to Phyl and Ross. The tears they cried were of sadness and relief that their lives were no longer a scandalous secret.

Readers of a certain age will probably wonder why the story was such a big deal. A prominent clergyman being revealed as a secret dad and lover today would still probably make front page news but would not be so shocking or groundbreaking. But history would show that the Cleary story added to the gradual process of eroding the Church's influential grip on Irish society. In particular it prompted people to question the hypocrisy and double standards in relation to the Church's attitude to celibacy and women.

The story caused a maelstrom of reaction. It became the main topic of news and conversation across the country. The paper sold out everywhere on that blistering hot day that I will never forget.

I was interviewed for the six and nine o'clock news broadcasts. I fell into the role of defending the story and became a de facto spokesperson for Phyllis which goes with the territory. At the time our strategy was to deny that we had paid her any money. The decision was taken because that would become the story, and it would have been used to undermine her motives which were always genuine. We knew there would be a lot of powerful people determined to use their influence to dismiss the revelations.

The initial reaction of Cleary's famous friends was to deny and refute the story. Others went on the offensive to discredit the woman and the muck-raking sleazy tabloid rag. But as the shock wore off the realisation set in that there was no way in hell a newspaper would run such a story without rock solid information and corroboration. Over time shock and anger eventually gave way to reluctant acceptance that their friend was no more infallible than anyone else.

However, the next day Michael's sister, Patricia Moynihan, spoke to RTÉ news to express her 'great disappointment at these fantasies and allegations being made'. She said: 'We totally deny them; they are absolutely untrue. There is no credibility to them, good, bad or indifferent.' She added that 'charity prevents me from saying anything more that might hurt Ross or Phyllis.'

Bishop Thomas Flynn the spokesman for the Irish Church hierarchy bluntly said they did not believe the story, declaring it to be 'a complete fabrication'.

Father Brian D'Arcy told RTÉ that his friend had always denied the rumours. He was understandably angry and upset with us. In the first days after the story broke Brian considered resigning from the newspaper. There is no doubt that he was coming under pressure from his own hierarchy and had been placed in a very difficult situation. Brian was adamant that the references to him in Cleary's letter to Phyllis did not mean that he was aware of the secret relationship. Phyllis and Ross, however, claimed that he did know.

While he made no apologies for the exposé Michael Brophy used all his powers to convince Brian not to resign. The role of the media is to tell the truth without fear or favour, no matter how unpalatable or personally hurtful it may be. Brian was clearly hurt by the revelations and Brophy gave him a right of reply in the following week's paper.

Under the headline: 'In defence of a dead friend who can't reply' Brian wrote:

> It has been one of my worst weeks ever. A good friend in life, Fr Michael Cleary has had his corpse picked over by a marauding media. He has been callously maligned without a right of reply. He has been labelled a hypocrite by sometimes sneering, lewd people.

In the days that followed the first publication Cleary's family and friends briefed reporters of the existence of Felicia as proof that Phyl was a 'loose woman' who'd had children with different fathers. We had purposely held that part of her story for the second week's instalment because we knew that it would be used to undermine Phyllis.

The front page that Sunday featured Ross's story, accompanied by a picture of him with his father. It also carried a simple headline: 'I called him Father but never Dad – By his son, Ross'. Also on the front page was the story about Felicia alongside a picture of Phyl with the child. We ran it with the child's eyes blacked out to protect her identity. The picture had been taken when her friends had brought Felicia to see Michael and Phyllis in Harold's Cross a few years earlier.

As part of the coverage for the second week psychiatrist Professor Ivor Browne took the unprecedented step of entering the fray. Phyl had been a patient of his since she was first admitted to St Brendan's psychiatric hospital as a child after suffering sexual abuse in the 1960s. I had consulted the pioneering psychiatrist as part of my research in the weeks before publication. Like Peter Lennon, Ivor Browne was one of the heroes of the story. He was prepared to risk his professional reputation to come to the aid of his long-suffering patient. It said all that could be said about that remarkable man who passed away in January 2024 at the age of ninety-five.

When the furore blew up he said he was prepared to go public to defend Phyllis. He confirmed on the record that he had known of the secret relationship for decades. Before he could go public, however, he needed a letter from Phyl that officially authorized him to speak publicly.

He told me: 'Michael always admitted to me that he was the father of Phyl's two boys. He was always honest with me and there was no time when he denied that he was the boys' father.'

Browne had also been aware of the rape incident. Such powerful testimony coming from such an unimpeachable source quickly silenced most of the detractors and deniers. But the establishment then went after him.

A year later the Medical Council censured Browne for alleged breach of confidentiality and ethical standards but ruled that he acted in the interests of his patient. Many were astonished by the censure. Ivor commented: 'I still believe that my ethical duty was to do what I could to protect my patient. If the same circumstances arose again, I would do the same thing.'

In the weeks that followed I secured a publishing contract with Mainstream Publishing in Scotland. The ghostwriting process was a learning curve as I had to delve into the hidden depths of the story and tell it in Phyl's words. I spent long hours interviewing her about the different chapters of her life.

A book requires a lot more information and detail than a newspaper article. It can hold over 100,000 words while the maximum that can appear in a newspaper is a fraction of that. It meant pursuing information in minute forensic detail. That process also produced some startling revelations. One in particular still stands out in my mind. When Phyllis fell pregnant with Ross, Cleary's friend Eamonn Casey had strongly advised him to organize her to travel to the UK for an abortion. It elucidated the hypocrisy and lies at the centre of the Church.

Phyl also revealed how at one stage her mother Philomena had learned of the secret relationship. Philomena was a staunch Catholic, a daily mass goer who never drank or smoked. She was the very opposite to her husband, a drunk, a gambler and a child abuser. Phyl recalled how they had a loveless, acrimonious marriage. She also described how Philomena regularly beat her and was not a very loving mother. One day she received a letter in which her mother called her 'a tramp, a hussy and a whore'. It caused serious distress to Phyl when her mother threatened to expose the 'evil' relationship to the bishops, the media and even the Pope. However, she was later convinced by her daughter to remain silent about the relationship.

Other more quirky details slipped out. I found a recurring reference to someone called 'Salvador' which appeared in several of the letters Michael had written to her over the years. One of the letters was from 1974 when Cleary had gone to visit his sister in Canada. His brother-in-law, a doctor, had diagnosed a malignant growth on his thyroid gland.

Before he came home to start treatment Cleary spent a few days gambling in Las Vegas. The letterhead was from the famous Stardust Casino in Vegas. But apart from the shock news of his cancer another paragraph caught my eye:

> There's a big fellow called Salvador here and he's coming to Ireland soon. He'll stay in 'Ballyer'. I told him you would look after him well – he's looking forward to that. He's an excitable sort of guy but I think you'll enjoy him.

On another occasion when Phyllis was visiting family in the US he mentioned the mystery man again: 'Salvador is driving me mad wondering when you will come home.'

From the way the references were written I became concerned that Phyllis may have been in some kind of relationship with this man. It would only be a matter of time before someone would point this out in an attempt to discredit her. My suspicions were raised when she became coy after I asked the question and she refused to elaborate. I emphasized that it was important to her credibility to clarify this before it became a problem.

Finally, she revealed the secret. Salvador was Michael Cleary's secret code for what she described as 'his physical desire for me'.

He also used to sign cards and letters with the number '8' which was the number of letters in the phrase: I love you. All of that went into the book.

Then there was another bizarre postscript that occurred a number of weeks after the *Sunday World* stories were published and I had begun working on the book. I was contacted by a former nurse who had cared for Cleary when he was being treated for thyroid cancer. The woman, who lived in Coolock in north Dublin, said that at one stage in his treatment, when he thought he was going to die, Michael confessed his relationship with Phyllis. She could provide proof that she had been his nurse and was happy for me to use the information in a story but didn't want her name mentioned. I spoke to her on the phone and arranged to call to her home the following day.

When I got there she told me that a priest had called to her home unannounced a few hours earlier to tell her that he heard she had been talking to me. In a thinly veiled threat he suggested that if she revealed what Cleary had told her twenty years earlier she could find herself in trouble legally. The priest was due to call back again the following day. The former nurse was concerned that I had told someone about her making contact. I had said nothing and could not work out what was going on.

With the woman's agreement, we decided to plant a recording device in her home to capture the conversation when the priest returned. I arranged to also have two photographers hidden in the area to snap him when he did. It would provide important evidence that the Church was actively working to undermine the story about their famous priest.

But then I got another call from the woman who was very anxious and scared. The priest had called her on the phone and told her she was a 'a very naughty woman for helping the *Sunday World* and that reporter'. It was clear that he knew what we were doing. I later discovered that a private investigator had been hired by someone in the hierarchy to eavesdrop on my mobile phone. At the time it worked on the old analogue system and could be picked up on a scanner.

However, to do that specialist equipment had to be used within a mile radius of my phone which meant that I was being followed from a discreet distance. I had become very security conscious over the previous year or so and would have spotted someone tailing me. It was an astonishing development. I was shocked that the Church was prepared to go to such lengths.

A senior garda source attached to Garda HQ contacted me to confirm they had also somehow learned about the spook operation. I later discovered the identity of the private investigator who had been hired by the Church. I have always known the identity of the priest involved – he is still alive.

It was another important learning curve for me. The PI had obviously picked up on my initial conversation with the woman. I had also phoned a colleague in the newspaper and asked him to bring the bugging equipment to the woman's home. It was a stupid mistake but also an important lesson. I was much more careful after that. A year later we started using GSM digital mobile phones as technology moved on. They could not be picked up on scanner.

Despite the scare the woman was happy for me to use the information she had given me. She didn't hear from the priest after that. When I eventually finished the book I recall thinking how I was glad to be returning to the murky world of covering crime. At least I knew what I was dealing with there.

The Cleary investigation put the *Sunday World* on the map as a serious tabloid. After that it was no longer looked down on by the rest of the industry. In October 1995 we received the vindication and approbation of our peers at the National Media Awards when I became the first tabloid journalist in Ireland to receive the award for Outstanding work in Irish Print Journalism. The judging panel was comprised of the most respected journalists and editors in the business.

The judges' citation read that the account of the relationship between Cleary and Phyllis:

> ... made compelling reading, revealing a liaison that was at once loving, fraught, sad and indicative of a dilemma for the times. The impact of the series was heightened by the fact that it coincided with the public debate on priestly celibacy.

It was a huge honour. I dedicated it to Phyl and Ross and my *Sunday World* colleagues who had made it possible.

Veronica Guerin also received an award at the same ceremony in recognition of her being shot and injured in her home earlier that year. The judges created a special award of distinction to commend her 'courage and tenacity that goes beyond what most journalists would consider reasonable'. A month before the award ceremony, on 14 September, she had called at the home of John Gilligan to seek an interview about the source of his inexplicable wealth.

The diminutive thug viciously attacked the journalist and later made sinister threats to have her murdered and her young son abducted and raped. As a result he was facing serious charges for assault. I remember, over several gin and tonics that day, Veronica describing how she was more traumatized by Gilligan's attack than the shooting. But she still found time to joke about the award. 'Imagine getting a fucking award for being shot and not writing a story,' she laughed. It was the last time that I met Veronica in person. Eight months later she paid the ultimate price when she was murdered by Gilligan and his mob.

The memoir *Secret Love: My life with Father Michael Cleary* was released in the same month and was an instant bestseller. Significantly Phyl's first big TV interview to promote the book was with Pat Kenny on his popular Saturday night chat show, *Kenny Live*. Everyone had decided that it probably wasn't a fit for Gay Byrne.

I made another small bit of publishing history as a result. For a number of weeks *Secret Love* and *The General* swapped positions at the number one and two slots in the non-fiction bestsellers list. I was able to buy my own computer after that.

Around the same time I met one of my heroes, *Father Ted* star Dermot Morgan. The first episodes of the iconoclastic comedy had started on the UK's Channel 4 in April 1995. To say that it angered the Catholic Church would be putting it mildly.

I had always been a fan of Dermot who I believe still holds the distinction of being Ireland's greatest comedian and mimic. He was the driving force behind *Scrap Saturday*, the weekly Saturday morning satirical, cutting-edge show on RTÉ radio which mercilessly targeted some of the most powerful people in the country, particularly Charles Haughey when he was Taoiseach. It was the most listened to show on Irish radio. The powerful elite got their revenge on Dermot when RTÉ caved in to pressure and dumped the show. After that he was forced to seek work in the UK and landed the iconic role in *Father Ted*.

I was introduced to Dermot over a few pints in one of his favourite watering holes, Doheny and Nesbitt on Dublin's Baggot Street. We became friends after that until his untimely death three years later. He often spoke of how he had felt betrayed by RTÉ for dumping his show. I remember him phoning me one day to tell me to keep an eye out for the next series. There was a scene in one of the episodes where Father Ted is seen reading *Secret Love*. He thought that was great craic.

For most journalists some stories are the equivalent of what old cases are to police detectives – evolving over several years like the stories of the Monk, Christy Kinahan, the General and the five years I spent covering the aftermath of the Guerin murder. I also spent fourteen years covering events in Limerick. Other stories seem to crop up just when you are about to assign them a space in the attic for stories that have reached their finale. The Cleary story falls into the latter category.

Immediately after the story went public in 1995 Peter Lennon initiated the legal challenge to have Ross lawfully recognized as the son of Father Michael Cleary. He fought tooth and nail to obtain a tissue sample belonging to Cleary which he discovered was held in St Vincent's Hospital. In 1999, after a four-year struggle, the tenacious lawyer finally obtained what Phyl always wanted for her beloved son – the DNA tests confirming Cleary was in fact his father.

Less than a year later in January 2001 Phyllis Hamilton died from cancer. She was just a few weeks away from her fifty-first birthday. Colm MacGinty and I attended the funeral. I hadn't been in touch with Phyl for a few years and visited her when I discovered that she was ill. She told me:

> I don't mind dying really. All I ever wanted was to have my boy accepted in this life for who he is. I just want to have things right for him. I always knew that I was right. I had the truth and despite everything the truth will win out in the end.

It was an honour to know such a valiant lady and to have been given the privilege of telling her story to the world. But time hasn't allowed her to be forgotten.

The story resurfaced to bring back vivid memories in 2007 when I took part in the RTÉ documentary, *At Home with the Clearys*, which was produced by Amy Millar. Amy had lived for a time with Cleary and his secret family in the early 1990s when she was studying to be a film maker. As part of her class exercises she had recorded several hours of footage of the unofficial family although she had no idea of their relationship until the *Sunday World* broke the story. She later discovered the films in a box in her attic and pieced together a compelling movie.

In the meantime there had been further posthumous controversy around Michael Cleary's legacy when it was revealed he had been guilty of covering up for Tony Walsh, a notorious paedophile priest. Walsh was a member of Cleary's *All Priests Show* and had been assigned to Cleary's parish in Ballyfermot.

It emerged that as early as 1979 Cleary, who was then the senior curate in the parish, was aware of serious allegations against Walsh who was later exposed as one of the most vicious serial child rapists in the history of the Dublin Archdioceses. His savage assaults on children spanned at least two decades, until he was finally caught. In December 2010 he was sentenced to 123 years in prison for rape and sexual abuse committed against three schoolboys. In 2018 he received an additional three-and-a-half-year sentence for assaulting a teenage boy with a crucifix while under Cleary's supervision. Then in 2022 Walsh received another four years imprisonment for indecent assaults on three boys during the 1980s. The Michael Cleary story was resurrected again in 2014 when out of the blue Dublin priest Arthur O'Neill launched a scathing attack on the 'lies' written about his former colleague twenty years earlier. In the June newsletter for St Brigid's Parish in Cabinteely, south county Dublin, he exhumed the original revelations and described them as 'exasperating', 'unproven' and the result of 'shoddy practice' by twenty named journalists, including myself.

I remembered O'Neill from the time I first broke the story. When the book was launched I had a major confrontation with him on Joe Duffy's morning radio show that had partially replaced Gay Byrne's programme. On that occasion I took O'Neill to task for the patronizing sneering way he referred to Phyllis and her allegations.

Despite all the incontrovertible facts of the case including DNA, Fr O'Neill challenged us to prove that one of the most sensational stories in the Irish Catholic Church's history was true. He suggested his former clerical colleague had suffered a serious injustice: 'The burial of a person's legacy deeper than their body just isn't fair – if it's based on a falsehood.'

In a sign of how much the world had moved on since those first explosive revelations two decades earlier, the then Catholic Archbishop of Dublin, Diarmuid Martin, strongly dissociated himself from Fr O'Neill's outspoken comments. His newsletter disappeared after that.

As a consequence of O'Neill's very public attack Felicia, the daughter who had grown up in Florida contacted the *Irish Independent* where I was then working. Felicia gave us an extensive interview in which she said she wanted to establish through a DNA test if in fact she was Cleary's daughter. Phyllis had often told me that she was never 100 per cent sure if her daughter was the product of the rape or was Michael's. Felicia reached out to Ross, but no DNA test was taken.

Then in 2024 Cleary's former best friend, Eamonn Casey, was the subject of another RTÉ documentary. In *Bishop Casey's Secrets* it was revealed that five women had made allegations that he had sexually abused them as children. One of the victims was his niece, Patricia Donovan. She alleged that she had been raped by Casey when she was five years old and that the abuse had continued for more than a decade.

It also emerged that Casey had been formally removed from public ministry in 2007 by the Vatican after the child sex abuse allegations first became known. The restriction remained in place until his death in 2017 but was never publicly disclosed by the Church. As part of the documentary the famous clips of Casey and Cleary at the Pope's Mass were aired again to illustrate the subterfuge and hypocrisy. In July 2025, as a consequence of the disclosures, the Catholic Church removed Casey's remains from the crypt of Galway Cathedral.

When the scandalous story broke about the allegations in 2024 I went back to my old Cleary files and found the material I had about Casey advising his friend and Phyl to have an abortion almost fifty years earlier. It was subsequently published in the *Indo*.

Around the same time a woman contacted me on the *Irish Independent* to say that she also believed that she was the daughter of Father Michael Cleary. The charismatic priest had been very close to the woman and her mother until his death. Although it was widely rumoured and talked about in her family circle her mother, who has since died, never admitted that she was Cleary's lover.

The woman had learned from other close relatives that at the time of the Pope's Mass her mother travelled to the UK for an abortion. She believed that the child was also Cleary's. The woman, who is in her fifties and an accomplished professional, didn't want to go public with the story. She just wanted to know how she could confirm or rule out her paternity. The only way that she could do so was if Ross agreed to provide DNA. I hadn't seen Ross in twenty years so I couldn't really help. We left it at that and agreed to talk again sometime in the future. At the time I was in the throes of writing *Crooks*.

In July 2025 as part of the research for this book I dug out the boxes of old files on the Cleary stories that were gathering dust in my office. I thought it would be a pretty straightforward process of recording for posterity the background to one of the biggest stories I ever worked on. But as I scanned the transcripts and notes I suddenly spotted something that quirked my interest.

There, in the midst of the files, was a reference to the mother of the woman who had contacted me a year earlier. I recalled how Phyl absolutely hated this woman and appeared to be very jealous of her. She said that Cleary had an affair with the woman. Thirty years later I was finally putting two and two together.

I phoned the woman and told her that I thought there was indeed substance to her claims. She has agreed to sit down and be interviewed about her life with Michael Cleary.

Three decades on the Cleary story has sprung back to life again.

CHAPTER THREE

TRACKING DOWN THE PIMPERNEL OF INTERNATIONAL ORGANIZED CRIME

In journalism, especially crime journalism, I have learned one important rule: to always expect the unexpected. On the quietest of days throughout my career, when there was nothing dramatic happening to report on (which was rare enough), it was always a source of reassurance that at that moment someone somewhere was doing something illegal which I'd eventually get to hear about it and then give it the investigative scrutiny and front-page treatment it deserved.

Most stories begin life as a tip off or a passing comment casually made by a contact over a few pints. Think of a story in terms of a plant. The tip-off is the seed. It begins the process of germination when it is first brought into the light before undergoing a process of photosynthesis in the form of hard information and corroborative evidence. The published story represents the successful end product of the process.

A garda contact phoned me one day in 1996 and suggested that I should 'take a closer look' at an upcoming inquest. He was one of the officers who was involved in providing protection at my home. The inquest was into a horrific car crash which had resulted in the death of a taxi driver.

I had no idea that the tip off 'seedling' would synthesize into something completely unexpected. I had effectively stumbled onto one of the most fascinating crime stories I had yet covered.

What started off as a routine hearing in the Coroner's Court put me on the trail of the drunken driver responsible for the tragedy and opened an unexpected door into the highest echelons of international organized crime. Although I didn't realize it at the time, it would also give me an exclusive inside track on what later became the biggest supergrass trial in the history of Britain's criminal justice system.

As a result of the inquest, I discovered that the drunken driver was a gangster, who had at least a dozen aliases with matching false passports and was the kingpin of an international criminal empire. He was conservatively estimated to be worth over €400 million in today's values. By the time I caught up with the secretive mobster he had been living anonymously in Ireland for over two years.

Born in London to Irish immigrants and having obtained Irish citizenship, the most wanted crime boss in Europe was proud of his roots. He also found them extremely advantageous. From a luxury mansion in County Kildare, he had been quietly running his vast narcotics empire organizing multi-tonne shipments of cocaine and hashish into the UK market and several EU countries including Ireland.

In appearance he was unremarkable and didn't stand out in the crowd. Of medium height, bespectacled with a receding grey hairline and a podgy belly he looked older than his fifty-four years. His cockney accent suggested he came from a working-class background which burnished his backstory of a rags to riches ascent in life. He told people that he made his fortune as a used car salesman which fitted the profile.

Since arriving in Dublin in 1993 he had become a well-known face on the social circuit, wining and dining friends and international criminal associates in the city's most exclusive restaurants and bars. His circle of friends included a number of ex-pat UK criminals who had come to the same conclusion as he had: Ireland was a sleepy backwater where they were safely out of reach of the law. A secret garda intelligence report that I subsequently obtained revealed that in reality he was under surveillance and had been regularly observed meeting with 'numerous Irish, UK, European and US drug traffickers'.

The mystery villain was also a regular patron in the city's premier nightclubs, where he and his entourage of associates and young women were given the red-carpet treatment because they flashed cash and swilled only the most expensive champagne. He mingled with unsuspecting celebrities, VIPs and the nouveau riche hedonistic Celtic Tiger pups with a fondness for cocaine. He even hobnobbed with the likes of the lads in U2.

But behind the cultivated facade of a fun-loving, generous-tipping middle-aged gentleman lurked a feared gangster who had no problem resorting to extreme violence, even murder, if some of his business associates tried to rip him off.

He was wanted by law enforcement in the US, Britain, France, Spain, Belgium and Holland. He was on the target list of every customs and police force in Europe, as well as Interpol, the US Drug Enforcement Agency (DEA) and the FBI. Intelligence reports identified him as having direct links with the US Mafia and the Colombian drug cartels. But every time it seemed that he was about to run out of road and end up behind bars he somehow managed to slip the net.

That was why law enforcement bestowed on him the sobriquet the 'Pimpernel' of international organized crime. Like the London villain's favourite comedic character, Del Boy in *Only Fools and Horses,* he would say he was the 'crème de menthe' of gangsters.

By comparison he made the homegrown villains I was writing about look like a bunch of second division amateurs. His name was Michael John Paul Green, better known as simply Mickey Green.

But exposing Green to the world was going to be much more difficult than any other gangster I covered.

My initial investigation of Green first spanned a number of months but eventually stretched out over several years. I became a de facto expert on the life and crimes of the Pimpernel. It was my first foray into the shady world of international organized crime.

Despite the obstacles put in my way, over time I pieced together his fascinating story. What I uncovered was the stuff of a gangster movie. In fact, it is claimed that Green's story inspired the movie *Sexy Beast* which was released in 2000. It featured Ray Winston and Ben Kingsley.

My investigation uncovered a story of international conspiracies and intrigue. It involved what were, even by today's standards, mind-boggling sums of cash. It also shed light on the dirty game and blurred lines between informants and corrupt cops. Initial enquiries covered two phases: piecing together the Pimpernel's life and crimes before his arrival in Ireland; and what happened in the intervening period leading up to the inquest. It would take me another five years to put all the pieces of the jigsaw together.

Mickey Green first arrived in Ireland to set up a new life when he stepped off a flight from the US to Dublin on 17 December

1993. He had no difficulties with immigration because he was the proud holder of an Irish passport. It was the only legitimate one of the twenty passports he possessed.

By then he had been playing cat and mouse with international law enforcement for over two decades. He was tired of running and had decided to make Ireland his forever home. It marked the end of a long journey.

But when I began digging into his past it would eventually make his life considerably less comfortable in his adopted refuge from justice. This is what I found out.

Mickey Green was born on 23 June 1941 in Edgware, North London, at the height of the Second World War. His parents had emigrated from Ireland in search of work before Hitler set the world on fire.

Green was part of the first generation of a new breed of criminal who emerged in Britain's post-war era. His criminal record shows he became involved in crime as soon as he reached puberty. Green's long journey to the big time began on 3 April 1956 when he received his first criminal conviction. The fourteen-year-old delinquent was fined £2, the equivalent of €50, and bound to the peace for two years for being drunk and disorderly.

Three months later he was before the juvenile courts again, this time for housebreaking and stealing. As he got older a string of other charges followed, mostly for breaking into shops, factories and warehouses around North London. Green received his first prison sentence of one month at the age of eighteen for shop breaking, stealing and possession of housebreaking implements. In 1963 he was jailed for 18 months for robbing a warehouse and in 1965 he got two years for receiving stolen goods. By then it was obvious that he was destined to be a career criminal.

The 1950s and 1960s were the golden age of London's gangland. It was the era of the celebrity bad guys, such as the Krays, the Richardsons and the Great Train Robbers, whose stories have been immortalized in books and movies. Long before narcotics became the stock and trade of the underworld, London villains made their ill-gotten loot through protection rackets, nightclubs, prostitution, pornography and armed robbery.

Many of them were aided and abetted by cops in the City of London police and the London Metropolitan police which were riddled with corruption especially throughout the 1970s and early 1980s. The success or failure of the gangs depended on how much they paid the cops to tip them off about impending raids or to simply look the other way. The police code for a bribe was 'taking a drink'. Thankfully, such systematic institutionalized corruption was never a feature of Irish policing.

Mickey Green soon became what was known in 1960s gangland parlance as a 'face' or an armed robber. Faces were swaggering playboys who had no interest in territory or turf – just money and a good time. In one of his excellent books on the era, English crime writer Duncan Campbell summed up their philosophy.

> Their only interest was instant cash. Sawn-off shotguns in a Wembley bank followed by a spell of sawn-off jeans on a Marbella beach. When they had spent all the cash on flash cars, nice suits, birds and booze, they just went back and robbed some more.

The police called them 'blaggers'. The criminal gangs were known as 'firms'. It was a boom time for armed robbers.

In Ireland armed crime had also begun to emerge from the beginning of the 1970s spearheaded by the Provisional IRA who robbed to fund their so-called war and in the process led the way for a new generation of young gangsters. In Dublin the Dunne family were the most infamous firm on the block. Some of the Dunne brothers, particularly Shamie and Christy senior, had previously lived in the UK where they learned their trade running with firms in London and Manchester. They were the first well organized armed robbery gang who introduced others, such as Martin Cahill, the General, to the art of blagging.

By his early twenties Mickey Green was a key member of the notorious Wembley Mob, a loose team of ten to fifteen North London villains who were responsible for a string of big payroll and bank robberies over a four-year period. According to Scotland Yard records the gang made off with the equivalent of €24.5 million in today's values. At the time Green's only legitimate work between heists was as a used car salesman in Edgware. He also managed a seedy nightclub.

But the Wembley Mob's luck ran out when they held up a security van delivering cash to a bank in Ilford, East London, in February 1970. Wearing stockings and helmets to disguise their faces and armed with sawn-off shotguns, the eight-member gang grabbed six bags containing the equivalent of €3.5 million today in cash.

But this time Scotland Yard's anti-robbery Flying Squad, also known as The Sweeney, was hot on their heels. The gang had become so notorious the cops would not be 'taking a drink' in this case. The police made a breakthrough when a messenger at the bank recognized Green's picture in a police photo album of suspects. He had been hanging around outside the bank earlier that morning as staff arrived. It later transpired that most of the planning of the job had been done in Green's flat.

The Pimpernel and three other gang members were charged with the robbery, along with two security guards who had provided Green with the information for the heist. A newspaper report of his trial recorded that when he was arrested Green said to the police: 'If I go down for this I'll get a lot of bird [time], won't I? I'm in the first division now.'

On 5 November 1970 Mickey Green's boast was acknowledged when the jury in the Old Bailey found him guilty and he was jailed for eighteen years. His co-conspirators were also convicted and received stiff prison sentences.

A short time later Mickey Green was escorted from Parkhurst Prison to seek a decree of divorce from his first wife, Carol. Giving his evidence from the witness box while handcuffed to a prison officer he told the court that he and his wife, whom he had married when he was twenty and she was sixteen, had been 'living apart for a few years' and their relationship had broken down. He would marry a second time but that also ended in divorce. He had a string of girlfriends and fathered three children with his various partners.

As I dug into his past a source revealed that Green was released on license from prison on 26 March 1979, after serving nine years. The armed robbery sentence was to be his last serious crime conviction. The condition of his release was that he did not participate in crime and was of good behaviour. Green had convinced the parole board that he was a changed character. But the gangster had no intention of going straight.

Shortly after his release Green got involved in a multi-million-pound VAT fraud operation, smuggling large quantities of gold into the UK. The venture, which ran from 1979 to 1981, turned over the equivalent of €44 million today but was closed down following an investigation by HM Customs and Excise.

A number of people were arrested and charged, and a warrant was issued for Green's arrest. Customs officers identified him as the main financier behind the scam and estimated that he personally made £2 million (€9.9 million today) from the racket. But Green was determined not to return to prison, and he fled to Spain in 1981. In January 1982 his temporary release licence was revoked and an order made that he serve out the rest of his sentence for the Ilford bank job. Green would spend the rest of his career trying to stay one step ahead of the law.

In 1978 a 100-year extradition agreement between Britain and Spain had collapsed making it a particularly attractive destination for fugitive hoodlums. Marbella and Malaga in the Costa del Sol had quickly become home to scores of runaway English villains. It became known in the British press as the Costa del Crime, the little part of Spain that 'fell off the back of a lorry'. It was the perfect location, a paradise in the sun and a short plane ride away from home and family. The fact that local Spanish police were open to accepting bribes was an added bonus. In more recent years it became the home from home for many Irish ex-pat gangsters, most notoriously the Kinahans.

Green loved the sunshine and quickly settled in. Spain would prove to be the land of opportunity.

By the time Green got his freedom the underworld had undergone dramatic change. Former faces had a new way of making a dishonest crust – drugs. The Costa del Crime was ideally suited to the new stock and trade of organized crime.

A short boat ride across the Mediterranean Sea was Morocco and a plentiful supply of cannabis resin. Soon the Costa del Crime became Europe's second most important hub of the drug trade after Amsterdam. Mickey Green had found himself a nice little earner. He was heading into the first division of drug trafficking in Europe.

Green established himself as a major hash supplier to the UK market. It was through Green and his associates that the Dunnes became the first Irish mob to begin smuggling cannabis into Ireland. Later Green and his associates were amongst the first European traffickers to get involved in the wholesale cocaine trade, developing direct contact with the Colombian drug cartels who were anxious to establish a new European market.

I discovered that, like all major villains, Green lived a lavish lifestyle. He bought a luxury villa in Marbella and owned a Rolls Royce, a convertible Porsche and a number of powerboats. The Pimpernel was joined by former partners in the Wembley Mob and Ronnie Knight, the colourful ex-husband of the late Barbara Windsor, the star of the *Carry On* films and *EastEnders*. Knight, a former Soho nightclub owner, arrived in the Costa del Sol in 1983 on the run from the police after the famous £6 million (€23 million today) Security Express robbery in London. Another recruit to this nest of infamous thieves was former Great Train Robber Charlie Wilson who was assassinated in Marbella in 1990 in a disagreement with another UK drug dealer. Green was not involved in the row.

After a dive into old newspaper clippings and information from sources in the UK and Spain I discovered that in 1986 the Spanish national police, the Guardia Civil, began a major operation to target the English drug cartels on the Costa del Crime. They targeted the crime organization they called *El Pulpo*, the Octopus, because of its many operational arms. The head of Octopus was identified as Mickey Green. In February 1987 Spanish police arrested six Britons and seized Stg£2 million (worth €7 million today) worth of cannabis, eleven powerboats and yachts and several high-performance cars including Green's Porsche and his Roller.

But the Pimpernel managed to again disappear before the Spanish could grab him. The police described the swoop as their 'greatest success ever' in breaking the link between the Spanish and British gangs. Both Green and Knight were captured a few weeks later. But on 15 March 1987 a Spanish magistrate ruled that there was insufficient evidence against them.

A few months later Green was again in the frame following the arrest in London of US-based drug trafficker Nicholas Chrastny and the seizure of cocaine worth €16 million in today's values, which had been smuggled by boat from Colombia. The arrest was the result of a joint US Drug Enforcement Agency (DEA) and Scotland Yard operation. Chrastny, who dealt directly with Pablo Escobar's Medellin cartel, had agreed to turn against his partners in crime and tell police everything he knew.

He identified Mickey Green as a member of the UK cartel who had arranged the shipment. Chrastny said he had a number of meetings with Green in Vienna in 1986 where they hammered out a deal for the coke. But the Pimpernel got off the hook yet again when Chrastny subsequently escaped from custody and vanished.

After his escape the DEA described Chrastny as 'one of the most wanted men in the world'. He was never seen again and there is speculation as to whether he was murdered or became a high-level

DEA informant with a new identity. His disappearance meant that the authorities could not pursue Green any further.

As I pieced together his history I found out that he had another close call in 1990. Three of his associates were arrested after a British financier involved in money laundering was kidnapped in France. He was smuggled out of the country and brought to a house in Mijas on the Costa del Sol where he was held for three weeks. A ransom had been demanded for the man's safe return. Police discovered that Green had ordered the kidnapping after money had gone missing. The Pimpernel fled just before the local Spanish police swooped and went into hiding. It was likely that a corrupt cop had tipped him off. He was never charged in connection with the incident.

Records I unearthed showed that a year later two of Green's associates were arrested by Her Majesty's Customs (HMC) in possession of 250 kilos of hashish. The evidence against Green centred on the movement of large sums of cash from the UK to a Swiss bank account that he controlled. He was named on indictment but again the Pimpernel evaded justice. Extradition was never sought because Green's exact location could not be established.

As a result of the bust Green moved to live in Morocco with his girlfriend where he carried on business as usual. He began shipping hash from his new bolt hole to the Netherlands. One shipment of 1100 kilos of cannabis and cocaine was intercepted by French customs following a surveillance operation.

A French undercover officer had infiltrated the operation. The officer had been present at meetings attended by Green in Paris while finalizing preparations for the shipment. One of the keys to the Pimpernel's success in evading the police was that he always kept a safe physical distance from the narcotics he was selling. He was not in France when the drugs were seized, and an international warrant was issued for his arrest on trafficking charges. On 6 November 1991 a court in Lyon sentenced Green to twenty years imprisonment in his absence.

Green then resurfaced in Amsterdam under a false identity where he established a new base. Intelligence reports I later gained access to revealed that he had flown to Colombia using one of his many aliases to organize a new supply route for high quality cocaine that was first smuggled to Holland and then onto the UK and other European countries. The reports revealed that the cartel included associates from Holland, Spain, Belgium, Denmark and the UK. But the successful operation soon came under the spotlight of Green's old enemies.

In 1991 HM Customs arrested two of Green's associates in the UK after they took delivery of 40 kilos of cocaine. The two men were subsequently convicted and jailed for twelve years each. The British identified Green as the supplier of the drugs but amazingly, yet again, there was insufficient evidence with which to charge him. The Pimpernel was earning his sobriquet.

Between 1992 and 1993 HM Customs and the Dutch police set up another operation codenamed, Operation Lucrativo, to smash Green's syndicate. During a three-month surveillance operation three of Green's Dutch associates travelled to London where they deposited a total of Stg£7.5 million (€18.7 million today) at a Thomas Cook exchange bureau. The three were also connected to the cocaine trafficking operation between Colombia and Europe.

About half of the money was then moved through a complex laundering operation to the USA. Over Stg£1 million of the cash was traced to accounts in the name of Brian Perkins and two companies, 'Flagship Racing' and 'Chequered Flag'. The DEA discovered that Green was using a false passport in the name Brian Perkins. They also uncovered evidence that he had used the two companies to launder drug money. The companies had been set up in the US by Green's money launderer, an English accountant living in Miami, Florida.

On 3 November 1992 the Dutch police seized 1100 kilos of cocaine and 1000 kilos of cannabis in a warehouse rented by Green's cartel. The drugs were destined for the English market. The total street worth of the haul was estimated at over €290 million in today's values.

As part of the operation police searched an adjoining warehouse that was being rented by Green for his own personal use. In it they found 126 kilos of gold bars, a BMW, a Bentley, a Porsche, a jeep, a Mercedes and a Ford Mercury. All the vehicles were registered under various aliases used by the Pimpernel. The three Dutch nationals were subsequently arrested and convicted for their part in the huge operation.

However, the Pimpernel's legendary survival instincts paid off and he fled to the US just before the cops came knocking. This time he resurfaced in San Francisco where he rented a mansion formerly owned by rock star Rod Stewart. By this stage the French, Dutch and British authorities were hot on his heels.

The DEA placed him under surveillance and monitored several trips he made to meet with his suppliers in Colombia and in Miami. In February 1993, armed with a Dutch extradition warrant, the DEA arrested Mickey Green as he lay by the pool at his new home. It looked like his run of good luck was coming to an end.

Green was found in possession of three false British passports and the official Irish passport he had obtained several years earlier. The DEA also seized 950 bearer bonds worth $1.5 million.

The Pimpernel was remanded in custody while the extradition was being processed. The French also made an application to the US courts to have Green returned to Lyon to serve his twenty-year sentence. As I followed his trail I was stunned by the sheer scale of Green's operation.

While digging further into the story I discovered another extraordinary character. Michael Constantine Michael was the ultimate gangland Mr Fixit. A physically large, handsome and charismatic man of Greek Cypriot extraction, he was involved in fraud and ran a chain of brothels across London. Born on 25 November 1957, his parents ran a fish and chip shop in Islington, North London. But frying chips was not how he envisioned making his fortune. After setting himself up as an accountant and a mortgage broker he began dabbling in fraud rackets before moving into the brothel business which made him very wealthy.

Michael was a particularly talented organizer and would eventually become the bagman and logistics manager for twenty-six drug syndicates in the UK, organizing transport, distribution, cash collection and money laundering.

Behind the scenes, however, Michael had been secretly recruited as an informant by Scotland Yard's Regional Crime Squad based at Tottenham Court Road in Central London. Michael Michael's career as a supergrass began after he set himself up as an accountant and a mortgage broker. In 1989 he was arrested by the Serious Fraud Office (SFO) and charged with mortgage fraud. In return for a lighter sentence Michael began passing on information to the SFO relating to other mortgage fraud scams. When Michael began associating with drug traffickers the SFO handed him over to Scotland Yard. It was to prove to be a mutually beneficial arrangement. In return for information about various drug trafficking clients the cops would turn a blind eye to his lucrative brothel business which was making him an average of over €3 million per year in today's values.

Several years later Michael would be described as the most prolific supergrass in the history of Scotland Yard when he testified against his former drug clients in the Old Bailey in 2000. One cop called him the 'super supergrass'.

It was around this time that I first learned the full details about Michael Michael's background and involvement with Green. A sensitive UK law enforcement source with whom I became acquainted as part of my investigation of the Pimpernel handed me a large dossier containing fifty-four statements Michael made to HM Customs after they arrested him on drug trafficking charges in 1998. Michael had decided that it would be in his interests to turn Queen's evidence. He agreed to testify against Green and the other crime syndicates he had served.

His handlers in the Regional Crime squad provided him with two pseudonyms, Andrew Ridgley and Chris Stevens. In 1991 he was introduced to his main handler, Detective Constable Paul Carpenter. For the next seven years he worked for Carpenter while also becoming a central player at the highest level of London's criminal drug rackets and Mickey Green's trusted bagman.

His first introduction to the drug trade came about when he acted as an accountant laundering money for two drug trafficking associates of Mickey Green's ex-wife, Anne. Michael's wife Lynn was a long-time friend of Anne Green. It was through this connection that he became involved with the Pimpernel. The relationship was encouraged by his police handlers who were particularly interested in penetrating Mickey Green's operation.

A few weeks after the Pimpernel's arrest in the US in 1993 Anne Green contacted Michael and asked him to raise money for Green's bail and legal fees using a property they owned in Wembley. Michael later flew to Malaga and met Anne Green with three of the Pimpernel's Dutch associates.

He reported back to his handlers that the seizure of Green's gold in the warehouse in the Netherlands had been discussed. One of the associates, a Dutch lawyer, advised Anne Green to swear a false affidavit stating that the gold really belonged to her and was not the proceeds of crime that linked the Pimpernel to drug trafficking.

When Michael reported this meeting back to Scotland Yard they were excited. At last they had a conduit to one of their top targets. The game of cat and mouse had begun. Sometime later Mickey Green phoned Michael from the US prison where he was being held on the extradition charges. It was the first contact between the two men.

The Pimpernel asked Michael to travel to his villa in Marbella, Spain, and remove incriminating paperwork and photographs which he did. His police handler then gave the future supergrass information to pass onto Green in a bid to further ingratiate himself with the most wanted villain.

DC Carpenter provided Michael with the names of three UK criminals who had been reported visiting Green in Miami before his arrest. Michael passed on the information to Green and it had the desired effect. Green was impressed that the bagman had access to such high-level intelligence but was also concerned that he had been so closely monitored by the US authorities. The Scotland Yard detective then gave Michael information that proved to be crucial to Green's extradition case.

The investigations had been the subject of debate between the Dutch, French and British authorities. At a joint conference it was decided that the Dutch would drop their case in favour of the French matter as it was a secured conviction with a twenty-year stretch. In any event the Dutch had decided that there would be insufficient evidence with which to prosecute Green.

DC Carpenter also revealed to Michael a fatal flaw in the French extradition case which was to be hugely beneficial to Green. The undercover customs officer central to Green's case had since been arrested and charged with a criminal offence. Michael contacted Green and his American lawyer with the information.

Green's lawyers later successfully won compensation from the Dutch government for the ten months he had spent in prison on their extradition warrant. A district court in Dordrecht meanwhile ordered the return of the gold and fleet of vehicles to the Pimpernel's representatives in Amsterdam.

The Dutch case was duly withdrawn as agreed. But then Green's lawyers successfully argued that the French extradition case was fundamentally flawed after the arrest of the police officer. On 22 October 1993 the US District Court of the Northern District of California dismissed the French extradition request on the grounds that there was insufficient probable cause or insufficient evidence.

Green was also in dispute with the US authorities concerning the passport offences for which he had been fined and his assets frozen. But DC Carpenter tipped Michael off that one of Green's associates had just been arrested in the Netherlands and was likely to implicate the Pimpernel in a drug trafficking case. Fearing that the Dutch were about to come after him again, Green cut his losses and made a deal with the US Government by which they took half of the $1.5 million in bearer bonds they'd seized at the time of his arrest. The other half was returned to him.

In December the US authorities ordered Green's release from prison and his immediate deportation to Ireland because he was the holder of an Irish passport. As he boarded the flight to Dublin on 17 December 1993 Mickey Green was a happy man. He had beaten the DEA, and the Dutch, French and British authorities.

Green was about to start a whole new life. This time he was determined that he would never have to run again.

I later discovered through Irish sources, both civilian and police, that the Pimpernel celebrated his freedom by throwing a lavish party in Dublin's former Burlington Hotel (now the Clayton Hotel Burlington Road) on the weekend he arrived in Ireland. The Garda National Surveillance Unit (NSU) had been alerted to Green's arrival in the country by their UK counterparts and were watching the festivities.

The party was attended by several of his criminal associates from London, Spain and the Netherlands. Among them were drug traffickers Steve McGoldrick and Clifford Hobbs with whom Green had formed a new cartel. Members of the notorious London crime families the Adams, the Rileys and Arifs also came to celebrate their old pal's extraordinary run of luck. It was the first time that such a gathering of international villains had congregated in Ireland. From then on they became regular visitors.

In his subsequent statements Michael Michael revealed that he flew from London with two of his most talented prostitutes to ease the Pimpernel's pent-up stress after his sojourn in a US jail. It was the first time the two men met face to face. Green was greatly impressed with the secret informant, and he immediately began to trust him. After all the Pimpernel thought he owed Michael his freedom.

Michael also attended a champagne reception and party thrown by Green to mark his mother's birthday on 14 May 1994 which was also held in the former Burlington Hotel. Apart from friends and family, several gangsters from Spain, England, the Netherlands and the USA flew in for the weekend long party.

The brothel boss quickly became an essential cog in the Pimpernel's international drug business. In one of his subsequent statements the supergrass revealed that Green had summoned him to a meeting in Dublin in early 1995. Over dinner in the fish restaurant of the upmarket Westbury Hotel, Green introduced him to two of his business partners, Steve McGoldrick and Terry McMullen. McMullen, a major drug trafficker from Liverpool, had also moved to live in Ireland. The syndicate was establishing another drug trafficking operation between the UK and continental Europe.

From his base in London Michael Michael organized everything from the storage and distribution of drugs to laundering the proceeds. He recruited transport managers to bring the narcotics into the UK. They were normally moved in a fleet of cars, a bus and a chemical tanker lorry.

After Green negotiated each deal the drugs were sent from Spain, France and Holland. Michael also used several people, including his brother, his wife and two sisters-in-law to move millions in cash. He recruited a Lebanese crook called Houssam Ali who owned a bureau de change in central London to launder the cash. In early 1996 the pair even set up their own bureau de change on the Edgware Road to handle the dirty money. Ali also acted as an interpreter between Michael and their French suppliers.

Michael Michael became Green's equivalent of a Mafia *consigliore*. Green relied on Michael more and more as his new operation rapidly expanded to become one of the largest and most sophisticated in Europe.

The supergrass even organized hotel accommodation, flights and false documentation to enable his new boss to move around the world undetected by the various law enforcement agencies who wanted him behind bars. And all this was happening with the full knowledge of Scotland Yard as Michael provided detailed reports to his handler about everything he was up to.

From Michael Michael's statements I discovered that DC Carpenter was supplying his informant with sensitive information from the ongoing HM Customs investigations. The detective had revealed that HM Customs had garnered detailed intelligence about the people involved in Green's money laundering operation and how it worked. The steady stream of high-quality information being provided by Michael via his police handler in London helped Green to modify his operation to avoid law enforcement's prying eyes.

On one occasion in early 1995 DC Carpenter showed Michael a picture which had been secretly taken by garda surveillance officers as he left the Conrad Hotel in central Dublin in the company of Mickey Green and Paul Boulton.

Boulton, from Baldoyle in north Dublin, had befriended Green after he arrived in Ireland. He had become Green's chauffeur, de facto personal assistant and general gofer. Boulton was a member of Fianna Fáil, the majority party in the coalition government at the time, and was close to a number of senior party figures, one of whom was a prominent Dublin city councillor. Using Boulton's connections the drug trafficker ingratiated himself with the political establishment, rubbing shoulders with the great and good of Fianna Fáil. I later established that Boulton introduced Green to his party colleagues as a wealthy retired businessman with Irish roots. The elusive mobster made generous donations to the party coffers at fund raising events.

In November 1994 Boulton and his Fianna Fáil friends had invited Green to a party fundraiser in the former Burlington Hotel in Dublin. During the function one of the most wanted gangsters in the world got to shake hands with the then Justice Minister, Maire Geoghegan Quinn. It later emerged that senior gardaí had not informed the Minister of Green's true persona although they had him under surveillance at the time. The party's apparatchiks only found out the embarrassing truth about their new admirer when I finally outed him on the front page of the *Sunday World*.

Mickey Green was thoroughly enjoying his new life in Ireland. He had made influential new friends, and the drugs operation was running like clockwork. He wasn't getting any hassle from the police although, thanks to Michael, he was aware that they were operating in the background.

Green continued to keep a safe distance, hundreds if not thousands of miles away from the physical product. Living in a different jurisdiction from the one where he plied his trade provided an added layer of protection. Law enforcement agencies knew that the Pimpernel would never be caught hands on with a drug shipment. He was far too clever for that. He paid third parties like Michael Michael to take the risks.

After spending the first eight months of his stay in luxury hotels Green decided to put down permanent roots and purchased two new homes. In August 1994 he bought Maple Falls, a magnificent single-storey mansion newly built on four acres near the village of Kilcock, County Kildare, a short drive from the capital. He also bought a new three-bedroom penthouse apartment in Dublin's upmarket Customs House Docks development.

Michael Michael later revealed how he had transferred the money through a network of false companies to pay for the properties in cash. In all Green spent €1 million in today's values. Back in 1994, the sky rocketing property prices in Ireland had not yet begun.

Green fell in love with Maple Falls as a haven from where he could run his huge drug empire and entertain some of Europe's biggest criminal godfathers. Privacy was ensured as the perimeter of the triangular shaped property was lined with high hedgerows and walls to prevent prying eyes.

Some years later I managed to get into the property for a look myself. Maple Falls had three receptions rooms, a spacious kitchen and breakfast room, five bedrooms, four bathrooms and a gym complete with a full-size sauna. The house also had an indoor heated swimming pool and a snooker room. Green spared no expense on his dream homes. He spent a fortune on antique furniture and ordered handwoven custom-made carpets and the best Italian tiles.

In the grounds of Maple Falls he built a stable and paddock so that he could keep ponies for his grandchildren when they came to visit from London. An avid tennis player Green also built a floodlit tennis court. The grounds included a large pond situated in the middle of landscaped gardens. Green spent thousands stocking the pond with exotic Japanese koi carp fish which reportedly cost the equivalent of €1,200 each in today's values.

Next to the pond was a fully equipped bar and conservatory for entertaining guests. As I pieced together the story of Mickey Green I was told by an associate that the Pimpernel would spend hours on his own gazing into the pond as he planned his various business deals and scams.

I tracked down a former employee at Maple Falls who recalled Green's fascination for his fish:

> Mickey had great taste, and he loved the fish. He found watching them very relaxing and he would say that it helped him work things out. When he sat beside the pool he wanted to be alone, and he would not tolerate anyone interrupting him. It was his special place.

Numerous sources later revealed to me how Green's parties were raucous affairs as he hosted underworld pals from around the world, a veritable who's who of international organized crime. Booze and food were brought in and staff hired to run the bar. Prostitutes were hired from one of the country's most exclusive escort agencies, run by Samantha Blandford Hutton, to provide carnal entertainment for the lowlife guests.

One visitor subsequently spoke to me in February 2000 from the comfort of his cell in London's Belmarsh Prison. Houssam Ali, the Lebanese money launderer, was amongst the first of many to be convicted on Michael's evidence. He was given seven years for laundering the equivalent today of €67 million for Green's cartel. Ali made contact while he was on remand, and I later visited him in the prison. Needless to say he felt that a terrible injustice had befallen him. But even though he had been locked up over his connection to Mickey Green Ali spoke fondly about his visits to Maple Falls.

He recalled seeing four London hoods naked in Green's swimming pool with several women:

> It was just like the decadent stuff you see in the gangster movies and this was all very real. There were drugs, booze and birds. At Mickey's parties anything went and that's why everyone loved to be invited to Ireland. He was a great host, a right diamond of a bloke.

A source close to a bar worker who was hired to work at one of the gangland soirees revealed how she had witnessed an ugly side to the rowdy guests which had raised suspicions that they weren't the legitimate businessmen they pretended to be. She phoned her boss the following morning in tears. She told how she saw two men at the party taking a third man outside after a row broke out. They returned later covered in blood without the man. No reports of an assault were ever reported to the police.

To the local villagers in Kilcock, Green was an affable retired English businessman who tended to keep to himself. He visited the local shops and would have a sociable drink in the village pubs. The Pimpernel used a coin box in the village as he put various drug deals together. While organizing the details of a drug deal worth millions he would casually wave to the locals as they passed the phone box.

Only when he was exposed by the *Sunday World* did villagers finally work out why he needed to use a public phone so much. A local later told me 'It used to strike you that maybe Mick's phone was always on the blink. When we found out what he was really at then it all made sense.'

He also appeared to have found love. The charming womanizer began a relationship with a beautiful twenty-year-old woman called Anita Murphy from Coolock, north Dublin. Boulton introduced them. Murphy was thirty-five years younger than her gangster sugar daddy. Murphy later moved in to live with the Pimpernel.

But then an act of reckless behaviour jeopardized the Pimpernel's peaceful paradise. Ironically, for the first time in his long career, he was about to run into trouble with the law because of a crime he had neither planned nor anticipated. That was where he came to my attention. As a result he was about to lose his cherished anonymity.

―――

On Saturday 8 April 1995, Green and his entourage went on a 14-hour bender in Dublin. It had become part of his normal socializing routine. The night had been another long, wild party which started with dinner in one of the city's most exclusive restaurants, before moving on to the VIP section of his favourite club, Lillies Bordello, all fuelled by large quantities of booze and cocaine.

The group finally called it a night around 4.30 a.m. when the Pimpernel and four companions, two men and two young women, decided to continue the party back at Maple Falls. There would be champagne on ice and a large bag of coke sitting beside a warm swimming pool and a bubbling jacuzzi waiting for them. The early morning would be spent in a hedonistic haze of sex, drugs and booze.

Green had no compunction getting behind the wheel of his powerful UK registered Bentley Turbo R motor, as he often did on such party nights. The journey home took him along the deserted southside of Dublin's city quays on the River Liffey, heading west towards the M4 motorway. He turned up the music and put his foot down. The car reached speeds of up to 160 kilometres per hour as he raced along the river.

At the same time taxi driver Joseph White, a father of nine, had also decided to call it a night after starting his shift at 10 p.m. He had only recently started working as a taxi driver and was renting a Toyota Corona for the purpose. Saturday was the busiest night of the week and a good opportunity to make some badly needed money.

As the taxi driver made his way home to Crumlin on the south side of the city he crossed the Liffey at Queen Street Bridge. The lights were green and the streets were empty.

At the junction of Usher's Island and Bridgefoot Street on the south side of the bridge, disaster struck. Green ignored the red traffic lights on the Quays and Joseph White's car drove into his path. The family saloon car was no match for the awesome power of the speeding Bentley. Joseph White didn't stand a chance. The huge car smashed into the side of the taxi. The Bentley mercilessly bulldozed the car across the junction and sandwiched it against a telegraph pole. The rented Toyota was hit with such force that it was squashed like a tin can.

Still conscious the taxi driver lay trapped and dying from horrific injuries in the crumpled wreckage. In the confusion that followed, and in keeping with his survival instincts as a career criminal, the Pimpernel tried several times to re-start his car and get away. He had no concern for the other driver. While he was doing so one of his male associates walked over to the taxi and looked inside at the dying man.

He walked back to the Bentley and took Green by the arm. One of the passengers later admitted to me that Green told them: 'This is serious, let's get out of here.' His only concern was to get away before the cops arrived. He made no effort to call an ambulance as the taxi man lay dying in the mangled wreckage. Neither did his passengers. It demonstrated what a callous, heartless thug he really was.

The pair walked briskly away with the other three passengers, abandoning the dying driver. A passing motorist who came on the crash called the emergency services at 4.45 a.m.

It took firefighters 45 minutes to cut Joseph White from the wreckage of his car. He died an hour later from shock and massive blood loss. A half hour after the crash a uniformed Garda patrol that had responded to the accident stopped the Englishman and his companions a short distance away.

The officers reported that the women were hysterical, and Green was obviously drunk. He admitted that he had been the driver of the abandoned Bentley. Green was arrested on suspicion of drunk driving and leaving the scene of an accident. The Pimpernel, who had eluded law enforcement for so long, was brought to Kevin Street garda station.

At the station a doctor arrived to take a blood or urine sample from Green at 5.30 a.m. but he twice refused to co-operate. He was then charged with failing to provide a sample and leaving the scene of an accident. It later emerged that Boulton had tried to use his contacts in Fianna Fáil to quash the case against his boss. Green had also dropped the name of the Dublin city councillor to the arresting officers in the hope that it would get him off the hook. But this time he wasn't dealing with corrupt Spanish or UK cops.

Later that day the Pimpernel was brought before the Dublin District Court where he was formally charged and remanded in custody to Mountjoy Prison. Amazingly, as will become clear later in this extraordinary story, I discovered that the officers who arrested Green were not informed of his true identity or his long career in organized crime.

Unknown to them, senior gardaí attached to the Garda National Drug Unit (GNDU), who had been keeping tabs on the mobster at the behest of Scotland Yard, were also alerted and were closely monitoring the situation from afar. The young garda who had arrested Green had no idea that he had just made one of the most significant arrests of his career.

In his subsequent statements Michael Michael revealed that DC Carpenter rang him first thing that Sunday morning to inform him about the crash. In keeping with their ongoing surveillance of Green the gardaí had immediately informed their UK colleagues about the incident. But the Irish police had no way of knowing that the information they were providing was being fed back to the Pimpernel.

Green was held in custody until the following Wednesday 12 April when Michael flew to Dublin and posted the money for his bail. The Pimpernel's priority was to do everything he could to get off the hook. He showed no remorse for the death that he had caused. Nor did he ever express any regret to the taxi driver's heartbroken wife, Margaret. His main concern was that he would not be held liable to pay compensation. He also wanted to retain his hidden identity.

On 12 October 1995 in the Dublin District Court Michael Green pleaded guilty to the two charges of failing to provide a blood or urine sample and leaving the scene of an accident. Given the circumstances they were no more than token road traffic charges. A charge of causing death by dangerous driving was not preferred on the grounds that the charge was not provable because of the lack of evidence and eyewitnesses to establish who had been at fault.

Green had retained the services of a distinguished senior counsel specializing in the area of criminal law. The uniformed garda who arrested the Pimpernel gave evidence of what happened that morning. In reply to questions from Green's counsel the officer said that in the absence of his client's admission that he was driving, they could not have established ownership of the Bentley.

The garda also said that as far as he was aware Green had no previous convictions. The officer was telling the truth: there was no reference to the Pimpernel on the garda computer system. As I was to discover later, senior gardaí had gone to great lengths to keep Green's presence in Ireland and his criminal status a strictly guarded secret. The efforts to maintain Green's anonymity had worked. As far as the law was concerned he had never come to the attention of the police before and was a law-abiding citizen who liked to drink and drive.

Following submissions from counsel the judge noted that there was no prosecution for dangerous driving. For the purpose of dealing with the charges before the court he could not therefore take Joseph White's death into consideration. The judge said he accepted that this was a bitter pill for the family of the deceased. The taxi driver's wife Margaret had been left to rear her nine children alone. After her husband's death, her only source of income was a paltry widow's pension and child support allowances from the State.

It was clear that the judge was unhappy with the way matters had turned out in terms of the charges before the court. He imposed a fine of IR£950 and disqualified the Pimpernel from driving for two years. Mickey Green had yet again walked away a free man.

Green was also happy that there were no reporters in court, and the case received no media attention. The fact that he had pleaded guilty meant that he did not have to give evidence and risk being cross-examined.

I only subsequently learned about what had happened in court. The dead man's family furnished me with a contemporaneous report by the family's solicitor who was there to keep a watching brief on the proceedings.

I was determined that Mickey Green's days as an anonymous Mr Nobody were about to come to an end.

CHAPTER FOUR

REVEALING 'MR BIG'

When my garda contact tipped me off about the impending inquest into the death of Joseph White in February 1996 I knew absolutely nothing about Mickey Green – and neither did the garda. I had never heard as much as a whisper about Green which was unusual. The fact that such a major international criminal was living in the country should have been major news. Green's status as one of the biggest drug traffickers in the world and his arrest after a fatal car crash would normally have been the subject of open conversation in police circles, which in turn would inevitably leak out through the grapevine and grab the attention of a crime reporter like myself.

All that my informant knew was that there was a rumour circulating amongst his colleagues in Dublin's south-central division that this was no ordinary inquest hearing. The gardaí involved in the original case were angry that Green had not faced the more serious charge of causing death by dangerous driving. He had shown no regard for Joseph White and had walked away leaving him to die. They had huge sympathy for the victim and his family. In the years that have elapsed since then the road traffic laws have been amended considerably to avoid such anomalies.

Modern technology, especially the pervasive use of CCTV, also make it difficult to escape arrest.

The source was based in the Crumlin garda district and knew Joseph White and his family. The sole motivation to have the story told was that the driver's widow Margaret and their nine children, most of them under the age of eighteen, had suffered a dreadful injustice. They had been left in penury. They were decent people who deserved better from the law.

To add insult to the appalling misery they were already experiencing, Green had effectively gotten away with it. He had received a mere slap on the wrist with a fine and a driving ban. The original hearing where he pleaded guilty had not even made a few lines in the daily papers. My source told me that the individual responsible for the disaster was fabulously wealthy but was doing everything in his power to avoid having to pay any compensation. Green's parsimony would ultimately lead to his exposure.

An inquest is a public inquiry chaired by a coroner who is a medical doctor. It takes place after the criminal justice process has concluded. The powers available to the coroner are limited. An inquest cannot apportion blame or determine criminal or civil liability. Its function is to establish the facts surrounding a death such as the identity of the deceased and the 'what, when, where and how' of the death occurred.

The source suggested that the Coroner's Court would provide an opportunity to at least publicly expose the driver who caused the tragedy. He gave me numbers for Margaret White and a relative. My informant hoped that the publicity might shame Green into making some recompense to alleviate their plight. I was happy to oblige. That's what journalism is all about – exposing the truth and injustice to the public. I decided that whoever this guy was he definitely deserved a few lines in the country's biggest selling newspaper.

When I first spoke to Margaret White she was, like everyone else, completely in the dark about Green's sinister background. She told me the story of her husband and how the tragedy had left her and her nine children heartbroken. She was extremely angry that the man responsible for destroying her life had used his money to pay for the best lawyers to get him off the hook. Apart from the loss of her husband she worried how she would cope alone to rear her children in the years ahead. The grieving widow gave me a picture of Joseph, and we agreed to talk again after the inquest.

The hearing was scheduled for 8 February 1996 in the Dublin Coroner's Court which is a few feet from Store Street garda station in the heart of the city centre. From the moment I arrived in the building I sensed that there was indeed something very unusual going on.

As I stood in the corridor before the hearing commenced, my attention was drawn to a group of seven well-dressed men who looked completely out of place. They shuffled through the crowd talking on mobile phones and scrutinizing everyone who came in and out of the building. It wasn't a scene I expected to see at the court and there was an unmistakable sense of menace in the air.

The smart suits couldn't disguise the fact that they looked like hired muscle who were there to protect someone or alternatively intimidate someone, or both. They were clearly unconcerned that there were police looking on. The most noticeable figure in the group who appeared to be in charge stood out like a sore thumb.

He was a very tall, heavyset man with a head of thick black hair and a dark complexion. At first I thought that he looked Middle Eastern. The heavies on the mobile phones seemed to be taking instructions from him. I thought he must be a bodyguard. At the time you didn't encounter many characters like him hanging around Dublin. I later identified him as Michael Constantine Michael.

I spotted a young, uniformed cop with a file under his arm. I assumed that he was one of the officers who had arrested the driver of the Bentley and was there to give evidence along with his colleagues. I sidled over to him and confirmed that was the case. Then I said that I had heard that there was something unusual about this particular inquest.

I clearly recall how the garda first looked around before almost whispering: 'There's a rumour that the guy responsible, Green, is a big time drug dealer from London – the word is that he is fucking seriously heavy. Those guys hanging around are his minders. That big fella is the boss–'

That was all my new-found source had time to divulge.

Just then a detective sergeant whom I recognized appeared next to him. The officer, who was attached to the Drug Squad, happened to have been a supervisor on the uniformed unit that arrested Green a year earlier. He was also due to give evidence. He rudely interrupted the illuminating conversation in mid-sentence and pulled the garda aside. I heard him warning the cop to 'Shut to fuck up' and 'you don't fuckin' tell him anything'.

I have never witnessed such a scene either before or since. Senior cops tended to be more discreet than that when it came to shutting down an inquisitive journalist. By then I was well known to the gardaí through my work and having been the subject of death threats for the previous two years. I would have been considered what they called a 'friendly' hack. It was obvious that today I wasn't a 'friendly' and they were anxious that I got no information. To be fair I later discovered that the officer was merely following orders from on high.

The young garda looked ashen-faced and moved away. I decided that it was probably a bad idea to try to talk to him again because it would have caused him serious bother. But I'd got what I needed.

The sergeant gave me a dirty look that bordered on disdain. I remember thinking: 'Fuck you pal – we'll see if I don't find out what you don't want me to know.' If my interest hadn't already been piqued then it certainly was now.

I then met members of the White family whose attention had also been drawn to the presence of the thugs in suits. They too expressed feeling an air of intimidation but couldn't understand why the heavies were there in the first place.

I kept my eye on Michael Michael which was easy. His towering physique and expensive brown fur-lined overcoat meant that you couldn't miss him. He was there to monitor the proceedings on behalf of his boss. It would emerge later that Green and his bagman had been working hard to scupper the proceedings ever since the crash nearly eleven months earlier.

When the hearing commenced in the afternoon, gardaí and fire fighters gave evidence of what they encountered when they responded to the 999 call on the morning of the accident. Medical evidence of the horrific injuries suffered by Joseph White and the pronouncement of his death at St James's Hospital was also given.

A number of witnesses described how the driver of the Bentley had tried to restart the car. They recalled seeing Mickey Green and his companions walk away from the scene. None of the witnesses had seen the crash happening.

The senior cop who had interrupted my conversation earlier gave the bare facts of Green's arrest. He told the inquest that he believed Green was drunk when he was brought to the station. He said criminal charges had been brought and the 'matter was dealt with by the District Court'. He offered nothing more. As the hearing continued it became obvious that there was indeed something seriously amiss.

A man called Dermot Ball, with an address in Coolock in north Dublin, had come forward a number of weeks before the inquest claiming to have witnessed the tragic crash. Ball's story was that he had been driving behind the Bentley at the time of the accident. He suggested that Green was driving at a normal speed even though the damage caused in the collision had proved otherwise.

He said that he saw Green's car driving through a green light at Usher's Quay and that the taxi drove out in front of it. It was obvious to everyone in the court that he was trying to convince the coroner that it was Joseph White who had broken a red light and had therefore been at fault. Even to the casual observer with no knowledge of the background to the case, Ball came across as shifty and not credible.

When cross-examined by the White family's solicitor, Ball said he failed to stop at the scene because he was in a state of shock. He said he was with his English girlfriend, Janice Marlborough, that morning. Ball claimed that he didn't come forward at the time because his marriage was going through 'difficulties' and he did not want to get involved.

When asked why he had only come forward with his evidence after a date had been set for the inquest, Ball claimed that he was unaware that the gardaí were looking for witnesses. Janice

Marlborough, who was present in the court, was not called as her statement was deemed sufficient.

The barrister for the White family accused Ball of telling barefaced lies under oath and committing perjury. It was obvious from listening to Ball that his story was a confection of dissemblance. The 'witness' simply shrugged his shoulders and said he was telling the truth.

The inquest hearing was then adjourned until March. It was not reported in the newspapers the following morning possibly because it had not yet reached a conclusion.

The solicitor's suspicions about Ball would eventually prove to be correct. The truth was that Ball's testimony had been concocted by Green with the assistance of Michael Michael to blame the accident on Joseph White to avoid paying compensation. Three years later Michael confirmed his role in the conspiracy. This part of his supergrass evidence was never given in court. He revealed that following the original district court hearing, the Pimpernel had summoned him to a meeting in Dublin. Green was concerned about the upcoming coroner's inquest and had a plan to ensure that the family of his victim could not sue him. The callous, miserly multi-millionaire was still determined not to have to pay any compensation. It spoke volumes about the character of Michael John Paul Green.

At his behest Michael recruited Janice Marlborough to make the false statement claiming that she was in a car with an Irish 'boyfriend' – Ball – and they had witnessed the accident. Green had been introduced to Ball by Paul Boulton. I later discovered that Ball had underworld connections.

Marlborough, it ultimately transpired, was no random punter. She managed Michael Michael's chain of brothels and worked on the organization of Green's drug business in London. He brought her to Dublin to meet Ball and Green. The Pimpernel took the phony 'couple' to the scene of the crash to familiarize themselves with the area so that they could lie more accurately at the inquest. In January 1996 Marlborough and Ball made their false statements which were then furnished to the coroner.

Marlborough became one of the people later given up to the authorities by Michael Michael when he turned supergrass. She also turned Queen's evidence and testified against the drug syndicates. As part of her deal, she was sentenced to four years and then taken into the witness protection programme after admitting her involvement in the movement of 19 tonnes of cannabis and over a tonne of cocaine while working for Green's cartel.

Marlborough confessed her role in the ruse in one of several witness statements she made to HM Customs. She said Green 'didn't want to be left wide open to be sued by the taxi driver's family'. I was the first journalist to make this information public knowledge.

Michael Michael subsequently revealed that he had reported the perjury plot to his handler DC Carpenter in advance of the inquest hearing. The Scotland Yard officer had no interest in the criminal conspiracy because it was in a different jurisdiction. This important information was never furnished to the gardaí who were monitoring Green for Scotland Yard. If they had been informed then they could have launched a proactive investigation to rebut the evidence. The senior gardaí had no idea that they were dealing with a corrupt cop and that the intelligence being gleaned from the secret surveillance operations was being funnelled back to Green.

After the hearing was adjourned, I followed Michael Michael as he left the court amidst the phalanx of minders and entered the

Master Mariner pub next door. It was obvious they were on high alert. The heavies took up strategic positions around the bar. He sat down at a table with an older man who I later established was Mickey Green. The mob boss had decided to stay away from the court. I ordered a pint and sat watching from a discreet distance.

Also at the table was Terry McMullen who I didn't know at the time. He would go on to feature in a number of my gangland stories. On the other side sat a friend of Joseph White's family and a face that I did instantly recognize – that of Charlie Dunne, a member of the notorious crime family I had been writing about for years. The tip-off seedling had sprung into life and was growing fast.

Later on, when I studied Michael Michael's dossier of fifty-four statements, I found one where he revealed the sordid conspiracy. The purpose of the meeting between Dunne and Green was to discuss compensation for the dead man's family. Dunne, also from Crumlin, had known the dead man socially and was trying to help his widow and children. Neither Joseph White nor any member of his family was involved in crime.

I never established whether Dunne knew that he was dealing with someone from his own criminal milieu albeit at a much higher level in the gangland pecking order. There was a strong possibility that his brothers Shamie and Christy knew who Green was but by then their days as major villains had long passed.

When I read Michael's statement a few years later, I discovered that he knew who I was before I knew him. I suspected that maybe Dunne had identified me. He later said:

> When the inquest began in 1996 I travelled out to Ireland with Janice and we went to the court where the inquest was held and

met Dermot [Ball], Terry McMullen and Paul Boulton. Eventually Dermot was called to give evidence. During his evidence he was accused of lying by the dead man's family.

While the inquest was running a man called Charlie Dunne and a relative of the dead man met with Michael Green, myself and Terry McMullen in the pub next to the coroner's court to negotiate a compensation payment on behalf of the driver's family. Charlie Dunne tried to secure a payment of £50,000 for the family. Mickey Green offered £10,000. This was refused by Dunne. This meeting was observed by an investigative journalist called Paul Williams.

I was subsequently approached by the gardaí in 1999 and asked if I had ever seen the man in the picture they showed me – Michael Michael. When I confirmed that I had seen the face I was asked where I saw him. I told them about the coroner's court and the meeting with Dunne, Mickey Green and others who I didn't know at the time. The officers were asking on behalf of HM Customs, seeking corroboration of Michael's statements to establish the veracity of what he was telling them, although those precious nuggets were not shared with me. But I didn't need them.

By then I had been covering the story of Mickey Green for over three years and was aware through my sources that Michael Michael had been arrested and turned against his former partners in crime. But the gangland fixer's decision to become the 'super supergrass' was still a secret.

After the inquest hearing I returned to the *Sunday World* offices that evening knowing that I had the makings of a major story but my information was scant. The attitude of the senior cop meant that I wouldn't be getting any help from the police. I related what

I knew to my editor Colm MacGinty and he agreed that this was definitely something big.

The resources required to gather information and carry out physical surveillance would not be a problem. Unlike other newspaper bosses at the time Colm MacGinty and *Sunday World* managing director Michael Brophy believed in supporting long-term investigative projects. I immediately went to work. I had plenty of time to dig as the inquest had been adjourned until 29 March.

Back in 1996 there was no Google or other online sources available to check out a story. It required good old-fashioned legwork and piles of paper. When I began making discreet enquiries a few trusted police sources confirmed that a rumour was circulating since the accident that Green was a major gangster who was being secretly watched by the Garda National Drug Unit and the Crime and Security Branch in Garda HQ. But they knew very little else. The sources were just as perplexed as I was by the efforts being made to keep Green's background under wraps within the gardaí.

A source who looked him up on the antiquated garda computer system found that the only record of Green was the road traffic conviction. The only other information was his date of birth and Irish address. There were no accompanying intelligence reports including previous convictions to illustrate his standing in the pantheon of international gangsters.

It meant that he would come up clean if a suspicious cop ran a check on him. However, there was information on the system about other foreign gangsters who had come to live quietly in

Ireland, even if they had not come to police attention here. I thought it was all very strange.

Over the following weeks I gradually began to build a picture of the mysterious Pimpernel. Faced with a wall of silence from the police I pursued other avenues to find the information I needed. A civilian source that I was using at the time remotely accessed various databases including those of the UK police. He was probably best described as a hacker. He was the one who managed to procure Green's rap sheet of eleven convictions, dating between 1956 and 1970.

I recall my amazement when the keyboard wizard also resurrected a Home Office document revoking the Pimpernel's parole. It was as a result of the gold smuggling operation Green was involved in after being released from prison in 1979.

I never asked the source how he came by the information because I didn't want or need to know. All that was important was that it confirmed that Green had pedigree as a major villain and I was on the right track.

I also found more corroborative evidence in a fleeting reference to Green in one of Duncan Campbell's books which told the story of the rise and fall of the Wembley Mob. Campbell had interviewed former members of the gang who had ended up behind bars when their former partner in crime Bertie Smalls decided to do his civic duty in order to protect his own hide. In return for immunity from prosecution his evidence convicted twenty-one of Green's associates in the 1970s. 'Grass' is UK gangland slang for an informant – in Ireland they are known as 'touts'. Smalls was the first criminal to be dubbed a supergrass by the media. The term has stuck ever since.

In the days before online search engines and the computerization of records journalists had to rely on physical paper files containing contemporaneous clippings of original stories from the various newspapers. Every newspaper, including the *Sunday World*, employed a librarian whose job was to read the newspapers from front to back every day and cut out relevant stories. Before the digital age every media outlet had a library next door to the newsroom which was filled with filing cabinets full of clippings in alphabetical order dating back decades.

Each clipping was then filed under the subject's name or, in the case of crime stories, the particular high-profile crime or gang they were connected to. The same template was used for all categories of news, sports and features. For example, there were files on national and international political figures and well-known celebrities – anyone who featured in the news.

Despite being a hugely important function the filing didn't involve a particularly sophisticated process. All it required was a keen, conscientious eye on the part of the librarian and a pair of scissors. Also essential to the process was a roll of sellotape to stick the clipping onto a page of blank paper. The date of the original story was then written in pen on the page. To journalists of a certain age today it probably seems as archaic as the first printing press invented by Johannes Gutenberg in the 15th century.

A visit to the library was the first thing a reporter did when starting to work on a story. It was our primary research tool. When I joined the *Sunday World* in 1987 my news editor Sean Boyne taught me the value of keeping files on those I was writing about. Over the years they grew to fill several filing cabinets. After the inquest I opened a new file with Mickey Green's name on the front. It grew exponentially over the next five years.

The Press Association (PA) agency in London owned one of the most extensive libraries in the media business which stored clippings from newspapers from all over the world. The library also included photographs. The agency provided the service to newspapers for a fee which was charged per page. Armed with the information that I had gathered already I phoned the PA and requested anything they had on a Michael or Mickey Green, also spelt Greene. I gave them a list of his aliases and other subject headings to cross reference including the Wembley Mob, UK organized crime and the dates of Green's recorded convictions.

After a number of days, the PA faxed me a sheaf of fifteen pages containing everything they had on Green. It was from these pages that I found court reports of his armed robbery trial and how he'd received eighteen years in 1970. The pages included photocopies of stories that had been published in the UK revealing Green's other jousts with the law, all leading up to his arrival in Ireland.

The majority of the stories, which had mostly appeared in tabloids such as *The Sun* and *The Mirror*, were no more than ten or twelve paragraphs long. He was fleetingly described as one of the most wanted gangsters in Europe. One short piece referenced how he had been dubbed the Pimpernel because of his success at evading capture. However, there were no feature length, in-depth stories written about Green and the cuttings ended in 1993. The information provided great assistance in piecing together Mickey Green's backstory.

Armed with that information I used it to consult other sources, each of whom added a few more details to my growing 'Green' file. I contacted the DEA office in London and a source confirmed that he was a major target of theirs. I used the file details to convince one senior garda that I knew a lot more than I did. He provided more pieces to the jigsaw.

Around the same time I had become friendly with an officer

attached to the Crime and Security section at Garda HQ. His job involved monitoring bugs on the phones of criminals and terrorists.

Over the subsequent years this particular source used to keep a discreet eye on me and was able to tip me off when gangsters were discussing having me attacked or killed. We never spoke on the phone but would meet and chew the fat over a few pints in a certain pub. The information gleaned from the bugs tended to be kept secret for operational reasons while garda surveillance units watched me from afar. I called him my guardian angel, and he remains a dear friend today.

The guardian angel was selective in what he told me over the years: he never divulged sensitive state secrets, only ones that the public needed to know about. He confirmed that Green was a major target and that he was a serious international player. The source was able to reveal that his colleagues had secretly bugged a high-level meeting that had taken place between Green and his international business partners in a room in the upmarket K Club in County Kildare. The intelligence, it was confirmed, was being collected for Scotland Yard. I had the information I needed to publish the story.

The next phase was to carry out physical surveillance on the Pimpernel in order to get his picture and see where he went and whom he met. Our starting point was the only place I was certain to find him – Maple Falls.

Together with my long-time colleague and friend, photographer Liam O'Connor – the Loc – I reconnoitred the property. We had to ascertain if we could watch Green from afar and snap him without blowing our cover. It was the same methodology we had adopted and honed since the days of following the General, Martin Cahill and his gang members.

Alerting the Pimpernel had to be avoided at all costs because there was a good chance he would go to ground. As was my practice in other investigations I had no intention of confronting him before the story was published. It was always better to creep up on the publicity-shy criminals.

It wasn't going to be easy. One useful piece of information I had picked up over the weeks was that Green had received threatening letters claiming to be from the IRA. They were sent in the period between his conviction in the District Court and the inquest hearing. The letters had culminated with him getting a bullet in the post. That explained the presence of the minders which I assumed he still had. The letters demanded that the mobster pay compensation to the dead man's family. The family had no knowledge of the threats.

Separately, a local source in Kilcock revealed that Green had installed a state-of-the-art security system including CCTV cameras and motion detectors around the grounds of Maple Falls. Michael Michael had hired a top London security company to install the system because he didn't trust domestic suppliers. People living in the area found that strange in a time when such elaborate domestic security systems were largely unheard of except at the homes of VIPs and senior government figures perceived as potential targets for terrorists. Local gossips had wondered of what their English neighbour was afraid. One idea was that the wealthy Brit was afraid of being kidnapped for ransom.

Michael Michael later revealed that Green had asked Dermot Ball to enquire if the IRA were actually responsible for the letters. According to the supergrass, Ball contacted a friend called 'Gerry' who he said was known to have contacts in the terrorist group. He came back to say the Provos were not involved. The 'Gerry' he referenced turned out to be the Monk, Gerry Hutch. After that Green recruited Ball as a minder.

Hidden behind high hedgerows and walls, the triangular shaped property was situated in a cul de sac bordered by the old Dublin Road on one side and the end of the new M4 motorway on the other. One day we drove up the small avenue that bordered the front gates of Green's hideaway. We could only do this once because his minders and the security cameras perched over the closed wrought iron gates and high walls would be keeping sketch for suspicious cars. Watching the place from close quarters was not an option. During the brief reconnaissance mission we spotted a large black Mercedes car parked at the front of the house so at least we knew what transport he was using now that the Bentley had been written off.

We decided that the best opportunity of snapping Green would be when the inquest resumed on Thursday, 28 March. That morning the Loc and Padraig O'Reilly who comprised our small team took up discreet positions around the coroner's court. They could snap Green as he arrived. We also had two cars parked close by with drivers on board to tail him when he left. But our hopes were dashed when he didn't turn up.

At the hearing his legal team told the coroner that their client did not wish to give evidence due to the possibility of a civil liability, which was his entitlement. The Dublin City Coroner Brian Farrell said that he would not require Green to give evidence based on the fact that he would claim privilege. The jury returned the only verdict open to it: Joseph White died as a result of injuries sustained when his car was involved in a collision. The Pimpernel had again managed to avoid any serious sanction.

The facts of the inquest hearing were reported in the next morning's daily papers. It was the first time Green's name was mentioned in an Irish newspaper. No one else in the media knew about his gangland status so I reckoned there was no pressure of being beaten to the chase. He didn't have the kind of high profile that would draw the attention of the UK media either. We decided not to write anything about the inquest until we had everything we needed for a full exposé. I was in no hurry to publish what was going to be one of the biggest stories of my career to date.

But in the absence of Green's picture the extensive exposé we were planning would lack any impact. The public want to see the face of the person they are reading about. A picture is the most effective way of blowing someone's anonymity. The major criminals I exposed over the years were often more concerned about their picture being published than the contents of the articles.

The Viper, Martin Foley, who organized a bomb scare at my home in 2003, never forgave me for first publishing his garda mugshot in the paper in 1988. It was the catalyst for a long running campaign of intimidation against me and my family.

The early days of chasing the General had shown us the value of regularly carrying out photographic surveillance at gangland gatherings, especially funerals and weddings. In the most part we were tipped off about such events by gardaí and underworld sources. I also had a great contact who worked for one of the city's top funeral homes. He would tip me off with the funeral details when a well-known criminal or a relative of a serious gangster had died.

Gangsters tried to keep such information private to avoid unwanted intrusions from the likes of us and didn't announce them in the death notices of newspapers. It gave us an opportunity to watch the funeral home and the funeral mass where the bad and the not-so-good came to pay their respects. It was a rich source of intelligence. Putting names to the often unknown faces in the frames was a worthwhile starting point.

Once a face was identified I opened a file in their name and added whatever information there was to go with it, including the crimes they were involved in and their connections with other criminals. As time went on I added more information. It was slow, incremental work that grew exponentially. In the process we built up a comprehensive picture of organized crime.

That was one of the main ways we turned highly dangerous and feared psychopaths into household names. Having their names and faces featured in the biggest selling newspaper in the country meant that they could not move around with the same sense of impunity. It was the same with Mickey Green. When a criminal receives media attention other villains tend to steer clear of them to avoid finding themselves in the viewfinder of a photographer's camera or getting unwanted heat from the police. Some criminals became pariahs amongst their own when we revealed their more heinous escapades alongside their pictures.

Over the years the Loc and Padraig O'Reilly got so good that every time I confronted or met a gangster in a public place the hoods would instinctively look around for a hidden camera lens instead of punching me in the face – which was always a relief.

I always took great pleasure in the knowledge that surveillance-conscious criminals were freaked out to discover that they had been secretly watched by newspaper photographers. The prospect of putting killers, drug dealers and other social parasites off their cornflakes on Sunday mornings was a source of great job satisfaction. We knew it often drove them mad. It was our equivalent of what Martin Cahill called the 'game'.

To fill the gaps in our files, friendly garda sources provided mugshots and pictures that were seized in raids or taken by surveillance operatives. The motivation of the generous sources was entirely honourable even if it contravened garda regulations. They wanted the public to see the bad guys up close and personal. It made life difficult for gangsters which made the exercise worthwhile. As a result the *Sunday World* had the biggest library of gangster mugshots and intelligence outside of the gardaí.

Getting Mickey Green into that library was something of a challenge. There was no prospect of picking up a mugshot because there weren't any in the possession of the frontline garda units. The upper echelons had made sure of that.

I also wanted a bird's eye view of the Pimpernel's hidden paradise which could not be seen or appreciated from ground level. On 4 April, with Colm MacGinty and Michael Brophy's blessing, and much to the extreme annoyance of the *Sunday World*'s bean counters, I hired a helicopter to photograph Maple Falls from the air. We were the first newspaper to go to such lengths in the pursuit of a story. Hiring a chopper was very expensive. Today there is the much cheaper option of using drones.

'Choo, choo, Kid, just get it done. . . I'll deal with the boys upstairs. . . it's always better to apologize than seek permission,' MacGinty said, as he signed off on the cheque requisition that was going to blow a bigger hole in his editorial budget than a blast from a sawn-off shotgun at close range.

Assuaging the concerns of in-house financial controllers that we were not being profligate with company funds was an occupational hazard. As part of the Independent group the *Sunday World's* accountants were answerable to financial controllers who considered expense-guzzling journalists an overrated extravagance.

It sometimes entailed Brophy and MacGinty taking the paper's accountants to the pub and plying them with pints. The charm offensive was designed to make them feel that they were part of the unfolding drama. To get around them MacGinty and Brophy would convince the bleary-eyed accountant to shift the extra costs to the advertising budget and put it down as entertaining advertisers, the lifeblood of the business.

On more than one occasion during the years that I worked for MacGinty I heard him explaining the *Sunday World*'s raison d'être to the bean counters:

> We expose bad people who do bad things to good people and that costs money which we will get back when we sell more newspapers because the public want to read about it... it's pretty fucking simple really.

I loved him for that.

The investigation of the Pimpernel in 1996 came in a very busy period as I was pursuing a number of major crime stories at the same time. I was trying to unravel the mysterious disappearance of an informant of mine, a very likeable petty criminal called William Jock Corbally. (See *Crooks*.) The investigation led to an extremely violent drug dealer PJ Judge, the Psycho, putting a contract on my head.

Also, for the first time in March we had successfully followed and pictured the elusive criminal mastermind, the Monk, Gerry Hutch. I got a tip that he was to attend the funeral of fellow gang member Gerry Lee who had been shot dead after crossing the wrong people. A year earlier the Monk and his mob had pulled off the spectacular Brinks-Allied heist netting the equivalent of €6 million today. In the course of three record-breaking heists Hutch and his gang had stolen the equivalent of €13.5 million today, making him a household name.

It was the first time that the notorious godfather's picture, with a thin strip across his eyes, had been seen by the public. Under the front-page headline 'Public Enemy No. 1' the accompanying story was the first comprehensive exposé of the gangster published. It revealed his history of armed crime and connections to gangland murders. The article also focused on his controversial tax affairs. The Monk was so upset about the story that he broke his own code of *omerta* and gave an interview to Veronica Guerin, who was my main competitor.

Meanwhile I was determined that we would get value for the extravagance of hiring a helicopter. On the same day that we got an aerial shot of Mickey Green's hideaway, I asked the chopper pilot to fly over a second property I had an interest in which was conveniently about sixteen kilometres away: Jessbrook, the equestrian centre John Gilligan had developed near Enfield, Co. Meath, from the proceeds of his drug empire.

Like Green's Maple Falls, Gilligan's expansive Jessbrook estate could only be fully appreciated from above. It had cost millions to build even though the diminutive thug was officially unemployed and in receipt of the dole. He was due to appear in Kilcock District court on 14 May 1996. Gilligan was facing charges for assaulting Veronica Guerin a year earlier.

The picture was the best way to illustrate the sheer scale of Gilligan's extraordinary wealth as part of a major exposé I planned to publish once the case was over. At the time everyone was confident that he would surely be convicted and jailed. Tragically, it transpired that Gilligan had the same view, and we now know how that worked out.

We eventually published the picture on the Sunday after Veronica was assassinated by Gilligan's henchmen on 26 June 1996. It illustrated why the diminutive mob boss had her murdered.

In the meantime the priority was his low-key neighbour Mickey Green, whose drug trafficking operation dwarfed Gilligan's. We had the pictures of Maple Falls but to catch Green himself we would have to follow him and then photograph him on the street.

We had established that he went to Dublin most days for meetings and to socialize with his twenty-year-old lover, Anita Murphy. It would require patience and perseverance. To avoid alerting him to our presence the safest vantage point was to park at the entrance of a graveyard about a half kilometre away on the old Dublin Road between Kilcock village and Maple Falls.

We watched through binoculars as we waited for the car to appear and then planned to follow it. It took only about six seconds for Green's car to emerge from the cul de sac before it took an immediate right turn and disappeared from sight. The car then travelled along a short link road about 500 metres long leading to the motorway. We had no idea what time he would emerge from his fortress. If we blinked or were distracted we could easily miss him.

The first time this happened the powerful Mercedes had long vanished before we reached the start of the M4. We had no hope of catching up. Green's driver was as fond of speed as his boss and took off at speeds of up to 160 kilometres per hour. Apart from being in a hurry, this was also a security precaution in case the people writing Green threatening letters were intent on ambushing the Pimpernel on the road.

It would also shake off any undercover surveillance cops and, unwittingly, the interfering press. If traffic cops stopped them and issued a speeding ticket then so what. Back then there were no penalty points. His chauffeur could pay a fine and keep on speeding regardless. Green had already learned that it was easy to flout the Irish road traffic laws.

We decided that in order to tail him we would require a second team of two photographers parked in a car at the side of the M4 closer to Dublin. When Green's car appeared we would alert the other guys over a walkie talkie radio that he was on his way. At the time we were still using analogue mobile phones which were easily picked up on scanners and coverage was not that reliable outside the capital.

Once alerted the guys could start driving in the direction of Dublin. By the time Green's car caught up with them they would have gained enough speed to stay with him. People who are conscious of being followed tend to focus more on the rear-view mirror than on the road ahead. But our plan didn't work on the first occasion we tried it. Green's car drove past the second team with such speed that they couldn't keep up either. The next time we got a faster car and the guys parked even further up the road for a better head start. On 10 April the plan finally worked.

The second team stayed with him and relayed their position as Liam and I broke the speed limit to catch up. We caught up with the car as it drew closer to Dublin. As the car made its way slowly through the busy traffic the small convoy of *Sunday World* cars were in front and behind. He wasn't going to get away this time. We tailed Green's car to the Westbury Hotel where he held a lot of his meetings with other villains. Liam got a series of pictures of Green and his girlfriend Anita Murphy when they got out. The story was in the bag.

The final part of the process was to seek comments from law enforcement. I already had a comment from the DEA. To no great surprise the Garda Press Office told us they had never heard of Green. But then I unexpectedly struck gold when I phoned the press office at New Scotland Yard and asked about Green's criminal status. When a spokesman later phoned me back he was, to my absolute delight, very helpful. He confirmed: 'We have known Mickey Green for many, many years.' The officer on the other end of the line also confirmed that he was wanted in several jurisdictions and was a 'criminal of major international proportions'.

On Sunday 14 April the story of the Pimpernel was emblazoned across the front page under the dramatic headline: 'Mr Big – Cocaine king's Irish hideaway from the law'. The strap heading declared: 'Exclusive: We track down one of the most wanted gangsters in the world'. The story was accompanied by a picture of Green looking grumpy in shades and a designer black leather jacket. Inside we gave most of a page to the aerial picture of Maple Falls to illustrate what we were talking about.

The intro paragraph read:

> This is Michael John Paul Green, one of the world's most wanted godfathers of crime who we have tracked down to an Irish luxury hideout. The fifty-five-year-old gangster is linked to the Mafia and Colombian drug families and presides over a multi-million-pound crime empire. Today the *Sunday World* exposes the sordid secret world of this notorious gangster who is using Ireland as his refuge from justice.

Over four pages we told the public everything we knew about Green up to that point. It covered the circumstances of the accident which had caused Joseph White's death; Green's criminal past and various close shaves with the law; and why he was known as the Pimpernel of organized crime. The story revealed how he was wanted by several police forces and exposed his luxury lifestyle.

It was a spectacular story and a front page of which we were all very proud. It certainly justified the expense and time put into the exercise.

Shortly before I ran the story I contacted the White family to tell them what I had discovered. They were shocked. But given the nature of the information they had decided not to go on the record out of fear of retribution from the gangster. We ran a separate story about the father who had been killed by the mobster but without any quotes from his loved ones. The family was happy to see Green exposed but sadly they never received a penny in compensation from him or his insurance company.

In December 2001, after the supergrass trials in London were first made public and it was revealed how Green had scuppered the inquest hearing, Margaret White told a reporter:

> Gardaí never told me he was such a big criminal. I only found out when a journalist told me about him. I never went to the trial. I couldn't bring myself to. The last few years have been hard – very hard for the whole family. Green didn't even spend a day in jail for what he did. He knew how to operate. I can guarantee you that if it was the other way around and it was my Joe who did that, he'd be in jail to this day.

Magaret's comments underlined why the blanket media coverage was so important.

Meanwhile the reaction of a number of senior gardaí to the Mr Big exposé was extraordinary. Serious efforts were made to trash the story and downplay Green's significance. Despite the fact that the story contained extensive hard facts a few journalists were briefed that the story had been blown out of all proportion. A few days later a respected security correspondent reported in a daily newspaper how 'senior gardaí have utterly rubbished a story in a Sunday newspaper which claims that one of the world's biggest drug dealers has been living in Ireland.'

One colleague at the time, who trusted his sources, accused me in person of making the whole thing up. Other commentators also condemned the story as typical tabloid sensationalism. However, the detractors got their answer when, in October of the same year, I was awarded the gong for Campaigning Journalist of the Year at the National Media Awards. The judging panel gave the award based on the investigations into Mickey Green, the Monk and PJ Judge, the Psycho.

At the time Colm MacGinty and Michael Brophy were furious at the attempts to discredit the story and they got on the phone to their counterparts in the newspaper concerned to put the record straight. If what the cops were claiming was true then Mickey Green had the mother of all libel actions against us. We never heard from his lawyers. I later learned that the exposure left the Pimpernel stunned and angry. The public attempts to denounce and undermine our story provided a small bit of consolation for him.

In Green's case the denial was the result of a misconceived, well-intentioned strategy by a small number of senior officers to play down any mention of the Pimpernel or his significance. The thinking was that if there was no publicity and he wasn't known to frontline gardaí, Green would let down his guard and surveillance officers would obtain high quality intelligence. That information could in turn be used against him by their UK counterparts. I took pleasure some years later in exclusively revealing that their intel was being fed right back to Green.

The strategy characterized a police management narrative that had prevailed during the years since I first began writing about crime. Some old school senior gardaí denied that the phenomenon of organized crime even existed and tried to ban the use of the term. I was once admonished severely in the early 1990s by a senior officer involved in serious crime investigations for using 'organized crime' in stories. 'There is no organized crime in Ireland. . . you're exaggerating a problem that doesn't exist.' I can still hear his words. The same gardaí also went to great lengths in 1996 to refute the fact that there were 'millionaire' godfathers in the underworld.

There was clear evidence that the denials had no basis in fact. It was the cognitive, institutionalized denial that effectively allowed the multi-headed hydra of Irish organized crime to grow and prosper.

The police on the frontline were telling reporters that there was a growing culture of organized crime because no one else would listen to them. That was why cops briefed Veronica Guerin and myself about Gilligan's unexplained wealth.

Some years earlier Barry Galvin, the then State Solicitor for Cork, had put his head on the block when he tried to warn the establishment of the urgent need to combat the growing problem of drug-related crime. In his role he dealt with all criminal cases occurring in the country's second city and was witnessing at firsthand how it was rapidly increasing. But in speaking out he incurred the wrath of both the crime gangs and the Government.

The Criminal Justice System has never seen the likes of Barry Galvin either before or since. When no one in power listened to him the crusading lawyer went to the media and started talking. In 1992 Galvin got the nation's undivided attention when he appeared on the *Late Late Show* with Gay Byrne. Galvin revealed how wealthy foreign villains had been attracted as much by our lax criminal laws as the rugged beauty of West Cork. He described how the coastline was being used to smuggle huge amounts of drugs and that the authorities didn't have the resources to patrol it. Irish Navy patrols were mostly concerned with enforcing fishing regulations not hunting for drugs. They were only called in to intercept suspect ships when gardaí or customs had received solid information.

Galvin criticized the inaction of successive governments against the godfathers and their ill-gotten gains. The public was astounded at the amounts of money Galvin claimed the mobs were making. Most significantly he called for the establishment of a single agency combining the skills of customs, revenue and the gardaí, which would be organized along similar lines as the Drug Enforcement Agency (DEA) in the US, as the State should be going after the money.

The Government, embarrassed by the disclosures, decided to shoot the messenger – metaphorically. In media briefings the Justice Minister, Padraig 'Pee' Flynn, laughed Galvin off as a publicity-seeking crank with a hidden agenda. On the floor of the Dáil the Justice Minister sneeringly rebuffed Galvin. Flynn said Galvin had been 'questioned' and his claims found to be exaggerated. Stories were leaked to undermine the solicitor's comments including that he had been motivated by a political allegiance to the main opposition party Fine Gael. Nothing could have been further from the truth.

The reaction spoke volumes about government priorities. There was more effort expended to silence the State Solicitor than catch the godfathers he sought to expose. Several years later I obtained proof of this while I was researching my book *The Untouchables*, which told the story of the Criminal Assets Bureau (CAB). Together with producer/director Gerry Gregg we later made an award-winning six-part documentary TV series on the CAB called *Dirty Money*. I unearthed evidence that Flynn had instructed senior gardaí to dig up dirt which would undermine and discredit Galvin. The people who told me were the ones asked to do the digging. They found none and reported back to Flynn that Barry Galvin's assessment on organized crime was absolutely correct. The officers were pissed off with the hear no evil, see no evil stance of their bosses. The *Sunday World* exposé of Mickey Green further validated what Galvin had been saying.

Ultimately vindication of the messengers came in the worst possible way two months after the Green story when Veronica Guerin was murdered. That seminal event finally forced the State into action, and they turned to Barry Galvin to help establish the entity he had first envisioned – the Criminal Assets Bureau. He became the Bureau's first legal officer and did his bit in making crime no longer pay for a lot of criminals.

Barry Galvin has been a close friend of mine for thirty years and I have long regarded him as one of my heroes in life. In 2006 I first revealed how English drug trafficker Johnny Morrissey who had been living in Cork and was targeted by the CAB at Galvin's insistence, had a murder contract out on the courageous solicitor. Morrissey, who went on to become one of the top members of the Kinahan cartel, was joined in the plot by George Mitchell, the Penguin. When gardaí learned of the conspiracy they moved to stop it. Galvin became the only civilian in the history of the State to be permitted to carry a garda-issue firearm for his own safety.

Former Justice Minister Pee Flynn, along with other senior figures in Fianna Fáil, was subsequently disgraced following a public enquiry into corrupt payments made to politicians by property developers. Galvin and CAB chief, Detective Chief Superintendent Felix McKenna, also made history when their investigations led to the conviction and imprisonment on corruption charges of another former Fianna Fáil Justice Minister, Ray Burke. It explained why this particular cabal, led by the venal former Taoiseach Charlie Haughey, had always resisted going after the wealth of criminals and corrupt officials.

After the murder of Veronica Guerin there were no more rumblings from senior gardaí that I had made up the Mickey Green story. And the term organized crime was no longer taboo either. Almost thirty years later it remains a bitter pill that it took such a horrific act of narco-terrorism to change the narrative and wake the State up.

In the meantime the Mickey Green exposure had made life very uncomfortable for the Pimpernel. He had been stripped of his anonymity and was now recognizable in his local village of Kilcock and in the swanky clubs where he liked to party. The subsequent establishment of the CAB was to also have far reaching consequences for Green. The days of his nice life in Ireland were numbered.

Michael Michael later revealed that following the pseudo-IRA threatening letters Green had asked him to get a sawn-off shotgun and a 9 mm handgun which were to be smuggled to Ireland so he could protect himself. When the story appeared in the *Sunday World* Green cancelled the order fearing that the publicity might result in a garda raid on his home and the guns would be found.

The exposé of the Pimpernel went down well with the cops on the frontline. Now their bosses could no longer keep him under wraps. Like most stories of that type I began to get calls from a multitude of sources giving me more information about Green.

The secret Michael Michael statements that I subsequently got hold of revealed that a few days after the story appeared he visited his boss in Dublin. They had dinner in the upmarket La Stampa restaurant and Michael later described how Green was clearly disturbed by his outing in the newspaper. The realization that he had been secretly followed made him nervous and paranoid. A week later Green and Murphy travelled to Rome and then Cyprus to let the dust die down back in Dublin.

But it was still business as usual for Green. He was still confident that the Irish police could do nothing to him because his drug smuggling was into the UK and he never went near any of the shipments. A month after the story appeared Green negotiated a deal for two tonnes of Thai herbal cannabis. Michael Michael organized the delivery in London.

His subsequent statements revealed that over the next twenty months just one of Green's smuggling operations had shipped cannabis worth over €70 million in today's values. And that did not include the Pimpernel's cocaine smuggling business which was worth many times more than that.

Inevitably the assassination of a high-profile journalist like Veronica Guerin drew the undivided attention of the world's media. This was the first time that a journalist had been murdered by organized crime in Western Europe. Unfortunately, it would not be the last. I lost count of the number of media organizations who interviewed me in the weeks and months after the outrage including the CBS flagship current affairs show, *60 Minutes*.

In August 1996, in Veronica's memory, I agreed to take part in a current affairs documentary, *The Big Story – Tracking down the drug barons*. The one-hour special for the UK's ITV network was presented by Dermot Murnaghan and focused on the links between Ireland and UK drug gangs. When they came to interview me I had a story which clearly illustrated the links: the Pimpernel of organized crime.

On 21 August the film crew accompanied the *Sunday World* team when we travelled to Kilcock. Together with the Loc, another photographer Mitchell O'Connor and colleague Mick McNiffe we agreed to provide some drama by descending on the front gates of Maple Falls in two cars seeking to interview the elusive London gangster.

We knew that Green was spending a lot of time out of the country since the first article. I hadn't been able to track him down to get a comment since then. The timing, however, was now perfect. Four days earlier a huge haul of cocaine worth €92 million today had been seized by the Irish Navy on a Colombian registered freighter *Front Guider*. The haul was destined for the UK market.

Stories in the Irish daily newspapers quoted garda sources who speculated that one of the suspects was 'a British criminal now living in County Kildare'. The official narrative had changed a lot in just a few months. I was surprised by the speculation as he never used Ireland as a transit route. It later transpired that Green had nothing to do with the haul. But if he was home at least we would have something to talk about.

The TV camera crew followed as we walked up to the gates. The photographers were also there to record what happened. A gardener was working inside. I told him who I was and asked if Mickey was about, that I would like to talk to him. To my surprise the gardener said he was there and then went inside to relay my request. Five minutes later the Pimpernel emerged.

Wearing his trademark glasses, with green shorts, a T shirt and a baseball cap, he was covered in dust and looked like he had been working on his beloved home. The ITV team recorded the following conversation:

> PW: Mr Green how are you doing, sir?
>
> MG: I'm alright.
>
> PW: How are you doing? At last, we get to meet.
>
> MG: I'm doin' very well, who are you?
>
> PW: Paul Williams is my name. Mickey, we wanted to talk to you about this cocaine seizure.
>
> MG: Why do you want to talk to me about that?
>
> PW: Well, everyone is saying you had something to do with it, that it was your gear.
>
> MG: Who is everybody?
>
> PW: Gardaí, Drug Enforcement Agency, British police, British customs, Irish customs…
>
> MG: All I would suggest is that you bring the police here. I'd like you to bring them here, that's all that I can suggest.
>
> PW: What do you think of all this media attention you're getting recently?
>
> MG: You know it's up to you… you know, you got to do what you want.

He tried to look unconcerned and smiled but I wasn't buying it. Then I asked him about the seizure of a second haul of gold ingots that had recently been confiscated by the Dutch police which had been connected to him. He was even less forthcoming.

> MG: No concern of yours.
>
> PW: Is it not? It must upset you a little bit though, Mickey, does it?
>
> MG: No concern of yours, nice meetin' ya.

He turned to walk away. As he did so I asked if he liked living in Ireland and if he was going to stay. He said, 'I love it here' and that he was 'certainly' staying in Ireland.

That was the first and only time that I got to speak with the Pimpernel. He had come across exactly as I had expected. The likes of Green weren't the type to get into a row with a reporter. The encounter made for dramatic TV and got a huge audience in the UK. Several of the national newspapers in the UK followed up on the story. It made Green's life even more difficult.

Despite his intentions fate was to prove that he wasn't going to stay in Ireland much longer. He would soon be on the run again.

In the meantime Green's various drug operations went from strength to strength. But they also led him into conflict with some of his business partners who he accused of trying to rip him off. Michael Michael later revealed how Green had visited London a few times using one of his false identities in order to sort out the problem.

In March 1998 one of his partners, a gangster called Gilbert Wynter, vanished without trace from his North London home after incurring the wrath of the Pimpernel. A source told me that his body was rumoured to have been buried in the foundations of the Millennium Dome in London. A less exotic explanation was that his body was fed into a car crusher. Michael, who claimed he had no knowledge of the plot, subsequently revealed that Green never denied being responsible.

Eight months later Wynter's partner, Solly Nahome, was shot dead outside his luxury home. A lone gunman hit him four times at point black range before jumping on the back of a motorbike and disappearing.

In November 1997 Michael Michael celebrated his fortieth birthday with a lavish party in London's Dorchester Hotel. The centre piece of the bash was a cake which reflected Michael's lifestyle: with icing sugar copies of the three mobile phones he always carried, his Porsche, the stacks of £50 notes that bulged in his wallet and the cigarettes he chain smoked. Gangsters, drug couriers and hookers mingled with celebrities and football stars. There were messages of congratulations from the luminaries of organized crime including Mickey Green.

I later discovered, however, that behind the scenes the bagman and brothel keeper was heading for meltdown. He had developed a serious cocaine habit that exacerbated his already high stress levels. Michael had become paranoid and trusted no one. Operating the largest drug distribution business in Europe for some of the world's most dangerous gangsters would tax the coolest nerves. Leading a secret double life as a police informant added to the mounting pressure. Like so many other gangsters before him the pressure was becoming too much and he was cracking up.

His marriage was on the rocks and in his paranoia he feared that his wife Lynne would tell his business partners that he was a grass. He told an associate that he would have to have her 'disappeared' permanently. Michael Michael thought his relationship with Scotland Yard made him untouchable and he never gave HM Customs a second thought. During that period Customs and not the police was the most effective drug busting agency in the UK.

HM Customs intercepted a number of shipments of cocaine and cannabis belonging to Green throughout the winter of 1997. The house of cards finally fell apart in April 1998 when they raided Michael Michael's main warehouse in Hatfield, Hertfordshire, and seized drugs worth €26.8 million in today's values.

At the same time they raided Michael's nearby mansion. The last people he expected to come calling were the law. Michael thought that he was being attacked by a rival drug gang, produced a handgun and threatened to shoot the HM customs officers. It was the weapon that he had procured for Green to protect himself back in Ireland.

In a search the officers found the equivalent of Stg£2 million in cash. But more importantly they discovered that the fraudster had kept meticulous records of all his dealings on behalf of the syndicates. The details included codes for the various clients, smugglers and couriers, and the sums collected, paid and laundered. It listed names, dates, places and quantities of cash and drugs, the value of which could pay the national debt of a small country.

'Hap' was his code word for Mickey Green. 'I called him Hap which is short for Happy because he [Green] was always miserable and in a bad humour,' he explained in one statement. When HM Customs found the records they hit the jackpot.

After a night in the cells and realizing that the game was up, Michael underwent a Damascene conversion. He offered the Customs a deal in exchange for his assistance. He and his wife Lynne would get shorter sentences and be given new lives with their sons if he co-operated. HM Customs agreed. Then Michael began to talk. By the time he had finished he had recorded 250 hours of taped interviews and made fifty-four individual witness statements.

The man the gangsters and the police would describe as a 'super supergrass' implicated everyone from the top down. Every gangster, henchman and courier he'd ever met was offered up on a plate. Michael Michael was proving to be the arrest of a lifetime.

First on his list was Mickey Green, followed by a procession of the top echelon of London's organized crime gangs, a veritable who's who of the underworld. In all he exposed the business dealings of the twenty-six crime syndicates. His records showed the amounts of drugs they had dealt in and the money they had made and how they had laundered it. He even gave up members of his own family including his brother, wife, mother, two sisters-in-law and his mistress. The list included his money launderer, Houssam Ali.

Michael had a phenomenal treasure trove of information. He revealed his relationship with DC Carpenter in Scotland Yard which sparked a major corruption investigation in the Metropolitan police. Over the years Michael claimed that he had paid the cop over Stg£250,000 (over €285,000) in today's values in return for sensitive information.

As HM Customs began building their cases their witness was held in solitary confinement for the next forty-two months.

By the time it was all over a total of thirty-four people were convicted out of forty-nine charged – thirty of whom pleaded guilty – with combined sentences of over 170 years being handed down by the court. Michael's wife Lynne, brother Xanthos and brothel madame Janice Malborough also agreed to turn Queen's evidence in the biggest supergrass trial in British history. The case was only surpassed by the Mafia super trials in Italy.

As soon as HM Customs hit Michael Michael's operation a huge chunk of the UK drug trade came to a shuddering stop. In an ironic twist the development gave Christy Kinahan and his associates a major opportunity to fill the void. As a result, Kinahan quickly became one of the biggest drug suppliers to the UK market.

When the bagman they had become so dependent on vanished the various crime groups began to panic. One of them was Mickey Green. The sparse information coming from the UK convinced the Pimpernel that it was time to disappear again.

In Kilcock the Pimpernel and his mistress hurriedly packed and left Ireland within weeks of Michael's arrest. He was never to return. Now fifty-seven years of age Green was doing what he had always done best – running from the law.

I heard from a source that the couple travelled to South America and then back into Europe through Italy and into Spain. The Pimpernel used his many passports and identities to keep his head down, while at the same time frantically trying to find out exactly what was happening back in the UK.

The courts in London imposed a blanket reporting ban on the case as gangster after gangster was arrested, charged and remanded in custody. Bail laws were not as lax in the UK as they were in Ireland. Three of Green's closest associates were lifted and charged with laundering his drug money.

My sources later revealed that in Spain the Pimpernel met with the other crime gangs where it was agreed to place a £1 million price on the head of the supergrass. Over the following months as more criminals were arrested the bounty was increased to £4 million and included Michael's wife and children.

Back in Ireland there were more problems on the horizon for Mickey Green. In June 1997 the Criminal Assets Bureau officially launched a major investigation with a view to seizing the godfather's assets including his beloved Maple Falls. When Michael Michael was arrested the CAB became involved in the international investigation. In July 1998 CAB officers attended a conference with HM Customs in London to discuss the case. HM Customs shared details from Michael's statements covering the Irish connection.

Later that month CAB officers raided four premises in Dublin and Kildare including Green's two properties, his solicitor's office and the home of his chauffeur, Paul Boulton. I was tipped off about the operation and reported the searches.

By December 1999 the Criminal Assets Bureau armed with affidavits from HM Customs and the information given by Michael Michael, obtained a High Court order freezing Green's Irish properties. Several months earlier I had heard about Michael Michael's arrest but had been asked not to write about it by both CAB and HM Customs. I honoured the agreement with my sources on both sides of the Irish Sea not to publish anything. The impending UK trials were the subject of a blanket reporting ban imposed by the courts. The UK court order, however, did not carry any weight in Ireland. It was the kind of reciprocal agreement that many journalists enter into. The quid pro quo was that I was given an inside track on the biggest gangland case in Europe. I was the only journalist to be given the voluminous dossier telling the inside story of Green and Michael Michael's partnership.

By then the Michael Michael cases were proceeding behind closed doors and maximum security at Woolwich Crown Court in London. The Crown Prosecution Service (CPS) had issued an international arrest warrant for Green on drug trafficking and money laundering charges. The problem was that, yet again, no one knew where he was. But the CAB was about to solve the mystery. They were confident that Green would break cover as soon as he learned that his beloved Maple Falls was going to be taken.

As predicted Green decided to fight the CAB tooth and nail. And that was his mistake. As part of their enquiries the officer in charge of the Pimpernel case, Detective Sergeant Paul O'Brien, discovered that Boulton was in direct contact with Green. By keeping tabs on Boulton, the Irish detectives then discovered that he was living under a false identity in the Barcelona area of Spain. They later narrowed it down to the Ritz Hotel and informed HM Customs. In the first week of February 2000 Mickey Green was arrested by Spanish police and remanded in custody to a prison in Madrid. It appeared that the Pimpernel's number was finally up. From his jail cell Green began fighting the HM Customs extradition case in London and the CAB case in Dublin.

Back in London a succession of those named by the super supergrass were being convicted before the courts and sent down. During one of the trials Michael was accused of being a 'polished liar' by a defence counsel to which he replied:

> Yes, I had to lie even to my family. It is the business of informing and dealing... being disloyal comes with the territory. My friends, family and lover are all awaiting trial because of me.

His Scotland Yard handler DC Paul Carpenter was also investigated but no evidence was found of the cash Michael claimed to have given him. HM Customs then arrested and charged the cop with conspiracy to import drugs. In court he was accused of being one of the most corrupt officers ever to serve in the London Met. The relationship between Michael and Carpenter was described by an Old Bailey judge as 'completely corrupt'.

But then Green's extraordinary luck kicked in. Michael Michael's career as a supergrass came to an abrupt halt in May 2001 after the court ruled it could no longer rely on his uncorroborated testimony. As a result the charges against Mickey Green and his closest associates were dropped. The charges were also dropped against Michael's police handler.

Mickey Green's release coincided with his sixtieth birthday which he celebrated in style. Once again the Pimpernel had lived up to his extraordinary reputation.

The incredible story of Michael Michael only became public on 18 December 2001 when the courts lifted the reporting ban on the case. I travelled to London for the penultimate chapter in the fascinating story.

Michael's was the last of the cases to come before the court. He pleaded guilty to five charges of drug trafficking, money laundering and possession of a firearm when he was originally arrested. As he stood in the dock, flanked by police officers armed with machine guns, Michael Michael looked nothing like the towering figure I'd first spotted in the Dublin coroner's court back in February 1996. Now he was a shattered, gray-faced man. As he handed down a sentence of six years Judge Michael Carroll told the supergrass that he would spend the rest of his life as a marked man.

Commenting on Michael's relationship with DC Carpenter Judge Carroll said:

> I have no doubt whatsoever that for the purpose of this sentence you received assistance and encouragement from a corrupt person to carry out and carry on the plan. I am satisfied, however, there were mutual benefits for both of you over that arrangement.

A few months later Michael Michael and his family were whisked away to a life in the witness protection programme. One of the HM Customs officers involved in the case told me how sometime after he had agreed to be a witness for the Crown Prosecution service, he asked Michael to draw up a list of the gangsters most likely to have him whacked. Mickey Green's name was at the top of the list.

Mickey Green meanwhile read the newspaper reports as he sipped champagne at his poolside in Marbella, Spain. One of Green's associates told me that in an act of defiance the undisputed

Pimpernel of international organized crime had taken over Michael Michael's villa on the Costa del Crime. 'Well, that bastard is hardly likely to come back and ask me to leave is he?' Green told one of his Irish visitors to the luxury residence.

The collapse of the trials meant that Green was untouchable. The UK sources I spoke to openly admitted that they would probably never be able to catch the elusive gangster. In the end the Irish police became the only law enforcement agency in the world to land a blow on the Pimpernel and the *Sunday World* was the only media outlet that ever exposed him. In 2002 the CAB sold off Maple Falls and his other Irish property for the equivalent of almost €2 million today. Sources close to Green said that it was one of the bitterest pills he had ever had to swallow. 'He really was sick when that happened... Maple Falls meant everything to him,' one of his associates later told me.

In 2003 I told the story of the Pimpernel and the super supergrass in *Crime Lords* – it was the end of an extraordinary journey. When the BBC current affairs programme *Panorama* dedicated an episode to the Michael Michael case their primary sources were CAB chief Felix McKenna and me. My investigation of the Pimpernel has been the source material for news reports and podcasts ever since. It was the ultimate scoop.

There was speculation that Green continued in the drug trade after the trials but by then he was determined that no one would ever get so close to him again. He had already made his fortune and still had it.

I only came across him once after that. It was in the El Corte Ingles shopping mall in Puerto Banus where I was browsing the shops with my son Jake while on holiday. I spotted him with a young child whom I presumed was one of his grandkids. As ever the world's slipperiest gangster didn't stand out – he was just another doting granddad.

Although tempted, I decided not to interrupt. My job was done.

In the end it was the Pimpernel's love of the sunshine that did for him. Over the years he had fought skin cancer and seemed to have beaten that enemy the same way he had the law. However, it was reported in July 2020 that he had died from it. He was seventy-nine years old.

CHAPTER FIVE

MIKEY KELLY – THE GANGSTER POLITICIAN

In November 2024 Gerry Hutch, the Monk, the mastermind responsible for the largest cash heists in Irish criminal history, came tantalizingly close to pulling off the biggest 'stroke' of his colourful career. Hutch jettisoned his traditional modus operandi by emerging from the comfort of the underworld shadows and announcing to the world his boldest conspiracy yet. The strategic plan didn't involve depriving a bank of its millions or trying to wipe out the Kinahan cartel. The gangland celebrity grabbed the rapt interest of the public and sent shockwaves through the political system when he decided to contest the General Election.

The Monk's decision to seek election to the 34th Dáil as an independent TD was, to say the least, a spectacular development which made him the biggest story of GE24. Declaring himself the 'people's choice' he sought to represent his beloved inner-city neighbourhood where he grew up in the Dublin Central constituency. The fact that the leader of an international organized crime group came close to winning a seat was sensational news. The joke at the time was the old trope that the Dáil was already full of crooks and he would be with his own.

When rumours began circulating in September 2024 that Hutch was considering the life changing transition from law breaker to law maker, I, like many of those who had chronicled his criminal career over the years, thought it was a wind up. Around the same time, he was arrested in Spain as part of an international money laundering investigation and was held in custody before being granted bail. We were sure the rumours were a joke, but it turned out he was as serious about it as his fellow gang members were about storming the Regency Hotel in 2016.

Like everything else he does in his life Hutch had carefully formulated his strategy. He capitalized on his image of being the Robin Hood of the inner city. But it was a big gamble: by putting himself in the public eye he shed the aura of mystique that had burnished his reputation. The Monk was the one who had fought the law – and won. We wondered if the humble man of the people had been blinded by his own publicity and succumbed to ego and hubris.

Hutch's subsequent cleverly orchestrated campaign used the oldest political cliché in the book – he wanted to bring about 'change'. You can't get more change than a notorious gangster seeking election. Throughout the campaign, which he largely conducted on social media, the Monk never explained what that change would entail.

Everything about his shot at politics demonstrated his strategic acumen. He announced his candidature jointly in the *Sunday Independent* and the *Sunday World*, two of the biggest selling newspapers in the country. He did a lengthy interview for the *Crime World* podcast with journalist Nicola Tallant. At the time there was criticism that Hutch had been given such a powerful media platform and that he wasn't challenged robustly enough about his criminal past and in particular the evidence presented at his trial in the Special Criminal Court in April 2023. Hutch had been accused of murdering Kinahan gang member David Byrne in the Regency Hotel attack.

His friend and associate, and former Sinn Féin golden boy, Jonathan Dowdall became the State's star witness which proved to be an unmitigated disaster. Hutch was acquitted of the charge. Given Dowdall's suspect evidence, and the fact that the State based their case solely on his testimony, it was the only verdict the court could arrive at.

I don't think that the criticism of the podcast was justified. It was a massive journalistic scoop which was reflected in the record number of downloads. It had one of the biggest audiences ever recorded for an Irish podcast. The public wanted to hear the Monk's story. Compromises and parameters are always a feature when a contentious high-profile figure breaks their silence and agrees to give an exclusive interview. The podcasters should have been congratulated rather than ridiculed – to hell with the begrudgers. In any event the listeners can make up their own mind. After the podcast Hutch avoided the rest of the media who backed off from asking any awkward questions.

I was one of the people who he didn't want to talk to. Hutch and his family hated the bestselling biography I wrote about him in 2020, *The Monk: The Life and Crimes of Ireland's most Enigmatic Gangster*. They attacked me for months on social media. I was happy with that response because it proved I had told the full story, including the unpalatable bits Hutch didn't like. I was told later by a source that he had the front jacket of *The Monk* covered in paper so that he could read it on a flight from Spain without the other passengers seeing what he was reading.

No one who knows the Monk believed for a minute that his move into the political fray had anything to do with 'change'. The most likely motivation for seeking election was to add a further layer of protection from his enemies. Assassinating a gangster is one thing but killing a democratically elected member of the Irish parliament is quite another.

Despite his claims to the contrary, it was also likely that Hutch wanted to give a metaphorical punishment beating to Sinn Féin and its leader Mary Lou McDonald, who represents the same Dublin Central area of the inner city. The Hutch clan had traditionally supported Sinn Féin but they perceived that the party, which was already tainted by associations with criminals, turned its back on them in 2016. The Monk's entry into the race certainly cost McDonald votes.

Then there is the possibility that Hutch wanted to double down on humiliating the authorities who had tried and failed to put him behind bars. The State was left hugely embarrassed after the Regency trial when the inexplicable decision was made not to charge Hutch with membership of an organized crime group and possession of firearms. There was plenty of evidence there to merit a conviction on both counts, particularly as he had been secretly recorded on garda bugs incriminating himself. That decision raised a lot of eyebrows in law enforcement circles and remains a mystery. Perhaps Hutch reckoned his lucky streak might extend to a seat in the Dáil.

In the end Gerry Hutch failed to be elected. However, he did exceptionally well and came fifth out of the thirteen candidates who contested the four-seat constituency. Political and sociological analysts are still trying to work out why so many people voted for him. The support he got certainly illustrated Ireland's ambivalent attitude to crime and criminals.

There were others who believed it was all a conspiracy. Far-right candidate Malachy Steenson, who initially welcomed Hutch's entry into the race, proffered the ludicrous conspiracy theory that the Monk was planted by the State to keep him out. Similar nonsense was promulgated by Daniel Kinahan following the Regency attack. Kinahan preposterously claimed that the attack was the product of a grand conspiracy between the Hutch gang, the police, the media and Fine Gael to damage Sinn Féin in the general election that took place three weeks later.

When Hutch failed to be elected there was widespread relief across politics and for good reason. On the international stage it would have caused considerable reputational damage for Ireland. Imagine the scandal of a man becoming a TD who had been secretly recorded plotting to hand over the murder weapons from the Regency attack to dissident Republicans in Northern Ireland?

In bugged conversations between Hutch and Dowdall, recorded by gardaí in 2016, the Monk said he was handing over the AK47s to the terrorists in the hope that they would then be used to murder PSNI officers. In such an event ballistics tests would match the guns to the weapons used in the Regency attack which in turn would lay the blame on the republican terrorists and divert suspicion from his gang.

The metaphorical ski mask slipped to give a very rare glimpse of the real Gerry Hutch when he arrived at the election count centre in the RDS, south Dublin. He was accompanied by a camera crew who were making a documentary about him, with his full cooperation. Outside he smiled when he stopped briefly for reporters and commented that he believed he'd achieved a large vote because people wanted 'change'. It was obvious that Hutch really believed that he had successfully whitewashed his past. But when it became clear that vote transfers were going to push him out of the running for the last seat, the only change visible was to his sunny disposition. It transformed into a scowl when RTÉ's intrepid crime correspondent, Paul Reynolds, suddenly appeared with a microphone beside him. Paul was the first journalist ever to grill the Monk in a robust face-to-face interview sixteen years earlier. Unlike many of the younger hacks in the media pack, Reynolds has been a crime reporter for a very long time and knew the background stories.

He asked the Monk about the evidence heard during his 2023 trial, especially his recorded comments about supplying the murder weapons to the IRA. Hutch took one look at Reynolds and his cocky smirk faded to a frown. As he turned to walk away he dismissed the reporter with a wave of his hand. 'Get away Paul Reynolds,' he snarled and then accused the reporter of being a 'dying wasp'. But Reynolds persisted with his questions.

Hutch was clearly angry. At one stage, in front of the cameras, the Monk turned to glare menacingly at Reynolds. It was a look that if it happened in a secluded spot late at night with no else around the recipient would start praying. Using a trope often used by the far right, Hutch accused his interrogator of being a puppet for the police and the State: 'You get paid from the State and RTÉ, that's what you do. The State is paying you to say this. . . go back to the Special Criminal Court and ask the court.'

There was pandemonium in the count centre as Hutch was swamped by reporters and photographers. As Reynolds persisted with his questions Hutch angrily tried to dismiss him: 'This is an election, go away Paul.'

When Hutch left the count centre in the midst of the media frenzy he was asked if he would run again. He smirked: 'Yes. I'm runnin' all me life. I love running.' And to prove the point he broke into a jog and headed for the gates of the RDS followed by reporters.

Inevitably comparisons were made between Hutch's bid for power and the election of Pablo Escobar to the Colombian Congress in 1982 when he was one of the world's most notorious narcos. Hutch was not the first Irish criminal to enter politics and seek a Dáil seat either. That record belongs to a notorious Limerick crime boss called Michael 'Mikey' Kelly.

Kelly managed to get a lot further in politics than Hutch when he was elected to Limerick City council. During his tenure Kelly demonstrated why electing criminals is an affront to democracy. He did everything in his power to undermine the legitimate political system by creating chaos in the council chambers.

Above all he used his elevated position to cover up a huge criminal enterprise and undermine the police. In doing so Kelly paved the way for the brutal gang war that later engulfed the city for over a decade and claimed over twenty lives. The mayhem left scores more people injured and maimed. Hundreds of innocent victims, including children, were left traumatized for life.

In the run up to the general election in 2002 Kelly was considered a favourite to win a Dáil seat. Kelly would later blame me for derailing his political ambitions. It is an accolade of which I will always be very proud. For once in his violent corrupt life, Mikey Kelly was telling the truth.

Mikey Kelly grew up in the sprawling working-class suburb of Southill in Limerick, an area that for generations was blighted by high unemployment, crime, anti-social behaviour and interfamily feuds. Knife crime was a particular problem. The city and particularly Southill had the highest murder rate outside Dublin in the 1980s and 1990s. Apart from Dublin the bulk of serious crime stories emanated from Limerick. I spent a lot of time in the Treaty City over the decades.

Kelly and his younger brother Anthony, who also had a reputation as a violent criminal, played a major role in the mayhem and helped severely tarnish the city's reputation. The exploits of the Kelly brothers earned Limerick the unflattering media tagline Stab City.

Mikey Kelly was a violent thug with a string of convictions for serious violent crime including wounding, robbery, demanding money with menaces, possession of firearms and shooting at a person with intent to maim and endanger life. He spent over twelve years in prison, with his last recorded conviction in July 1986.

A few years earlier, in 1982, twenty-seven-year-old Kelly was the prime suspect in the murder of another local criminal, Ronnie Coleman, who was associated with two families who were feuding with the Kellys at the time. One night Coleman smashed a pint glass into Kelly's face in a city pub. On 12 October that year Mikey got his revenge when he stabbed Coleman to death in the street. Kelly was tried for murder but was acquitted by the jury.

Two months after the Coleman murder Anthony Kelly, who was twenty-two, ran into Sammy and Tommy McCarthy in the Treaty Bar in Thomondgate in the shadows of King John's Castle. The Kellys were also feuding with the McCarthys. The brothers produced a knife and attacked Anthony Kelly. When it was over the McCarthys had been stabbed to death. Anthony Kelly was subsequently charged with the killings but was acquitted after testifying that he was acting in self-defence.

Mikey Kelly was a clever manipulator of the media and from the late 1980s successfully portrayed himself as an ordinary decent criminal who had retired from a life as a violent brute and wanted to give something back to society. He proclaimed himself a peace maker. It was around that time that I first took an interest in Kelly.

The mobster loved to tell the story of how he underwent his transformation from street thug to model citizen when a local priest called Joe Young visited him in his prison cell in the mid-eighties. Kelly, who was serving a sentence for armed robbery, had beaten up a number of prison warders and there was a standoff at his cell. Father Young arrived to mediate and asked him if he was alright. Kelly claimed that he told the priest to 'fuck off' whereupon Young replied: 'No. You fuck off.' And that, according to Mikey Kelly, was all it took to convert one of the country's most violent thugs into a born-again model citizen. He exploited his 'conversion' for all that it was worth. When he got out of prison Kelly claimed that his only ambition in life was to repay society for the wrongs he had done. The 'reformed' prisoner used his new status living on the coat tails of Fr Young who was a curate in Southill, hiding his criminal activities behind the façade of a community activist.

In 1988 he helped to supervise the Garda Activity Programme in Southill. It was a local community project organized by the gardaí at the local station at Roxboro Road. The aim was to break down the barriers between the police and the local youth. Kelly had discovered the perfect front. He was photographed in the local newspapers at various meetings with senior police officers and began rubbing shoulders with members of the political and business establishment in Limerick.

Kelly's apparent transformation was soon paying dividends. Mikey and Anthony took full advantage of their newfound respectability and set up a security company, M and A Security in 1991. The poachers turned gamekeepers inveigled lucrative contracts from businesses and the Corporation. Break-ins and vandalism were reduced when there was a Kelly sign over the door. It was nothing more than a hugely profitable protection racket. Accepting Kelly's lies effectively gave organized crime a foothold in Limerick whose motto is: 'A city well versed in the art of war.' It proved to be a dreadful mistake that the city would rue for decades.

By making Kelly a bit respectable the Corporation had sent out a toxic signal – in Limerick crime paid. The reality was that the gangster was a parasite. He even used his newfound status as a protector of the people to collect protection money each week from the ordinary, hard-pressed citizens of Southill.

Kelly was an attractive character for the media because he was probably the only criminal ever to speak so frankly about his exploits. The media attention added to his respectable image. I was one of the reporters taken in by the ruse. I first met the gangster and his brother when I interviewed them in 1994. He told me over a cup of tea in his home:

> We both did a lot of very bad, violent things in our past. You name it and we did it – armed robbery, GBH, using firearms with intent to endanger life, the lot. But now crime or violence plays no part in our lives except for the fact that we are in the business of preventing crime and violence through our security

> business. We have made a lot of money but every penny of it has been earned through honest hard work, but we know that some people here in Limerick don't believe that.

In the article I naively wrote about how the two 'reformed' villains prided themselves on their ability to 'deter' other criminals from attacking property or people in their crime-troubled hometown. 'No one messes with us, we take no bullshit from anyone but when we deal with problems we don't break the law,' declared Anthony who confessed that in his criminal days he 'was not as mad as Michael'. I wrote:

> Michael sees himself as a sort of social worker in his hometown and counsels kids about the downside of a life of crime. He wears a lord mayor's chain which was presented to him by the local community for his social work with kids and the old folk.

Kelly told me: 'We tell young people that crime is not the answer to anything and that the only way to be successful in life is hard work and honesty.'

Such frank on-the-record admissions by notorious criminals made for great copy. But over the intervening years I discovered that I, like the rest of the media, had been duped. Every word that came from Kelly's mouth was lies and dissemblance. The gardaí in the city, who knew the real story, had to look on in silent frustration as their top target was rendered virtually untouchable

Kelly's whitewashing operation reached its apex a year later when RTÉ broadcast a flattering documentary about his life, entitled *The Hard Man*. In it he bragged about his past as a 'vicious, dangerous' criminal who had been addicted to booze and violence. But now he had changed.

From then on, he used the media to nurture the image of himself as a reformed criminal battling a system which refused to accept that he had gone straight or, as he would say himself, was 'crime free'. The godfather hid in plain sight using a unique mixture of lies, media leaks, malicious allegations, legal actions and intimidation to protect himself. If anyone dared to question Kelly's scams and lies, he would hold a press conference to declare that there was a 'vendetta against the peace-making Kelly family'.

But later in 1995 Kelly was at the centre of a major criminal investigation when a former associate revealed that he had plotted to murder a local garda. The uniformed officer, Garda Brendan Sheehan, incurred the wrath of the Kelly clan when he took an interest in a pub that Anthony Kelly bought from the proceeds of the brothers' successful security company.

The Hunt Bar on Wickham Street, central Limerick, became a popular haunt for the city's criminals. Anthony openly flouted the licensing laws because the Kellys believed they were above the law. Garda Sheehan had a different view. He insisted that the pub shut its doors at closing time, the same as every other establishment on his beat.

A small-time crook, James O'Gorman, tipped-off gardaí that guns were smuggled in from the UK to carry out the hit on Brendan Sheehan as he drove home after duty. The gang had carried out surveillance on him and knew the route he took. O'Gorman also gave details of fraud and protection rackets Kelly was running at the time. The threats were taken seriously, and a firearm was recovered in a search of the home of one of Mikey Kelly's associates. That summer Brendan Sheehan was transferred from Limerick to Ennis. The garda had to sell his home and move his young family. Like so many other victims of crime that I encountered over the decades Brendan became a friend. He sadly died of natural causes in 2010.

Following the incident Kelly launched a damage limitation offensive and organized a press conference to protest his innocence. I had interviewed Kelly about the allegations and attended the media event which was held in a Limerick hotel. A video was shown of O'Gorman retracting his earlier claims as he sat across a room from Mikey. He made counter allegations that the gardaí had used him to set up the Kelly family.

During the choreographed show Mikey bawled his eyes out and accused the police of not accepting that he was a reformed man. The Kelly family was being victimized. I remember feeling that it was blatantly obvious that O'Gorman had been under duress: the whole thing was a set up by Kelly.

What Mikey or Anthony did not share with the media was that O'Gorman's change of heart occurred after his brother Paul in Manchester ended up on a life-support machine taking his food through a straw. Anthony was arrested and later charged in connection with the assault by the Manchester police but the case was dropped after Mikey visited Paul O'Gorman's girlfriend. O'Gorman then signed an affidavit stating that Anthony Kelly had not beaten him.

The case subsequently featured in a special *Primetime* programme which was broadcast by RTÉ in September 1995. It was a lot less flattering of Mikey Kelly than the previous documentary. In the programme James O'Gorman retracted the supposed confession he'd made in the video with Mikey Kelly. He confirmed that he had plotted to kill Garda Sheehan. Paul O'Gorman also spoke about his assault. Around the same time I also interviewed the O'Gorman brothers who reaffirmed the truth of what had happened. Kelly threatened to sue RTÉ and the *Sunday World* but never proceeded with either case.

Two months later Kelly was hired to force an innocent man, Sean Mescall, to leave Limerick following a custody battle with the mother of his child. I interviewed the victim about the incident some years later. Mescall told me how he had been summoned to Kelly's home. He had never met the infamous gangster before but recognized him from TV. Kelly was sitting behind a desk like a modern-day Don Corleone. Mescall told me:

> He said: 'Sean, you know who I am. Now as regards your situation I know more about it than you think.' He then said that there was someone out looking for me, but he [Mikey] could stop it. I was shocked and didn't know what to say. Then Kelly said to me: 'My advice to you is to leave the country for four or five years and if you want to see your son you can come through me.'

When Mescall didn't comply, he was abducted by two of Kelly's henchmen. They slashed his face with a knife and pistol whipped him. He went to the police and the associates, Pat Nash and Alan Wallace, were subsequently convicted. The woman's brother who had hired Kelly (unbeknown to her) was also charged and got a suspended sentence. I subsequently interviewed him and he admitted hiring Kelly to intimidate Mescall.

Kelly was also arrested but the Director of Public Prosecutins (DPP) decided there was insufficient evidence with which to charge him.

As he continued his life of crime two of Kelly's associates went missing and gardaí believed he'd had them murdered. One was believed to have been buried in the foundations of Kelly's home. When I later put the allegation to the mob boss he denied it with a flick of his hand saying: 'Sure let the police dig it up.'

As all this was going on the local media in Limerick continued to lap up everything Mikey had to say. He gave them plenty of juicy copy. Over time Kelly grew more confident and mounted campaigns to undermine the police at every opportunity for the benefit of the emerging crime gangs in the city. He used the local newspapers and an illegal pirate radio station to announce that he was setting up a private police force in Southill because the gardaí were not doing their job.

His typical modus operandi bore many similarities to that of US president Donald Trump. He made outrageously false allegations in the local media against unnamed local politicians, businesspeople and police officers who had crossed him or his family. There would be no evidence to back up his insidious claims which he invariably dropped once the seed of doubt had been sown in the public mind.

Inevitably the man of the people turned his attention to politics. In the 1999 local elections he was elected to the city council, He topped the poll and earned the title of Alderman, from then on referring to himself as 'Alderman Michael Kelly'. His election was made possible when the previous incumbent in the Southill area opted out of politics after being the subject of a false smear campaign circulated by Kelly. Organized crime had won a major victory.

Kelly wasted no time in causing chaos in local politics. Shortly after his election in September 1999 Kelly presented an unidentified boy to a number of journalists and told a chilling story about how he and other boys had been paid for sex by a paedophile ring that included well-known local politicians.

The sordid allegations made front page news in Limerick and featured in the national newspapers. A former mayor who was married with children was forced to deny the sex smears in the *Limerick Leader*. But by then the non-existent rent boy sex ring story had consumed the city. The shit had stuck.

When I interviewed him about the claims Kelly promised that the case would be brought before the courts because the boys concerned were under his 'protection'. He then called for the resignations of two politicians he named. But he couldn't produce a shred of evidence to back up the claims. I put pressure on the mobster to allow me to meet the boys to hear their stories which he promised to do. He never produced them. The case disappeared and so did the youngster. From then on I had no doubt that he was a dangerous charlatan. Kelly had learned the value of the sex smear.

The lawlessness continued as Kelly helped sow the seeds for one of the worst gangland feuds in Irish criminal history and did everything in his power to nurture them. In 2000 the notorious Dundon family arrived in the city from London and teamed up with their cousins the McCarthys. Together they became the most dangerous crime gang ever seen in Ireland. I dubbed them Ireland's Murder Inc.

The McCarthy/Dundons became embroiled in a series of bitter and complex feuds with other criminal families including the Caseys and the McNamaras. But they later settled their differences when Wayne Dundon, the leader of Murder Inc., married one of the Caseys.

The two sides then joined forces and went after the McNamaras. It led to a string of shootings, assaults and abductions as up to four extended families got involved. Houses and cars belonging to each side were burned out and shots were fired through front windows. Luckily no one was killed.

Members of other families, including Anthony Kelly, also got involved in the mayhem. Kelly was charged with shooting nineteen-year-old Paddy Casey in the face.

The local gardaí were determined to bring the situation under control. An inspector in Roxboro garda station, Jim Browne, set up an operation to put an end to the feuding. Browne would later find himself on the frontline in the war against the Limerick gangs. He is still remembered as one of the heroes in the battle against organized crime in the city.

The gardaí charged up to twenty of the combatants from the different families, with serious offences including criminal damage, assault and possession of firearms. Such were the myriad charges that the victim in one case could also be the accused in another. Due to police objections to bail most of the thugs were locked up while awaiting trial which restored a degree of calm to the city. But then Alderman Mikey Kelly stepped in to make matters much worse.

Amid much public fanfare Kelly established his own version of a 'peace process'. The motivation was to pervert the course of justice and get Anthony off the charge of shooting Paddy Casey. Kelly 'brokered' peace between the various protagonists and victims in a bid to undermine the garda investigations. As a result all the victims who had given statements to the police in the various criminal cases shook hands and withdrew their evidence.

Kelly organized choreographed press conferences for the local media where the former enemies posed for pictures and shook hands. As each case came before the courts the charges were struck out as none of the injured parties were prepared to give evidence. At one stage Kelly was getting more publicity than all the sitting TDs and ministers in the city combined.

Mikey's strategy was a spectacular success. I covered the extraordinary developments as they unfolded between 2000 and 2001. It was incredible to witness how one man could do so much to undermine the rule of law in full public view while the gardaí could only look on in sheer frustration. The Alderman was turning Limerick into his own version of Gotham City.

Kelly began to consider himself to be omnipotent. Every time a member of the family or an associate was stopped or arrested Mikey organized protest vigils outside Roxboro garda station. He was openly intimidating the local gardaí. The main target of Kelly's venom was Inspector Browne.

Long serving local TD Willie O'Dea, who had represented the people of Limerick since 1982, was one of the only public figures unafraid to take on the gangster politician. In 2001 he had a public showdown with Kelly at a charity function in the city. At the time O'Dea was Minister for Education and Science. He later became Minister for Defence. During speeches the Alderman grabbed the microphone and made a bitter personal attack on O'Dea. The furious minister got to his feet and in front of 300 witnesses called Kelly a 'liar, a criminal and a scumbag'.

Kelly instructed his equally dodgy solicitor, John Devane, to send Minister O'Dea a letter demanding an apology the next day. Minister O'Dea wrote 'see you in court' on the letter and sent it back to Devane. That summer I also received a letter from Devane alleging that I had libelled the Alderman in a story I had written in the *Sunday World* about how he was undermining the rule of law. Our lawyer Gerry Fanning sent back a 'fuck off' letter and, like Willie O'Dea, said we would see him in court. Previously Kelly had received a cash settlement from the paper when his picture was mistakenly used in a different crime story. I was determined that he wasn't going to get any more payouts.

In the meantime, however, it appeared that nothing could stop the political ambitions of gangland's equivalent of Donald Trump. He made no secret of the fact that he was going to contest the General Election in 2002 as an independent candidate. All the opinion polls indicated that he was on course to win. But then in August 2001 the wheels began to come off Kelly's bandwagon.

―――

Kelly's wife Majella had endured an appalling marriage with the monster since she first met him at the age of fifteen. For twenty years he had subjected her to an ordeal of constant beatings, psychological abuse and coercive control. On 24 August 2001, after yet another assault, she decided that she could take no more and went to Inspector Jim Browne and his officers to make a complaint of assault. In her initial statement to the police she described what had happened:

> He [Michael] started roaring abuse at me, calling me a bastard, saying he was now ruined because of me. He kicked me and I fell on the ground. He kicked me into the head and at my legs. He pulled me back up and started digging me in the face. He said to me, 'You bastard you, I should finish you.'

With Browne's help she obtained a barring order in the local courts. Two days later the gardaí arrested Kelly after he breached the barring order and assaulted Majella in the family home. He was charged and held in custody for two days.

On 29 August Kelly was brought before the court. Majella announced that she was withdrawing her complaint. Inspector Browne, who represented the State at the hearing, asked Majella if her husband had assaulted her. 'I was assaulted,' she replied, 'but I also assaulted my husband. It was both ways.'

The charges against Kelly were dropped. He had succeeded in thwarting the law again. As he left court the Alderman told reporters that the case would not harm his political campaign in the forthcoming national elections. He would be a voice for the city's downtrodden. He later went on the illegal pirate radio station and made allegations that his wife was forced by the police to smear him. He typically claimed to being the real victim. But the matter had not ended there. That was where I got involved.

Two days later, on Friday 31 August 2001, I got a call from Willie O'Dea. I had known Willie ever since I first started working in the *Sunday World*. He is a politician that I have always had huge respect for and consider him a friend. Willie O'Dea has always exemplified the qualities of what it means to be a public representative which is why he holds the record of consistently being the biggest vote-getter in the country.

O'Dea knew that I was one of the reporters who had been investigating Kelly. He told me that Majella Kelly wanted to talk to me about the abuse she had suffered. She was angry that her husband was circulating a claim that the local gardaí had forced her to make the original complaint.

On the pirate radio show that he used as his own propaganda platform, Kelly had demanded a tribunal of enquiry to investigate a police conspiracy to damage his political career. The legitimate, licensed Limerick radio station, Live95, had nothing to do with propagating his lies. Mikey said that he had merely slapped his wife's back during an asthma attack. I completely agreed that it was time that Kelly was exposed as an abusive thug.

Willie gave me a number for Jim Browne who I didn't know at the time. Although wary of the call from an unknown reporter he confirmed that Majella had told him that she specifically wanted to talk to me. She didn't want to talk to a journalist from Limerick because she feared that the local press was too friendly with her husband. Majella also knew that I had previously locked horns with Kelly.

The senior garda told me that she was anxious to put the record straight about her husband's allegations. He said that she was in hiding and then gave me her number. She had told him that she could take a call that evening around 5 p.m.

I later phoned Majella Kelly. Given the sensitivity of the case and the fact that she was living in fear of her husband I decided that it was wiser to record the conversation. There was a risk that if she was prepared to go on the record and I published the story, her husband could force her to recant. He would then sue us.

I was conscious that she had done a similar volte face a few days earlier in Limerick court. Browne told me that she had made a statement to gardaí already, repudiating her husband's claims that she had been forced by them to make her initial complaint.

I had planned to attend the removal that evening of Vinnie Ryan, the father of DJ Gerry Ryan. The brilliant 2FM shock jock extraordinaire, who passed away in 2010, was a good friend. I had to cancel my plans. Gerry of all people understood the importance of getting the story. It was to prove to be a very significant decision – particularly for the gangster politician.

The following is an extract from the transcript of my phone call to Majella Kelly.

PW: Majella how are you doing? I am sorry to be talking to you in these circumstances; things have gone a bit sad for you?

MK: Ah well.

PW: How are you feeling?

MK: I am grand yeah.

PW: I believe you are hiding at the moment, are you?

MK: Well, I came back to Limerick today only to make a statement of my whereabouts on the night the house took fire. [There had been a fire in the family home around the time that Kelly was arrested. Gardaí suspected he had caused it as a distraction.]

PW: Now tell me this, it is quite obvious from looking at the reports and from talking to people that you are in fear.

MK: Yeah.

PW: That you made the allegations against Michael that he was beating you and then you withdrew them.

MK: Yeah.

PW: Did he threaten you? Why did you withdraw them?

MK: Just two reasons now, Paul: one was that my kids begged me, one of them threatened that he would do away with himself and one threatened that he would run away if I got their father locked up. And secondly, at the end of all this I was just thinking that this was an everyday thing.

This is the first time I actually went to the Guards about the beatings. I know I was in shock. I was terrified. I know he threatened me and the whole shebang but when I sat down and thought about it – I wouldn't like anyone locked up. I wouldn't see him locked up – do you understand? I mean my opinion now is that I get on with my life and he gets on with his life.

PW: How often did he beat you?

MK: Well, I met him twenty years ago.

PW: Was it under the influence of alcohol that he did it or was it just a normal occurrence? How did he beat you?

MK: He used his hands and legs. Kicking me and digging me.

PW: What kind of things would set him off?

MK: Anything, Paul, anything could trigger him.

PW: Would he take out his frustration on you that something had gone wrong during the day for him?

MK: In drink. Now if it was something that was said to him in the pub, he would come home by night and take it out on me.

PW: Is it true that you had to go the Accident and Emergency unit at the local hospital last week after the beating, the last beating?

MK: I did go to the hospital, yeah.

PW: And what kind of injuries did you have, Majella?

MK: All the left side of my jaw and my eye was swollen. It still is now but it's not very bad now. It is gone down now but I still can't chew with it.

PW: What are you going to do now? I saw himself [Mikey] and Anthony on TV the other evening and they did look quite intimidating.

MK: Imagine when you are in court against all that, Paul, and all his family there and nobody with me?

PW: Are the police protecting you at the moment?

MK: Well, I tell you now, they are very good to me. People think they are intimidating me and forcing me to make statements, but they are not. I am my own person. I am capable of doing what I want to do. Do you know what I am saying? And Michael said on the radio that he gave me a slap on the back because I got the worst case of an asthma attack and that they hadn't seen anything like that in medical history.

PW: Is that true or is it a lie?

MK: It is a spoof. I did get an asthma attack like, you know, it was a severe asthma attack like you know. But I mean asthma is asthma, you know, you have your good days and your bad days.

PW: But I don't think you would put a woman in an Accident and Emergency Unit trying to give her a slap on the back to help her cough. That is a bit of a strange excuse, isn't it?

MK: His excuse there was that I was hysterical, Paul. I was not hysterical. I was shaking. I will admit when he came up to the room I was shaking.

PW: There are a lot of serious question marks over Michael's business dealings, and that anyone who falls out with him in business tends to have their places burned down afterwards and all kinds of accidents happen.

MK: This is what I heard. I have only heard this in the last few days.

PW: Did you ever hear your husband plotting any kind of criminal activity?

MK: No and I am telling the Gospel truth about that; no, I never, but if there was a meeting going on I would automatically get up and walk out. I am not one to listen, Paul, I don't and that is the truth. Now don't get me wrong, I used to look after the business – things to do with the business – getting contracts and things. The business side of it was mine. But I signed everything over to him after the last argument. I signed everything over to him.

PW: And he has been beating you for twenty years and this is the first time you ever went to the gardaí?

MK: Yeah, the first time – I really wanted out of the marriage this time. I really did and it is not because there was anything going on or I am not having an affair with anybody, or . . . it is nothing to do with that. I have just gone thirty-five years of age. I have been beaten since I was fifteen years of age. I don't need that life anymore.

PW: So, you are saying Majella that violence was part and parcel of everyday life with Michael Kelly? Was it both mental and physical torture?

MK: Yeah. Everything I done was wrong or stupid or you know, accidents would happen. Now let's supposing I spilled a drop of tea. He would shout, 'Look at that fucking eejit, can you do anything right?' You know if he was in bad form this is all I used to hear.

PW: Tell me about Kelly's business and his politics.

MK: He would not answer the phones, he would not answer the calls, the same with the public – he would not answer the people. It was me who had to answer them you know.

PW: And why was that?

MK: Because he was so wrapped up in drink. His king now is drink, drink, drink. He wants nothing to do with anything but drink. He gave up his family and he stayed for drink. Many a night, Paul, I stayed in the car. I slept in the car all night on my own regularly.

PW: Why is that?

MK: Out of fear that he'd find me you see. You would have to give him two or three weeks to mellow down until he comes to his senses and then he'll phone and say 'look, come home, I am sorry' and blah, blah and all that.

PW: Are you going to leave Limerick?

MK: Well, I am going for a protection order and a safety order on Monday right.

PW: Are the gardaí going to help you?

MK: Oh, they will, they will.

PW: Are you going to tell the judge why you withdrew your charges?

MK: No, I can't Paul. I can't tell anybody that. I'd love to pour my heart out to someone, but I couldn't tell anyone that.

PW: I think your safest thing is the publicity around the case because he will be terrified to go fucking near you because of the publicity.

MK: Yeah you see I can't tell anybody why I really withdrew them charges. My main concern was my kids, Paul, that genuinely my main concern was my kids. Now he is saying he was terrified. I am laughing at this. I can't get over this fact. He said he was terrified of me. He said he had to lock himself into presses. He said people often had to restrain me with the anger that I got into. I can honestly and truthfully say this, I never told the man to fuck off in my life; I never raised my voice. Now my eyes are opened.

Do you know when my eyes were opened, and this is the truth? The day in the court, the Monday in the court. He picked up the bible and swore on that bible he did not hit me. I said to myself, my God I can't believe what I am after hearing from that man.

I tell you the truth. I went up today and I made a statement to Jim Browne. I went to Jim Browne and I said to Jim, 'Look I say what I have to say that you didn't force me into making a statement.' I said you didn't put words into my mouth. I am of perfect mind and body and I said I made that statement from myself. 'You did not force me,' I said, 'you did not put words in my mouth,' I said. A detective came into me and asked me if I wanted to make a statement and I said yes.

PW: This is the statement you made to Jim Browne today about you withdrawing your statement.

MK: Jim Browne, the Kellys are saying that Jim Browne forced me into making a statement and put words in my mouth.

PW: So, you made a statement to the police about that.

MK: Yeah.

PW: And did you give them the same reason as you gave me for withdrawing the charges?

MK: No, I didn't explain why I withdrew the charges. I went in and said that Jim Browne did not intimidate me into making a statement or put words in my mouth. That I made the statement of my own free will. I am of sound mind and body, and you know, I think I am capable enough to make any of my own decisions.

PW: Yeah.

MK: But I mean why should that man fall in for it because they think he intimidated me. Do you know what I said to him? That 'you were doing your job', I said, and 'I am glad that you are there for me doing your job.' I said, 'I am glad that you were there for me.'

PW: Majella you have my home number, and my mobile number don't you? You can ring me at any time.

MK: I don't. I didn't take your numbers off him [Browne] because

> I will tell you why. If anything happens you see and if they get my phone there are numbers on my phone. I don't dial people.

Before the interview ended I asked Majella if she really wanted to go on the record and publish what she had just told me. I was concerned that it might push Michael Kelly over the edge and cause her even more harm.

As a journalist you have a duty of care to the people whose stories you tell. She said that she didn't want it published yet but wanted me to have a record of what she had told me. I remember thinking that she wanted to leave a record of her true story in the event that she ended up dead. We left it at that.

The months of August, September and October 2001 were an emotionally tumultuous time in my life. In July my dad, Benny, was diagnosed with terminal pancreatic cancer. We were told he had a few months to live. I was utterly heartbroken. Whenever I was on my own I cried uncontrollably and had a permanent pain in my chest. My mum and sisters were also distraught.

My dad was the ultimate cool dude in my life. Sometimes a soft American twang could be detected in his accent as he'd spent a number of years working as a long-distance trucker in the US. Quiet and extremely wise, he worked the rest of his life in the family business in Leitrim, quarry drilling, with his brothers Seamus and Larry. They had been very successful and at one time Williams Brothers was the largest privately owned drilling company in the country. Many years before, when my wonderful granny Ellen was alive, there had been an ambition that I might join the business. This was before journalism turned my head. The company ceased trading in 1996 when Dad and Uncle Larry retired. Benny loved a few pints and the craic with his family and friends. He was also a besotted granddad to my two kids.

The day after the 9/11 attacks on New York I arranged with Professor John Crown, one of the country's foremost consultant oncologists, to have him admitted as a patient under his care in St Vincent's Hospital in Dublin. A kind-hearted local detective from Crumlin garda station, who was involved in protecting my family at the time, collected my dad from the train with me.

Dad got a buzz when the officer put on the flashing blue lights and siren as we sped towards Vincents to get there in time. I remember how he laughed excitedly as the squad car weaved through the heavy afternoon traffic. It was to be his last jaunt in life. In reality Dad needed hospice care but there were no places available in the Northwest region.

When I consulted Professor Crown he effectively broke all the rules when he agreed to look after my dad until he passed away. He had Benny admitted through A and E. Our family will never forget him for that act of immeasurable kindness.

The attacks on the Twin Towers had claimed the lives of almost 3,000 people the previous day. One of them was John O'Neill, the FBI's former top terrorism expert on Osama bin Laden and al-Qaeda. I had known John for many years, and we had become friends. His death added to the dark clouds looming over my world. (See *Crooks*.) The *Sunday World* asked me to go to New York to cover the biggest crime story in the world, I was at first reluctant, but Dad insisted that I go.

Then on 28 September my *Sunday World* colleague and friend, Martin O'Hagan, was assassinated in Lurgan, Co. Armagh, by a loyalist drug gang. Marty was walking home from the pub with his wife Marie when a hitman shot him dead.

Just five years after the murder of Veronica Guerin his execution came as a numbing, heartbreaking blow to journalists everywhere but particularly on the *Sunday World*. I remember receiving the awful news from RTÉ's Paul Reynolds that Friday night, just after I had returned from visiting my dad in hospital. Paul said: 'I am sorry to say your friend has been murdered Paulie.'

I really felt like the world was falling asunder.

Dad bore his illness with a courage that astounded everyone who knew him. He was a very popular man and had a non-ending succession of visitors at his bedside. He would sit up in his hospital bed and every now and again ask me to phone different family friends back in Leitrim. It took all the power in my body to hold back the tears as I listened to him telling the person on the other side how thankful he was for their friendship and then saying a cheery goodbye. When some of my garda friends visited Benny they later told me that he asked them to make sure and mind my family and me. He showed no fear of death. He had lived a full and happy life.

Benny even gave us instructions as to who should carry his coffin. He also wanted former Fine Gael TD Gerry Reynolds, a close family friend, to sing his favourite song by the Fureys, *The Auld Man*. More importantly he wanted us to have a massive piss up in the Reynolds' family pub and in my friend Gay Prior's famous hostelry, Priors, in Ballinamore.

In the early hours of 21 October dad passed away peacefully as my mum Patricia, my sisters Caroline and Bernie and I sat at his bedside. He was seventy-four years old. His funeral was a huge affair. Our neighbours, friends and family gave him a right good Leitrim send off. There was no closing time in Priors that night.

I took dad's death very hard. I was devastated. In the days after the funeral an old garda friend who had experienced much worse grief in his own life gave me some solid advice. He told me to find a story to investigate and throw all my energies into it to distract from the grief. It had worked for him in the past. Fortunately, I had one at hand: an in-depth investigation of Alderman Mikey Kelly.

As it turned out events in Limerick had conspired in my favour. In September there had been an extraordinary development in Mikey Kelly's vendetta against Inspector Jim Browne and the police. Majella Kelly had come forward to make an outrageous claim that Browne had subjected her to sexual assault and sexual harassment. Willie O'Dea and my garda contacts had tipped me off about the claims that no one believed.

Majella alleged that Browne had sexually assaulted her at Roxboro garda station when she'd made her original complaint against her husband. She further claimed that the respected garda had sexually harassed her in repeated phone calls between 23 August and 17 September 2001.

It was as clear as day that Mikey Kelly had forced his wife to make the allegations which were the complete antithesis to what she had told me. The proof of that was that the recorded interview had taken place several days after the first alleged assault. According to Majella's current claims the sexual harassment by Inspector Browne was going on at the time that she spoke to me – but she never mentioned it.

It wasn't a surprise either that it was Kelly's solicitor, John Devane, who had initiated a private prosecution on Majella's behalf against Inspector Browne in the District Court. As a defence lawyer

Devane had an unhealthy, and at times unprofessional, association with Kelly and other criminals in the city, especially the McCarthy/Dundons. Devane saw himself as Kelly's *consigliore*.

At one stage Devane was suspected of using his position as a defence lawyer to relay information between suspects as they were being held in custody for serious offences including gangland murders. Some years later it was discovered he had advised members of the Dundon clan to pretend they had been sexually assaulted by a senior cop – Jim Browne.

It was yet another classic example of a Mikey Kelly-inspired sexual smear campaign. The wife-beating mob boss was determined to destroy the one Limerick cop he saw as a serious threat to him and his criminal associates.

John Devane had also submitted a complaint on Majella's behalf containing the allegations to the Garda Complaints Board in late September. It was quickly dismissed as vexatious on the grounds that Majella had made a full voluntary statement exonerating Browne and his colleagues at Roxboro Road of forcing her to make a complaint against her husband. That took place on 31 August, the same day that she spoke to me.

If such an allegation were made today the garda would be immediately suspended and left in limbo for years before the case was resolved. The Garda Síochána Ombudsman Commission (GSOC) – now Fiosrú – has a notorious record for taking years to complete investigations. A similar charge can be placed at the door of An Garda Síochána's own internal units who investigate allegations of malfeasance.

In similar cases the lives and reputations of gardaí who are eventually deemed innocent have been irreparably damaged. I am aware of a number of officers in the recent past who suffered nervous breakdowns only to be completely cleared of wrongdoing three or four years later. Unlike any other Irish citizen, gardaí are deemed to be guilty until proven innocent.

In this case I possessed incontrovertible evidence that Jim Browne was completely innocent: the recorded admissions of the woman making the allegation. There are some in the journalism profession, however, who promulgate that getting involved in such a case is outside the ethical boundaries of the job. I remember discussing it with Colm MacGinty and the *Sunday World's* solicitor Gerry Fanning. They agreed that I should follow my instincts and provide the tape to Browne's defence team. It was time that Kelly was properly exposed.

I still remember MacGinty's comment. He took a long drag of his cigarette, rubbed his head and calmly remarked: 'We can't allow a man to be destroyed by a lying thug like Mikey Kelly, especially if we have the evidence. That would be a dreadful injustice.'

I headed to Limerick a week or so after my dad's funeral to continue covering the ongoing internecine feuding and Kelly's effort to undermine the law. It was to be the first of many such trips to the Treaty City over the next six months. I phoned the office of Chief Superintendent Gerry Kelly who was in charge of the Limerick Division at the time and requested a meeting.

He was reluctant to give time to a reporter, especially as he was knee deep in feud-related crimes. I told him that it was as much in his interests as it was mine. When we met in his office in Henry Street station I got straight to the point. I said I wasn't there to talk about gangs. I wanted to talk off the record about the allegations against Browne.

The Chief Superintendent said it was a concoction of lies and Browne would be getting all the support he needed to fight the claims if or when they were brought to court. His main concern was that even if the case was dismissed or dropped, doubts about his top officer would linger and Kelly would continue to spread his lies.

I still remember the look of surprise on his face when I told him that I had a tape that could prove Browne's innocence beyond any doubt. I was happy to hand over a copy of the tape and said that, if subpoenaed, I was prepared to testify as to the provenance of the recording in court.

The following day I met Jim Browne for the first time. My revelation of the existence of the tape had been quickly sent up the line to the office of the Garda Commissioner Pat Byrne. Browne, however, was typically sceptical of journalists, as are most cops. When we met he was very wary of me and my motivations. He even checked to see if I was wearing a recording device. Given his experiences over recent months, I reckoned he was entitled to be suspicious.

Browne seemed shocked that I had come forward to help him. I handed him a copy of the tape. All of this was kept strictly under wraps because there was no guarantee that the Kelly engineered private prosecution would go ahead. If it didn't then we had decided to publish the contents of the tape in the *Sunday World* regardless. By making the allegations I believed Majella Kelly had negated any duty of care. Even if she was being coerced, which she undoubtedly was, she was still lying. After all she had freely given the interview. Mikey Kelly ensured that everyone in Limerick knew about the allegation. Even if the case didn't go ahead the damage to Browne's reputation had been done – mud sticks.

In the meantime I had requested permission from the Garda Press Office to go on patrol with the cops in Limerick as part of my ongoing investigation of crime in the city. I had also contacted

Mikey Kelly and informed him that I was preparing a major story about him for the *Sunday World*. I said I had a number of serious allegations to put to him and wanted to give him an opportunity to give his side of the story. Kelly, who considered himself a master of media manipulation, said he had nothing to hide. We had two very lengthy meetings.

The longest face-to-face interview took place in the Castletroy Hotel on 16 November 2001. It lasted about three hours during which I put to him every allegation and piece of evidence there was against him. I recorded the interview and so did the Alderman.

I had interviewed several people including Sean Mescall, the man he had abducted and beaten to force him out of the city. I also talked to the brother-in-law who had hired Kelly. I had information from businesspeople who had once used Kelly's security company. When they stopped using M and A Security in favour of other more legit security companies their premises were burgled, vandalized or burned. Of course he denied everything and blamed the police for spreading 'lies' to discredit him.

At the end of the interview Kelly handed me a subpoena to appear as a witness in the forthcoming private prosecution against Jim Browne. It was clear that he had this planned for a while. He knew that I had interviewed his wife. I questioned him about some of the things she had told me, but I didn't share the fact that it was all on tape. I was pleasantly surprised that he had sought a court order compelling me to give evidence in the case. It meant that Browne's side didn't have to. But being a witness for Majella Kelly also meant that her lawyer could not cross examine me. Kelly was walking himself into a trap.

That evening, along with photographer Padraig O'Reilly, we accompanied a special garda foot patrol through some of the estates in the south of the city worst hit by crime and feuding. Inspector Jim Browne, the best-known cop in the city, happened to be in charge. But it was very quiet with no incidents taking place. It was like every villain in Limerick had taken the night off. Around midnight Browne and two of his men were giving us a lift back to our hotel when another car came towards us. It was being driven erratically and at high speed. The cops gave chase. At last, we would have something to report.

After a short pursuit the squad car hemmed in the suspect car. Inspector Browne opened the driver's door and he fell out. He was blind drunk and was immediately arrested. The driver was charged with drunk driving and dangerous driving. He was later convicted.

When the gardaí then asked the passenger to get out for a drug search he became hostile and aggressive. One of the officers present told him to go home. When he continued to hurl abuse, he was also arrested. The passenger was charged with a breach of the Public Order Act. We took a picture of the arrest and went back to the hotel.

The following morning I got a call from Mikey Kelly. He said that he had another example of how the police were harassing his family. The previous night the cops had arrested his brother's stepson, David Roche. During the incident he claimed that the gardaí had deliberately targeted Roche to 'create publicity against his father Anthony and against me'.

It just so happened to have been the same incident that I had witnessed but I didn't know the name of the arrested man or his pedigree. When I told Kelly I was there he promptly hung up the phone.

A few weeks later in early December Majella Kelly's private prosecution case came before the District Court but it was adjourned, as it was on a number of occasions before finally being heard in March 2002. As I was entering the court building I was approached by Anthony Kelly.

Kelly handed me a subpoena to appear as a witness for the defence at David Roche's upcoming public order hearing which was a very minor case. Anthony had arranged for a local press photographer to record him handing me the document. It was duly reported in one of the local newspapers.

After that I made several trips to Limerick to attend the hearings which were also adjourned. Even though he knew that the cases were not going ahead on those days John Devane insisted on me being there anyway. When I confronted him about this Devane told me that if I did not turn up at the next hearing he would seek a bench warrant for my arrest. It was obvious that Mikey and his lawyer were using the law to harass me.

Gerry Fanning fired off a letter assuring Devane that I would turn up when the case actually came to hearing but would not be doing so when it was to be adjourned. He suggested that if Devane continued to abuse the court system to harass me then the *Sunday World* would refer the matter to the presiding judge and the Law Society.

When the public order case finally came to hearing on 31 January 2002 I was in court as ordered. Even though it was a minor offence Mikey Kelly and his solicitor Devane were determined to turn it into a publicity stunt to aid his political ambitions to achieve a seat in the Dáil. What happened next was bizarre to say the least. The Alderman wanted to make me the focus of the hearing.

The first witness called by Devane was Mikey Kelly who only wanted to talk about the interviews I had conducted with him a few months earlier. He said he had brought a tape of the interview from November. He claimed that it contained proof that the police had told me 'things about him'.

Judge Tom O'Donnell interrupted to say that he was dealing with a public order offence and nothing else. He told the Alderman to leave the witness box. As he did Kelly approached a journalist and offered her a copy of the said tape. Judge O'Donnell ordered him to leave the court.

The arresting gardaí gave their evidence of what happened. Devane accused them of trying to create negative publicity about the Kelly family – 'primarily Alderman Michael Kelly' – for the benefit of the *Sunday World*. Devane said that his client, Roche, believed he had been targeted because of a 'vendetta Inspector Browne is waging against the Kelly family'. It was all absolute nonsense.

When I was called to give evidence I told the court why I was in Limerick and what I saw. It also gave me an opportunity to put some of the information I had about Kelly on the public record. After all I was there as a defence witness. I was questioned by Devane about the accusations the Alderman had made before he was turfed out of the courtroom.

I confirmed that I had interviewed Mikey. I said: 'I put to him serious allegations that he was plotting to murder at least one or more gardaí in Limerick.'

In the end Judge O'Donnell fined Roche €300. In reference to the 'vendetta' line from Kelly he said: 'It is my view that nothing could be further from the truth.'

The judge said that it was 'coincidental' and 'fortunate' that a reporter had been there to give independent evidence of what happened, adding 'While all these coincidences occurred I am asked to believe it was a set-up to do the Kelly family down. I don't accept that.'

The whole circus demonstrated the Alderman's contempt for the law. It also showed him and his solicitor up to be idiots.

Majella Kelly's private prosecution case came before the District Court on 4 March 2002 and lasted three days. The case was heard by Judge Peter Smithwick who was the president of the District Court. It reflected the seriousness with which the case was being taken. The local Limerick judiciary had opted not to hear the private prosecution to avoid even more conspiracy claims by Mikey and his mob.

The transcripts of the taped interview were in the possession of Browne's legal team. I remember the quizzical expression on Devane's face when speakers were brought into the courtroom to play the tape that he knew nothing about. As Majella Kelly was the one who brought the prosecution there was no onus on Browne's defence to inform them of the evidence they would be presenting in court.

The court was packed with garda witnesses and the media. Devane and Kelly had been briefing the press for months and promised that the case would be sensational. Also in court that day were members of a CAB team who had been dispatched to investigate Kelly's ill-gotten gains by Detective Chief Superintendent Felix McKenna. Kelly was equally determined to thwart their efforts. Another team of detectives were also there from Cork. They had been assigned to investigate what amounted to Kelly's public intimidation of the gardaí in Roxboro.

Since first making Majella's claims public Kelly had distributed thousands of leaflets on Limerick Corporation headed stationary outlining the allegations against Inspector Browne and the terrible toll it had taken on his wife and family. Kelly also accused the police of conducting a conspiracy against him. It was an outrageous abuse of power which no one seemed to be able to do anything about.

The Kellys had also placed placards citing the allegations and demanding tribunals of inquiry on a van which was parked outside Roxboro garda station for several weeks. Mikey was determined to pull off the biggest publicity smear stunt in his career. He reckoned that it would surely propel him into the Dáil and destroy his garda nemesis in the process.

As the complainant Majella Kelly was the first witness. She took the stand, swore an oath to tell the truth and then told a tissue of lies. I knew in that moment that I had made the right decision to breach normal journalistic practice of impartiality. How could anyone stand back in the face of such a blatant attempt to destroy the life of an innocent man? I will never forget the anger I felt witnessing what was a manifestation of coercive control and spousal abuse in its most sinister form. The only reason she had left herself open to public humiliation was abject fear of her husband.

She told the court of the alleged incident that was central to her case:

> He [Browne] brought me upstairs to a room and told me they were after arresting my husband. I said I wanted to drop the charges, but he said I couldn't. He told me to sit on a chair in the room. He was standing behind me. He put his hand on my left breast and said I could do better than him [Kelly]. I caught his hand and threw it away. I asked him what the fuck did he think he was doing. I heard my brother-in-law Anthony whistling outside and told Jim Browne he was there. He flew around to the other side of the table.

She said she felt terrified: 'I was going through enough with a domestic dispute. I was going through a bad time with my husband.' Majella claimed that the injuries she had sustained were accidental. 'I had fallen against the bunk bed, because the floor was wet,' she said.

Jim Browne's defence counsel, Brendan Nix SC, cross-examined Majella for several hours over the next two days. As he did so he referred to excerpts from the tape transcript and questioned how her comments to me were completely at variance with what she was now saying in court. When John Devane learned that a tape was to be played he sought an adjournment to seek higher legal advice on its admissibility. The tape recording was perfectly legal and above board. The judge ruled that it could be used.

Before it was played I was called to testify how the recording came about. John Devane was put in a terrible pickle because he could not cross-examine me as I was after all a witness for the prosecution. I told the court how I recorded the conversation and when. I then commented:

> I had put to her the fact that she had told me a completely different story about the assault. Inspector Browne was being accused of extremely serious crimes and he could potentially be ruined. I decided to break from the normal journalistic modus operandi and hand over the tape. I could not sit by and see a man's life and family be destroyed.

Then Majella Kelly returned to the stand. I genuinely felt really sorry for her. She sat there listening as her voice streamed from the speakers telling a completely different story to the one she had just related to the judge. She showed no emotion and insisted that her allegations were true. It was excruciating to watch. I will never forget how you could hear a pin drop in the packed courtroom which was standing room only. It seemed like all of Limerick was there.

On the third day of the hearing Mikey Kelly took to the stand to finish giving his evidence which had begun the previous day. Needless to say Browne's defence team had put him through the ringer. For the first time Kelly had left himself completely open to be grilled on his lies and smear tactics. He said that since the case had begun 'my character, my credibility, my business, everything has been open to allegations and ridicule.' No one in the crowded courtroom could disagree with him. It was an example of well-deserved karma.

After all it was Kelly who had initiated the circus. He complained that his mother had suffered a 'cardiac response' when the CAB had raided her home on 24 October the previous year. Several properties associated with the Kellys had been searched at the time including his solicitor's office.

In his closing remarks Brendan Nix SC said that because of the contradictions in the evidence that Majella Kelly could not be believed. He said that she had been put up to making the false claims by her husband, commenting: 'This is a campaign by the Kelly family to obstruct and impede the gardaí at Roxboro from doing their duty.'

He said the only conclusion was that Jim Browne was innocent of the allegations. In reference to my involvement, which had been criticized by a number of other journalists at the time, he said:

> When this man discovered this conspiracy he courageously brought it to the attentions of the authorities and broke with his own right to privilege which I have not seen before in journalistic history.

John Devane attempted to clutch victory from the jaws of defeat by insisting his client was truthful. But by then the die was cast and the mendacious stroke had failed spectacularly.

In dismissing the case Judge Peter Smithwick said that he believed Majella Kelly was being coerced into making the claims by Mikey Kelly. Referring to Alderman Kelly Judge Smithwick said:

> People who physically abuse their wives can be manipulative and Inspector Browne was professionally correct in speaking to Mrs. Kelly. I don't believe this concocted allegation of sexual assault... I do not believe Majella Kelly when she said the incident occurred. I believe that she was telling the truth when she spoke to Paul Williams. It is plain to me that this is an evil conspiracy of the Kelly family to denigrate An Garda Síochána and particularly Inspector Browne who is innocent of the charges against him. The accusation, if it were true, would result in the complete ruin of Inspector Browne.

As the judge was delivering his scathing verdict Mikey Kelly kept talking loudly into John Devane's ear ordering him to object to the comments being delivered from the bench. In the earshot of everyone present, Devane turned around three times and angrily reminded Mikey that he was the solicitor. Exasperated, he finally told Kelly in a loud voice to 'fuck off'. The mob boss and would-be parliamentarian got up and sat at the back of the court beside his brother. The whole thing was an astonishing spectacle. The Kelly family and their lawyer left court humiliated and downcast.

Outside the court Inspector Browne's solicitor Dan O'Gorman issued a statement on behalf of his client:

> It is hard to imagine a graver allegation levelled against anyone than that levelled against Inspector Jim Browne. The judge called the prosecution an evil conspiracy. The judge's decision is a complete vindication of Inspector Browne and the force he serves. Heroes may live amidst the skyscrapers of Manhattan, but today Limerick can witness its own hero and be proud.

One of Browne's colleagues was blunter: 'Making allegations like that was probably better than Kelly getting a gun and killing the man.'

With the case finished, we were all set to put my extensive exposé of Mikey Kelly into print. It was time to show the world how a gangster could corrupt the political system. The weekend after the hearing the *Sunday World* ran a two-page spread on the case. A week later, on St Patrick's Day, I published the scathing exposé of Mikey Kelly over several pages.

It was the first time that the full unvarnished truth about the gangland thug was published. Colm MacGinty organized for the exposé to feature as the front-page splash for all editions sold in Limerick. I remember TD Willie O'Dea phoning me that day. He had been sitting on the same reviewing stand as Kelly at the Limerick parade. 'Jaysus,' he laughed, 'there were more copies of the *Sunday World* to be seen in the crowd than there were flags.'

Mikey Kelly never recovered from the trouble that was all his own making. If he had been as intelligent as Gerry Hutch then he could have been dangerous. But as this story proved, fools can also be extremely harmful. Kelly's despicable smear campaigns, particularly the way he targeted a much-respected local cop, turned him into a pariah in the law-abiding community. The criminals whose activities he had aided and abetted also saw him as a busted flush and moved away from him.

Kelly ran for the Dáil seat that he had once been tipped to win. In the end he secured a mere 700 votes and was eliminated on the third count. Then in November 2002 Kelly resigned from Limerick City council. Kelly blamed me for his electoral defeat and the demise of his political career. He told a local journalist: 'Those articles by Paul Williams destroyed my chances.'

But his troubles didn't end there. He was subsequently jailed for eight months for tax offences following an investigation by the CAB and his business closed down. In May 2004 he was found unconscious in his bed with a gunshot wound to the head. He never regained consciousness and died in hospital a month later.

Kelly's family claimed he had been murdered by the cops. Intelligence later emerged that he had most likely shot himself and someone had taken away the weapon to cover up his suicide.

Media speculation – not by me – suggested that the weapon might have been buried with Kelly. That prompted his family and others to carry out a macabre and illegal exhumation of his corpse to prove the story false. Gardai intervened to stop the exhumation and the family then obtained a licence from the environment department of Limerick County Council to proceed with it. When the casket was opened no gun was found.

Mikey Kelly's demise was mourned only by his closest loved ones who continued with the narrative that it was he who had been the victim. I don't know what happened to his long-suffering wife, but I hope that she found peace in her life.

In 2011 I wrote *Badfellas*, which told the story of the evolution of organized crime in Ireland from the beginning. The book was based on the 2010 documentary series of the same name which I wrote and narrated in collaboration with Emmy award-winning producer/director Gerry Gregg for RTÉ. Both the book and the TV show reflected Kelly's prominence in gangland. In October 2011 I was to do a book signing in Eason's in Limerick. However, Anthony Kelly warned staff that he planned to confront me about what I had written and said about his brother. I had no problem with meeting Kelly. Local garda chiefs told the store that they would send armed officers to ensure that the thug would not step out of line. The store's management were sufficiently intimidated to cancel the signing.

But by then Mikey Kelly's legacy was there for all to see.

CHAPTER SIX

EXPOSING GANGLAND'S JIMMY SAVILE

The TV news bulletin carried a special report about the fifteen-year jail sentence just handed down to one of Dublin's most notorious gangsters – Stephen 'Rossi' Walsh. The forty-five-year-old armed robber, fraudster, extortionist and arsonist had been convicted of blowing up a city centre public house – after the emergency services found him smouldering under the rubble. The trial before Dublin's non-jury Special Criminal Court (SCC) underlined his status as a dangerous criminal.

In November 1993 it was unusual for gangsters to be tried before the SCC which had been established to deal almost exclusively with terrorist groups, such as the Provisional IRA. The State had used Walsh's connections to paramilitary groups to justify having the trial held in the heavily guarded building that housed the court on Green Street in the north inner city. The prosecution wanted to prevent him using his favourite weapon, fear, to intimidate the jury in a normal court.

The Green Street courthouse had been in constant use since 1797 and was the most secure location for the non-jury court which consists of a panel of three judges from the District, Circuit and High Courts. Since the outbreak of the Troubles all terrorist related trials were held there. It had also been used to hear some of the more serious gangland cases

I had covered the trial from start to finish and watched as he was taken away to Portlaoise maximum-security prison, under military escort. The fact that the former member of the General's gang who was once considered untouchable, was going away for a very long time was a major crime story. Catching him had been a struck of luck. For the police the fifteen-year sentence was a major victory. The news came as a relief to the many innocent victims he had terrorized and bullied during his career.

Since I first got involved in crime reporting in 1987 I had taken a big interest in Walsh, especially because of his involvement with Martin Cahill. I had covered stories about Walsh's involvement in fraud and protection rackets. The violent thug had operated as a barrack room lawyer who advised criminals and terrorists on how best to undermine the police's efforts to convict them of serious crimes. He had provided plenty of material for an enthusiastic young reporter.

A dozen years later, when he had his time served, Rossi would boast in a *Sunday World* interview that he had been the 'real' Public Enemy Number One and not the psychopathic General.

In the south inner-city neighbourhood where he grew up, and which he treated as his personal fiefdom, Walsh was regarded as an ordinary decent criminal. A handful of his old neighbours I later interviewed were unperturbed by the gravity of his crimes. They were angry that the 'likeable rogue' had been jailed. The police had a different view. For several years he had been classified as a major figure in the emerging world of organized crime who used the legal system and fear to stay one step ahead of them.

Businesspeople who had to pay him protection money rather than have their premises burned to the ground saw him as a parasite and scourge. Some years later in my third book, *Gangland*, I exposed the life and crimes of the thug who had once been tipped to play soccer professionally in the UK. At that point I thought I knew everything there was to know about Stephen 'Rossi' Walsh. How wrong I was.

That same evening in 1993 an innocent nine-year-old girl had taken an unusual interest in the six o'clock news in her family's Corporation flat in Irishtown. As the child watched the image of Walsh being led away in handcuffs a chill of fear ran through her tortured and confused mind. She was one of the only ones who knew his dark, sinister secret – something that neither his friends nor foes were aware of.

In her eyes there was nothing ordinary or decent about the man who had been one of her dad's best friends and had played the part of the uncle figure who loved kids.

When she looked at the TV screen she saw a monster that none of the adults could see. The depraved creature that had hidden in plain view had threatened to kill her and her family if she ever revealed it. Walsh's secret would remain hidden from the world for another thirteen years until she broke her silence to tell a horrific story of sexual abuse and rape.

That little girl's decision set in motion a chain of events which led me to publicly exposing the shocking truth about what Walsh really was – a serial paedophile who used his criminal power to prey on countless children over the course of decades. By the time *Sunday World* lawyer Kieran Kelly and I finally got around the legal hoops and were able to name him we had identified at least a dozen victims.

The reality was that he had abused many more than that number. Stephen Rossi Walsh turned out to be the gangland equivalent of Jimmy Savile.

Walsh, who also used the alias Stephen Byrne, was born in 1949 and grew up in Dublin's south inner city, in the Pearse House Corporation flats. He was a key member of the new generation of criminals who emerged in the 1970s when the spectre of organized crime first emerged in Ireland. His associates included the likes of the Dunnes and the Cahills. In the process he earned a reputation as a prolific armed robber and became one of Dublin's most feared criminals.

One detective who knew Walsh told me:

> Rossi was a psychopath, and he loved the power that carrying a gun brought him. Every thug on his patch was absolutely terrified of him because of his violent nature. A lot of policemen were also scared of him. Rossi was one of the most dangerous criminals ever to have come out of that end of town.

Like the rest of the underworld fraternity his criminal CV dated back to his teens. His first conviction in 1965 was for stealing a bicycle. He was given probation and told not to do it again. Gerry Hutch, the Monk's inaugural conviction was for stealing a bottle of lemonade. John Gilligan's was for stealing a chicken. They all started off small.

Walsh could have easily taken a different route in life. He was a talented soccer player who throughout the 1960s was invited for trials by top English clubs including Arsenal. A nifty inside forward, he got the nickname 'Rossi' after the famous Italian centre forward Paola Rossi who scored six goals in the 1982 World Cup which Italy won. Ironically, the real Rossi was suspended from playing as a result of corruption.

The English clubs turned down Walsh although he played League of Ireland football for Shelbourne and later Liffey Wanderers for several years. Soccer pundits said that he could have played for Ireland had he put his mind to it. Former armed robber Dave Brogan, who once did 'jobs' with Walsh, told me: 'He never made it into professional football because he was so aggressive and arrogant, the Brits wouldn't put up with that kind of shite. Rossi was mad.' When his career as a soccer star faded Walsh pursued a more lucrative career off the field.

During the 1970s he was caught and convicted for four armed heists. But each time he received suspended sentences after pulling every legal stunt in the book to beat the criminal justice system. As a result of Rossi's many jousts with the law, new legislation was enacted to close the loopholes he had exposed.

In one case he was acquitted when the jury failed to reach a verdict. It was widely believed that he had intimidated some jurors to get the right result. The last time the police came close to putting him behind bars was in 1978 when he had been caught following a post office robbery. But before his trial commenced he had it transferred from the Circuit Criminal to the Central Criminal Court.

Switching trials from one court to another was the legal right of the defendant which was often used as a delaying tactic by criminals. It led to a change in the law during the 1980s. From then on, all criminal cases were conducted in the Circuit Criminal Court. Walsh was eventually found guilty and got eight years. But his luck held and much to the anger of the police, the sentence was suspended yet again.

The close shaves established his reputation in the underworld as a serious criminal who could play the system and appear to get away with it. From then on, he became a major player in gangland.

One of his most successful rackets involved the organized theft of containers of goods from the docks where a number of his associates worked. He also worked with John Gilligan's 'Factory' gang in the 1980s when the future drug trafficking murderer was the country's most successful large-scale burglar.

Over the next fourteen years or so sources told me that Garda intelligence pinpointed Walsh as the prime suspect for scores of serious crimes. In the same period he was arrested and questioned over twenty times as part of garda investigations of armed robberies, protection rackets and murder. But each time there was insufficient evidence to sustain a charge against the cunning gangster.

Walsh's local area of Pearse Street in the south inner city remained his stomping ground even though he had moved to live with his wife and three children in upmarket Sandymount in the 1980s. He paid cash for a substantial four-bedroom home despite being officially unemployed and in receipt of social welfare payments.

From my vantage point I could see how he portrayed the image of a mafia-style godfather who demonstrated staunch loyalty to his family and friends. Rossi was a man of 'respect' which meant that no one dared cross him. If one of his old neighbours had a problem they called Walsh instead of the police. He and his team of heavies, including two martial arts experts, enforced their own brand of rough justice in the complex of flats.

If anyone stepped out of line, he or she was severely beaten. Walsh had no qualms about beating up women which he often did. But he burnished his reputation as a local hero when he regularly splashed out to bring the elderly residents on day trips and organized parties for the local children.

In Pearse House he also organized and sponsored soccer tournaments for the kids. They looked up to Walsh and they wanted to be like him. As some of the children grew up he coached them on more than soccer. Off the field he helped guide them in their criminal careers.

When I was researching his background I heard a story of how in the early 1990s Walsh called to a local school to introduce a celebrity to the kids, someone famous they had all seen on television. That man was his long-time associate Martin Cahill, the General, who had become the first gangland celebrity in Ireland. (See *Crooks*.)

Long before anyone knew the sordid truth about him, people in the area argued that Rossi was a necessary evil. His fearsome reputation for violence and disapproval of heroin abuse ensured that dealers and junkies steered clear of the flats. He was seen as a protector of the local children to whom he had unfettered access. Hindsight would illustrate how this was the perfect cover for a serial paedophile.

Buoyed by his successes in the courts, Walsh developed his interest in the law and advised criminals on how best to utilize the system to beat the rap. Rossi would read books of evidence in cases and offer advice for which he charged his fellow rogues, as well as members of the IRA.

When the Government set up the Garda Complaints Authority in 1987 to investigate allegations of misconduct by members of the force, Rossi Walsh discovered a new tool for fighting the system. He advised gangsters who were caught and charged with an offence to immediately make a complaint against the arresting officers.

The Authority was statutorily bound to conduct an investigation into each and every allegation made, no matter how frivolous or vexatious. While an investigation was ongoing a trial could not take place. The more complaints there were, the longer it took to investigate them and this process significantly delayed trials coming to court, sometimes by years. In the interim villains had an opportunity to get at witnesses and help them develop amnesia. At one stage, as a result of Walsh's meddling, the system practically seized up, leading to a public outcry from the garda representative associations.

Walsh achieved such notoriety that he even took centre stage at one of the annual conferences of the Association of Garda Sergeants and Inspectors (AGSI). Delegates complained bitterly that gangland's Perry Mason was successfully making an ass of the criminal justice system. At the height of the complaints' blizzard Walsh boasted to his cronies that there were more cops under investigation than criminals.

In the early 1990s I ran a story about his unofficial paralegal work. I also revealed how he was operating a 'Fagin's school' for young villains from the converted attic of his home, although I couldn't name him at the time for legal reasons. I had been tipped off by local gardaí who were frustrated at the way he was undermining the law. He advised other hoods about their legal rights, the attitude they should adopt while in custody and how to arrange good alibis which would convince a jury of their innocence.

Throughout his patch Walsh continued to run his extensive protection racket extorting cash from pub and restaurant owners. I once reported how a particular pub which refused to pay up mysteriously burned down twice in the space of five years. He instilled terror in everyone who crossed him, whether criminals or innocent victims. The local gardaí regularly received reports that Walsh had threatened people with firearms but, out of fear, none of them would make a complaint.

In Ringsend, south Dublin, I was told how he got into a row in a pub once with a local docker who'd had enough of Rossi's bullying tactics. Walsh won the fight after sticking a gun down his opponent's throat in front of at least twenty witnesses. He had no worries about anyone going to the police. They were too scared.

Some years earlier Walsh had been arrested and questioned about the murder of a local barman, Jackie Kelly, at a time when gangland murders were extremely rare. A lone gunman had walked into Grace's Pub on Townsend Street in the inner city and shot Kelly at point blank range. One eyewitness later related that before he died Kelly was heard to say to the gunman: 'Rossi, ya bastard. . . ya shot me.'

Walsh was later released without charge. Sometime after the incident the soccer player was again arrested and charged for beating up Kelly's mother and sister after they confronted him about the murder. He used his knowledge of the law to wriggle out of the charges, seeking judicial reviews and using various other ploys to delay the case for almost eight years. The charges were eventually dropped by the DPP after his solicitors argued that too much time had elapsed since the offences took place.

I'd first become familiar with Rossi Walsh after joining the *Sunday World* in 1987 and investigating the General and his gang. Rossi was a key player in the mob and took part in the Beit art heist in 1986. At the time it was one of the biggest art robberies in the world. As I got to know more gardaí I began to hear a lot about the mobster who fancied himself as a legal whiz kid. The first time

I laid eyes on him was in the Four Courts in Dublin when a garda contact pointed him out.

In those years I spent a lot of time in the courts complex which at the time housed both the civil and criminal courts of justice. I loved the courts. It was a melting pot of cops, lawyers, defendants, litigants, victims and veteran court reporters from whom I learned a lot. All human life could be found under the green dome of the landmark building.

Walsh was a regular patron. He would strut through the corridors of the Four Courts in his trademark shiny tracksuit and runners, with a carrier bag full of legal books over his shoulder. I took an immediate and abiding interest in him after that. Walsh thoroughly enjoyed arguing points of law with defence barristers whom he described as snobs.

Rossi knew a lot of the angles, but some cops reckoned that he was overrated. 'Fellows who take Rossi's advice on how to approach their trials often end up getting longer sentences as a result,' my source revealed.

When Martin Cahill became a household name and began making a spectacle of himself for the cameras in the late 1980s Walsh moved away from him, as did several of the General's former gang members. By the time I first laid eyes on him Walsh was running a massive compensation racket involving staged accidents throughout the city. The racket was the indirect result of a devastating gas explosion in a block of apartments in Ballsbridge, south Dublin, a few months before I joined the *Sunday World*.

As a result of the explosion, which claimed the lives of two people, it was discovered that the city's gas pipeline system was leaking. A huge refurbishment and repair operation ensued which involved digging up hundreds of streets and sidewalks.

Rossi had found a Klondike. He used a group of up to twenty-three associates who took turns falling and driving into the holes and then making compensation claims. Over a three-year period the Irish insurance industry estimated that Walsh was behind dozens of staged accidents where compensation and legal costs of up to £2 million were incurred – or over €5 million in today's values.

Walsh's antics led to a major overhaul of how insurance companies and public utilities dealt with compensation cases. Companies began spending more money investigating the background to individual claims. A Claims Task Force and a database were established to analyse each claimant and to identify whether the individual concerned had made any previous claims.

Rossi's presence in the courts as a legal adviser and his association with so many compensation cases soon came to the attention of the judiciary. He had become a constant irritant and some judges had barred him from their courtrooms. In 1992 a judge threw out a compensation claim describing it as 'another Rossi Walsh production – fraudulent from start to finish'. Walsh had run out of road. That ruling gave us in the media the first opportunity to publicly name the gangster.

A year later the same judge, Frank Martin, threw out another case taken by three people who claimed they suffered whiplash injuries after driving into a hole. But when a witness came forward to say that the car had 'driven very slowly, very deliberately into the hole,' Judge Martin directed that the Fraud Squad be called in to investigate. The judge said he was perturbed at the number of bogus claims coming before him.

Behind many of them, he said, was 'the malign name of Rossi Walsh'. Judge Martin announced angrily: 'We've had him [Walsh] in here a few times where he was running fraudulent claims for people. He runs a dial-a-witness service.'

But Rossi Walsh's days as a compensation fraudster were coming to an end.

In the early hours of 12 September 1992, a massive explosion demolished Collins' public house on Ballybough Road in the north inner city. As firefighters and ambulance crews extinguished pockets of fire in the ruins, they heard a voice emanating from where the front bar once stood. 'In here. . . get me out,' the voice shouted. They were astonished that anyone could survive such a blast.

The figure they pulled from the wreckage was covered in blood and dust. His clothes, a tracksuit, were burned off and he had a gash on his forehead. The man's hair was singed and there were burns to his face, hands and arms. Miraculously the unrecognizable survivor was able to walk to an ambulance.

Later in the emergency room of the Mater Hospital, as nurses cleaned away the mask of blood, soot and dust, the police waiting to speak to him could not believe their eyes. Sitting in front of them was the gangster who had eluded them for so many years. One garda source told me that the joke went at the time that Rossi had handed himself up on a plate to his hated enemies – albeit rather well done.

A garda investigation later established evidence that Walsh had been responsible for the explosion. He and an accomplice had entered the building with two 25 litre containers with a petrol and diesel mixture. They also brought three gas cylinders and an electric fire. Inside they spread the fuel around. Once the liquid had vaporized through the pub the plan was that it would be ignited by the electric fire after they made their exit. The gas cylinders would also explode destroying the building. Unfortunately for Walsh the vapours were prematurely ignited by either a naked light or a spark from another electric appliance. Rossi was caught bang to rights. It was an amazing story.

When Walsh's trial came before the Special Criminal Court on 19 October 1993 I covered every day of it. He was facing charges for unlawful trespass, criminal damage, arson and attempted fraud. At the time there weren't very many gangland cases before the courts – and certainly nothing as colourful as this one.

Walsh's trial was almost as remarkable as the manner in which he was finally caught. It lasted for three weeks and needless to say Walsh denied all the charges. On the fourth day he sacked his legal team and took over his own defence.

I remember thinking how the lawyers must have been relieved. Walsh had constantly interrupted them while they cross-examined witnesses, frantically passing them hastily scribbled notes. At one stage the barristers were spending more time turning around to listen to Walsh than facing the witnesses.

Dressed in a tracksuit Walsh then conducted his own defence. He was the only one in the court who seemed to think that he was a capable advocate. He grilled the detectives who had investigated him, accusing them of tampering with evidence and questioning their professionalism. One of his assistants in the case, who also wore a tracksuit, acted as his notetaker for the rest of the trial. Each morning Walsh arrived in court with a large bag stuffed with legal books.

The underworld paedophile also targeted the judges. He accused them of being biased and improperly constituted. On one occasion he claimed that one of the three presiding judges had fallen asleep. 'It's an outrageous situation to say that a member of the court should lapse into a lack of concentration. I am calling on the court to have a retrial,' he demanded. After a short adjournment, the presiding judge, Freddie Morris, whose patience was obviously wearing thin, refused Walsh's application and assured him that the judge had not been asleep.

In his defence Walsh claimed that he had been walking past the pub when he was sucked into the blaze by a backdraught. In his closing remarks Walsh declared that he couldn't remember the events of 12 September 1992. 'I have absolutely no recollection due to the incident about it [sic]. That's basically it,' he said.

He asked the court for a not guilty verdict on the grounds that the State had not proved its case against him. However, on the 9 November the Special Criminal Court found the evidence against Rossi was overwhelming. He was guilty as charged.

Before sentence was passed Judge Frederick Morris told him:

> You, either acting alone or with others, deliberately assembled the paraphernalia of destruction in the licensed premises with the clear intention of destroying it without regard for the owners or members of the public. This type of conduct cannot be tolerated in a civilized society.

On the charge of arson Rossi Walsh was sentenced to fifteen years in prison and ten years each for causing criminal damage and trespassing with intent to cause criminal damage.

As soon as the sentence was passed Walsh was on his feet and applied to Judge Morris, in his capacity as a High Court judge, for a *habeas corpus* order under Article 40 of the Constitution.

Judge Morris had had enough of Rossi and curtly replied, 'No'.

Walsh was handcuffed and brought under armed escort to Portlaoise maximum security prison. He would remain inside for another twelve years.

I was sure we hadn't heard the last of him.

Just three weeks into his sentence I got a tip from a prison officer source in Portlaoise that Rossi had received a beating from some of his former partners in crime. He had tried to push his weight around on the E1 landing which housed the country's most hardened armed robbers and drug dealers, including members of the Dunne clan, John Gilligan's 'Factory' gang and the General's mob.

They were also doing long sentences and had no intention of putting up with Walsh's nonsense. He was then transferred to Limerick high security prison where he got a severe beating from another member of a hardened Dublin gang. Walsh was hospitalized and had to receive physiotherapy for the injuries.

A year later in April 1994 Walsh was back in the Dublin District Court to face five charges of beating up three women and two teenage girls. In May 1993 he had attacked the children after accusing them of assaulting his daughter. He punched one of them, a fifteen-year-old, in the jaw and slapped the other, a thirteen-year-old, across the face. He also threatened to smash their heads in with a hammer.

That night he got into another row with three women who confronted him about the earlier assaults on the two young girls Walsh punched one of the women four times in the face, breaking her nose and leaving her with two black eyes. When the second woman in the company tried to intervene, Walsh punched her in the face, breaking her nose and leaving a gash which required several stitches. He then turned and punched the third woman, a fifty-one-year-old, in the chest.

Despite his reputation and the fact that he was doing a long stretch the women testified against him. Judge Michael Connellan imposed a total of two years for the string of assaults which he ordered Rossi to serve at the end of his fifteen-year stretch for the pub explosion. 'You beat up young, defenceless women and children and this cannot be allowed,' Judge Connellan told him.

But Rossi Walsh refused to allow the Irish judiciary to forget about him. He channelled his energies into bombarding the legal system with dozens of appeals and submissions for the High Court and Supreme Court on behalf of other prisoners and himself. He made a lengthy submission on several points of law relating to his conviction at the Court of Criminal Appeal which were rejected. Walsh then appealed the decision to the Supreme Court. He also sued the State for the beating he got in Limerick and later received compensation.

In 1995 he even applied to the Supreme Court to be granted permission to represent other prisoners in court in Dublin. The spectacle of Rossi Walsh being escorted from Limerick Prison every day to represent his 'clients' in the Dublin criminal courts was a sideshow which the judges found too much to contemplate. The application was refused. Using the Irish version of his name, Stiofán Breathnach, he then mounted a successful constitutional challenge in the High Court and Supreme Court for prisoners to have the right to vote.

The State ensured that Walsh served the maximum length of his sentence. With mandatory remission he was eventually released from custody in July 2005. On his old stomping ground of the Pearse Street flats there were parties held in celebration. In an interview that month in the *Sunday World* with my colleague Niamh O'Connor, Rossi tried to portray himself as a likeable,

Robin Hood figure. He bragged proudly about his past criminal exploits like they were a badge of honour.

The fifty-seven-year-old thug even mocked his one-time partner in crime, Martin Cahill, the General. He gloated: 'I was the one followed 24 hours a day. I went on all of the jobs I organized. He [Cahill] didn't. It was embarrassing. He was a baby.'

Walsh boasted about his career as an armed robber, conjuring the image of youthful escapades by a rebel fighting back against an unjust system. He showed no regard for his many victims. He even claimed that the police were afraid of him:

> I was Jesse James, 100 per cent. A warrior. When I started out I wouldn't rob anybody's house, I thought that was petty anyway. So, my thing would be go and rob a bank. I had no transport, so I'd go in and rob the thing and run down the street. You see I was a flier as well into the bargain. The police would often come across us in the middle of something [armed robbery] and say, 'It's Rossi, go around the block' because they knew if they stopped it would be confrontational, and they wouldn't be winning because I tell you we were warriors.

The narcissistic gangster's interview in Ireland's biggest selling newspaper was his way of alerting the world that the boss was back in business. Shortly after his release Rossi began appearing again in the courts with his bag of legal tomes and his dodgy advice.

Elsewhere the story held more profound resonance for a young woman who, as a fearful nine-year-old child, had viewed Walsh through a very different prism. Ruth Dunne was now living in a state of fear that the monster who had raped and abused her was back and still a feared criminal with the power to harm her and her family. Her exceptional courage would soon eviscerate the image Walsh was fabricating of the amiable gangland warrior.

By the time Rossi Walsh was set free it was known in a small circle of cops and crime reporters that he had already been the subject of an investigation into child sexual abuse. The victim who was related to Walsh through marriage had been repeatedly sexually abused by him in the late 1970s and early 1980s. I had heard through police sources that she had gone to the gardaí and made an official complaint in 2003.

In October of that year Walsh was arrested and questioned about the allegations while he was serving the remainder of his sentence in Cloverhill Prison in Dublin. But the DPP decided not to proceed with a prosecution on the grounds that there were no independent witnesses to corroborate the victim's story. Members of her family had turned against her when she made the allegations. There was no way to progress the story, and it faded into the background.

Then shortly after his release rumours began to circulate in gangland circles that Walsh was a paedophile. I received several anonymous letters alleging that he had raped a young girl but there were no other details. Sometime in the middle of 2006 I got a phone call from a man who said he was the one responsible for the letters and the whispers about Rossi Walsh.

The caller was the best friend of Christy Dunne, Ruth Dunne's father (no relation to the Dunne crime family). Both he and Christy were close friends and associates of Walsh back in the day when he was at the height of his powers. But that friendship was no more. The man explained that Walsh had abused and raped Ruth on a number of occasions when she was nine years old. He immediately had my full attention, and I arranged to meet the two men.

Ruth's dad told me that he first found out about the abuse when his daughter broke down after Walsh's conviction in 1993. Like most parents in such cases, he and his wife were deeply hurt and angered. They felt guilty that they had inadvertently allowed their daughter to get into the clutches of a fiend. Since his release the two friends had been involved in a campaign of sorts to spread the word through the underworld and Dublin's inner-city neighbourhoods that Rossi Walsh, the much-feared godfather, was a depraved pervert.

They knew the unnamed woman relative who had gone to the police in 2003 when the DPP decided not to prosecute. The men were particularly concerned that there were many more victims out there. Since his release from prison Walsh was living with a woman and her young children in an inner-city flats complex. The two men had circulated leaflets about Walsh and told anyone who would listen to them.

Ruth, who was now twenty-two, had made a formal complaint to the police before his release in 2005. Detectives had interviewed her and the rest of the family, but nothing had happened since. The wheels of justice tend to grind slowly. Walsh, as far as they knew, had not yet been interviewed by the police.

When word filtered out in the Irishtown and Ringsend locality that she had gone to the gardaí, associates of Walsh and his family members had subjected the young woman to a hate campaign in the area where she lived amongst many of them. None of them believed the accusations. Ruth had been verbally abused in the street and her car was smashed up. Everything was being done to silence the terrified young woman.

I wondered aloud if the men were placing themselves in danger. In gangland sex offenders are despised as the lowest form of life, which is why they are housed separately in prison, away from the rest of the population for their own safety. I was concerned that a dangerous gangster, like a cornered rat, would use everything in his power to avoid being prosecuted in the first place.

In 1993, the same year that Walsh got fifteen years, I had witnessed firsthand the appalling ordeal suffered by the daughter of another member of the General's gang when she reported to the police that she had been raped by her father. (See *Crooks*.)

The gangster concerned, a violent criminal, was a long-time associate of Martin Cahill and Rossi Walsh. His daughter was fourteen when he raped and abused her in the family home. Her grandmother brought her to the police and her father was arrested and charged.

After a failed campaign of intimidation to get the girl to drop the charges Cahill arranged to shoot his associate, the child's father, in the leg to defer the trial going ahead. When it eventually did take place the girl testified against her sick father and he was convicted. The conviction was later overturned on a technicality. Rossi had been one of his advisors.

Around the same time that I was alerted to Ruth Dunne's case another child sex abuse scandal was about to explode in a vicious gang war in the north inner city. Two men were shot dead in December of that year. The conflagration broke out after drug trafficking crime boss Christy Griffin was accused of repeatedly raping and abusing his partner's young daughter. The feud also led to several serious assaults, shooting incidents and even a bombing.

1: A church scandal. Celebrity priest Fr Michael Cleary with his secret family – Phyllis Hamilton and their son Ross

 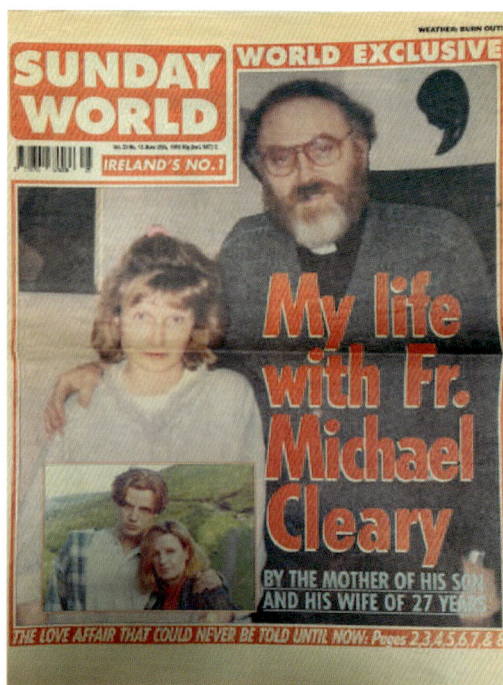

2: The front page stories that exposed Fr Michael Cleary's secret life and rocked the Catholic church

3: The book I ghost wrote with Phyllis

4: Michael with his son Ross

5: Me with *Father Ted* star and one of Ireland's greatest comedians, Dermot Morgan

6: Confronting Real IRA boss Alan Ryan

7: Face-to-face with international drug trafficker Mickey Green – the Pimpernel

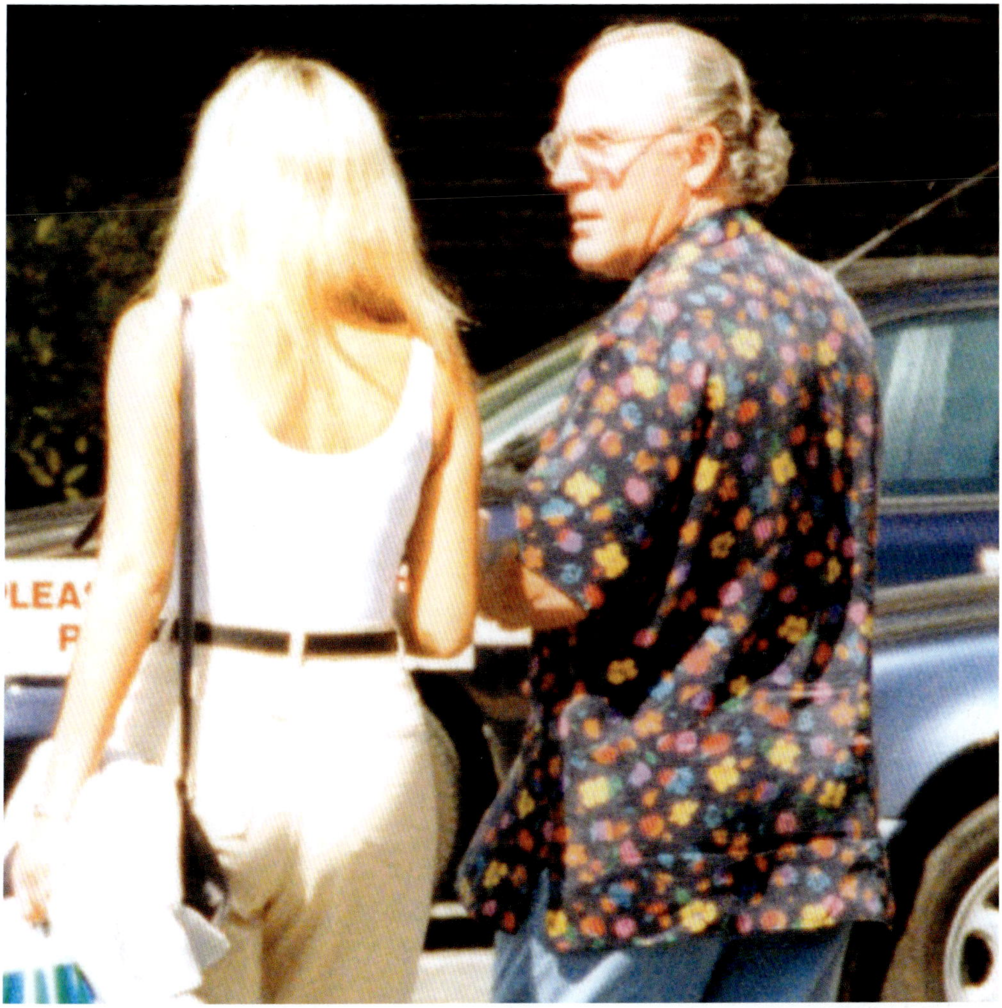

8: A surveillance picture of Mickey Green with his girlfriend on the streets of Dublin

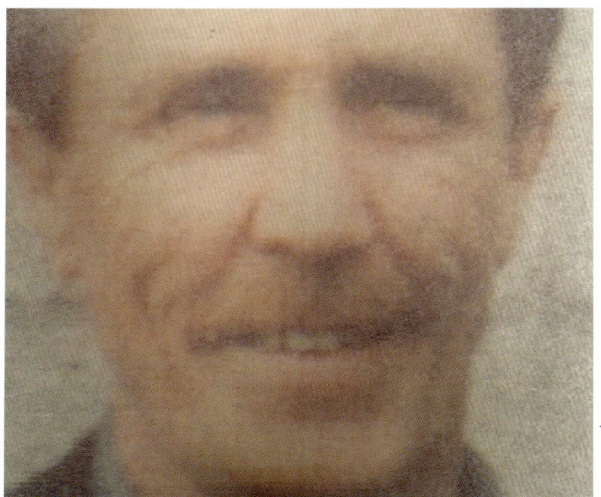

9: Taxi driver Joseph White

SUNDAY WORLD

IRELAND'S No.1

THE RACE FOR THE TITLE

RED FACES

UNITED SLIP UP ON THE GLORY TRAIL

EXCLUSIVE: WE TRACK DOWN ONE OF THE MOST WANTED GANGSTERS IN THE WORLD

MISTER BIG

By Crime Reporter PAUL WILLIAMS

Cocaine king's Irish hideaway from the law

Donor mum's tragic baby

EXCLUSIVE

LUXURY LIFE OF EVIL CRIME BOSS: Pages 4,5,6&7

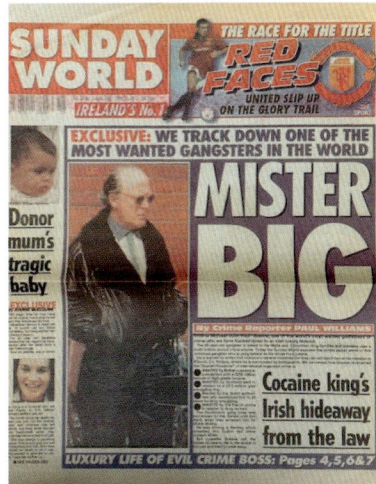

10: The front page exposé of Green

11: Michael 'Mikey' Kelly – the gang boss whose political career I helped thwart

12: Kieran Kelly and Colm MacGinty – two of the most inspiring people I ever worked with

13: Gerry Fanning – the legendary lawyer

14: Myself and Cathy Kelly joined the *Sunday World* at the same time

15: With former *Late Late Show* host and Newstalk presenter Pat Kenny, who launched *Crooks*

16: With my dear friend Joe Duffy

17: With Anne – who has put up with me and my crazy career for 40 years

18: Former *Sunday World* MD Michael Brophy   **19:** John 'Dot' Donlon – my mentor since 1984

20: With my wife Anne and our two children, Jake and Irena, who suffered a lot of stress over the years because of my work

21: Gangland's 'Jimmy Savile', the mob boss I exposed as a serial paedophile

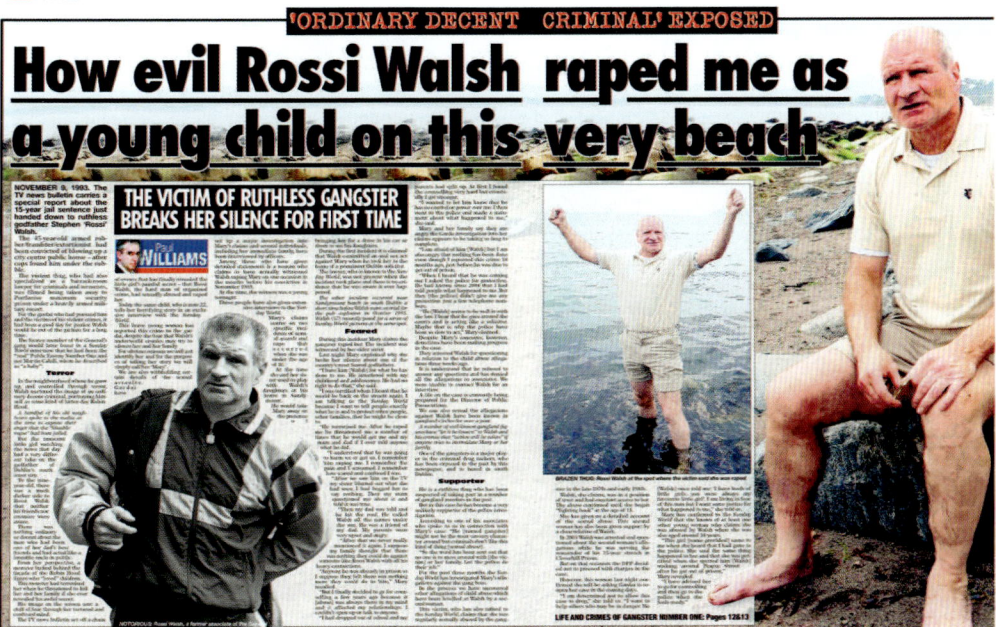

22: How we exposed Rossi Walsh – the twisted monster they called 'the Monkey'

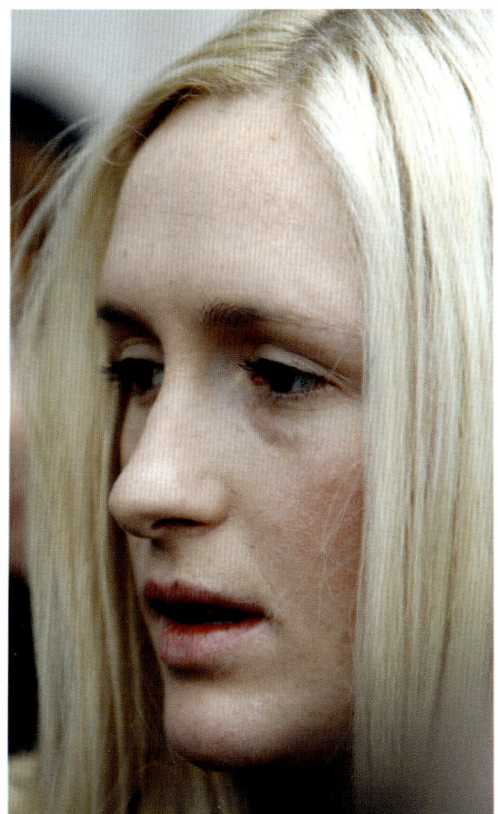

23: Ruth Dunne – one of the bravest young women I have ever known

24: Naming Wayne Dundon as responsible for ordering the murder of Roy Collins

25: Steve Collins – the accidental hero who helped take down Limerick's Murder Inc.

26: Interviewing former Det Supt Jim Browne – the top cop who took on the Limerick mobs

27: Me with Carmel and Steve Collins the night before they were forced to leave Ireland

28: One of the many front pages showing the garda war on Murder Inc

29: Breaking the sad news that Steve Collins and his family were being forced to flee Ireland

30: Happiness at last for the Collins family – at Steve's wedding with sons, Ryan and Steve jnr

31: On an exercise during my days as an army reservist – the best of my life

METRO EDITION

Irish Independent

IRELAND'S BEST-SELLING DAILY NEWSPAPER www.independent.ie Monday 24 June 2013 €1.90 (£1.25 in Northern Ireland)

Best writers on a day of drama in the GAA

36-PAGE SPORT PULL-OUT INSIDE

Inside Anglo: the secret recordings

Exclusive: Tapes reveal the lies and deception that led to the bank bailout

Paul Williams
Special Correspondent

TAPE RECORDINGS from inside doomed Anglo Irish Bank reveal for the first time how the bank's top executives lied to the Government about the true extent of losses at the institution.

The astonishing tapes show senior manager John Bowe, who had been involved in negotiations with the Central Bank, laughing and joking as he tells another senior manager, Peter Fitzgerald, how Anglo was luring the State into giving it billions of euro.

Mr Fitzgerald had not been involved in the negotiations with the Central Bank and has confirmed he was unaware of any strategy or intention to mislead the authorities. Mr Bowe, in a statement last night, categorically denied that he had misled the Central Bank.

The audio recordings are from the bank's own internal telephone system and date from the heart of the financial crisis that brought the State to its knees in September 2008.

Anglo itself was within days of complete meltdown – and in the years ahead would eat up €30bn of taxpayer money. Mr Bowe speaks about how the State had been asked for €7bn to bail out Anglo – but Anglo's negotiators knew all along this was not enough to save the bank.

The plan was that once the State began the flow of money, it would be unable to stop.

Mr Bowe is asked by Mr Fitzgerald how they had come up with the figure of €7bn. He laughs as he is taped saying: "Just, as Drummer (then-CEO David Drumm) would say, 'picked it out of my arse'."

He also says: "If they (Central Bank) saw the enormity of it up front, they might decide they have a choice. You know what I mean?

"They might say the cost to the taxpayer is too high . . . if it doesn't look too big at the outset . . . if it looks big, big enough to be important, but not too big that it kind of spoils everything, then, then I think you have a chance. So I think it can creep up."

Strategy

Mr Fitzgerald, the Director of Retail Banking, is heard saying: "Yeah. They've got skin in the game and that is the key."

Mr Bowe's comments in the audio recording reveal that Anglo's strategy was to lure the State in, leaving taxpayers with no choice but to continue to provide loans to "support their money".

The recording also shows Mr Bowe and Mr Fitzgerald laughing as they say how there is no realistic chance of ever repaying the loans.

For the first time, taxpayers get an exclusive insight into the banking shenanigans that cost Ireland our sovereignty.

FULL STORY: PAGE 2

ANGLO IRISH BANK

Anglo executives Peter Fitzgerald (left) and John Bowe

INSIDE ANGLO
Special Correspondent
Paul Williams

NEWS, COMMENT & ANALYSIS

PAGES 2-7 & 24, 25

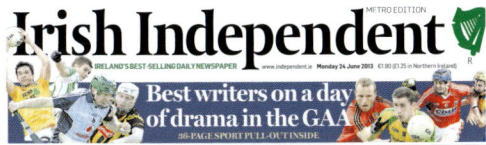

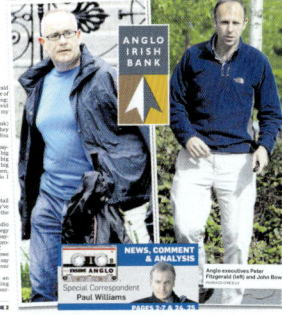

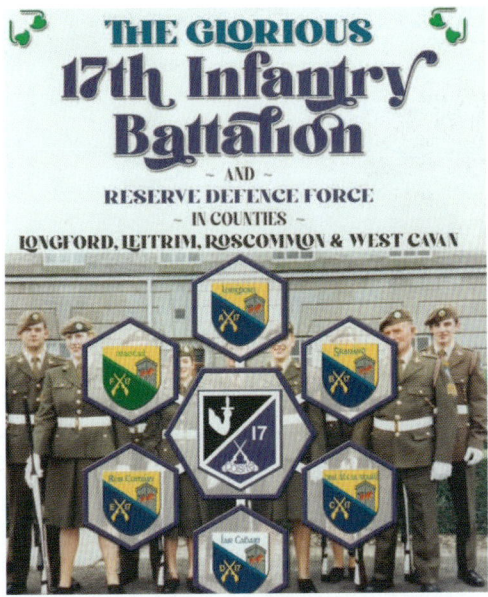

32: The front page that broke the Anglo scandal

33: The history of my old battalion by Hugh Farrell

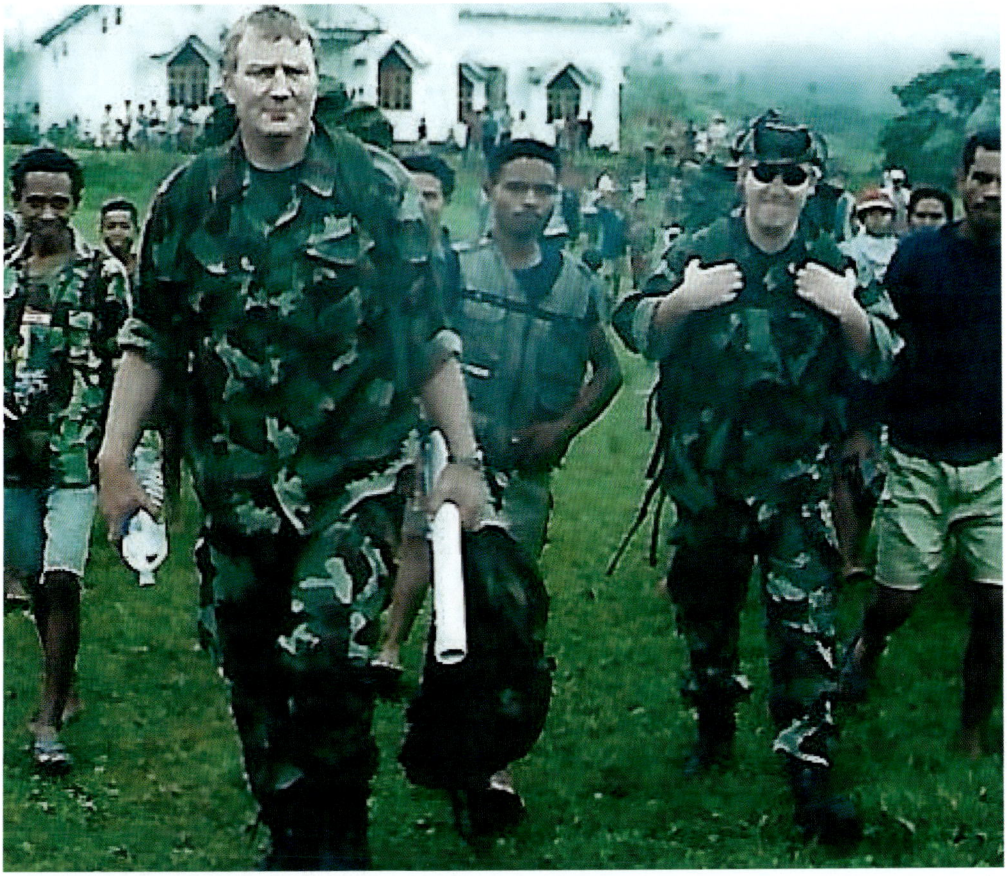

34: Eoghan Ó Neachtain and me after landing in East Timor

35: Army Rangers boarding a Huey chopper as we went on patrol in the East Timor jungle

36: Before and after – decked out for Operation Scribe and, above right, with my son Jake after four days in hell

When Griffin was subsequently convicted the victim told me her traumatic story which I gladly shared with the rest of the world.

Giving a voice to the victims of sexual abuse is an important function in journalism. Over the decades I told the stories of countless victims of sexual abuse and rape. In the hierarchy of crime, the abuse of children stands next to murder. It was always harrowing and upsetting to hear the ordeals of innocent children at the hands of monsters.

Some people angrily denounce paedophiles as animals. I don't agree with that. Animals don't possess the same capacity for unspeakable evil as humans. In such cases I think there is no room for impartiality. The journalist has a duty of care to the victim which often transcends the normal remit of the job. The victim must have trust in the reporter and be assured that they are believed.

Sex offenders are by their nature manipulative, devious creatures who prey on the victim's vulnerabilities. In practically every case of child abuse I ever covered the victim was told by their attackers that they would not be believed if they ever spoke out. Being believed is hugely important to restore their confidence and to eradicate the misplaced shame and reflected guilt so they can make the transition from victim to survivor. You have to be prepared to take on the role of the victim's advocate and defender. Exposing such evil and giving victims a voice was always a source of job satisfaction for me. That was my first instinct when I was approached by Christy Dunne and his friend.

The two men were fully aware of what they were up against in crossing a crime boss like Walsh. But they were not scared of their former pal and had given him a new nickname – the Monkey. After they began their campaign against Walsh they told me that a major gangland player had decided to give them moral support. He put the word out that Ruth Dunne and her family were not to be harmed. I wondered if Walsh might even live long enough to face a courtroom.

The two friends wanted to see the paedophile exposed to the public and the best place to do that was in the *Sunday World*. They also believed that it would force the gardaí to progress the investigation which appeared to be dormant in autumn 2006 even though Walsh had been free for months. There was also the pressing issue that the suspected deviant had unfettered access to children and anecdotally they knew that there were many more victims. The fact that he was being associated with two allegations certainly pointed to a pattern of deviant behaviour.

Publicly naming someone as a paedophile in the absence of them being charged or convicted was, in legal terms, extremely difficult. Being labelled a child sex abuser is probably the worst thing that a person can be called. In Ireland individuals who are accused of sex crimes cannot be named until after the trial process is over and only if they have been convicted.

The legislation is framed to primarily protect the victim. The naming of a sexual offender is not allowed if it leads in any way to the identification of the victim. In certain cases, an offender can only be publicly named if the victim agrees for them to be named or decides to bravely waive their right to anonymity.

I could have written a story which did not identify Walsh but that would not be as effective as naming and shaming the bastard. The story would have to be published before he was formally charged because after that it would remain *sub judice* in the time leading up to the trial which could take years. Nothing can be written about a case while it is *sub judice* for fear of prejudicing a trial. Before we could even contemplate writing anything about the Walsh case I said I would need to sit down and interview Ruth.

I was also aware from what her father told me that Ruth's sister Jennifer, who was a few years older than her, had witnessed Walsh attacking the child on one occasion back in 1993. I would have to formally interview Jennifer, Christy, her mother and anyone else who had any knowledge of the allegations just as the police had done. They would be our witnesses in the event that we published the story and Walsh sued for defamation of character.

Getting a story like that into print would require the involvement of our lawyer Kieran Kelly at every stage of the process. Kelly was unlike most media lawyers who have a mantra – 'if in doubt leave it out'. At the time, running a story which named the alleged perpetrator would not have been countenanced in any other newsroom. In fact it wouldn't be entertained today.

What I always loved about working with Kelly was that he believed in doing everything legally possible to get a story across the line. And, of course, my editor Colm MacGinty was firmly of the same mind. We pushed out the parameters and trod where others dared not on many occasions in those years.

If we did 'publish and be damned' then the newspaper would have to be prepared to face the prospect of defending a hugely costly libel action. This time we all agreed that this case would be a major challenge. But failure to expose Walsh would not be from lack of trying.

In September 2006 Christy Dunne said that his daughter wanted to speak to me and I was invited to the family's home in Irishtown one evening. I still recall that first meeting with Ruth and her father in his modest flat. The young woman I met on that occasion was extremely shy and obviously deeply traumatized. She was also terrified of what might happen to her loved ones if her story went public. I did everything in my power to put her at ease and reassure her. We would only talk if she felt up to it. On that occasion she left the room and didn't return. I understood why.

Experience had taught me that Ruth would have to feel safe and secure before relating such a profound trauma. It is the same approach the police take in such investigations. Empathy and understanding are paramount. I left telling Christy not to push his daughter. If she wanted to talk then she would do so in her own good time. I was only a phone call away.

In the meantime I made discreet approaches to garda contacts who were familiar with the case. I told one source who was a senior investigator that we were aiming to publish a story about the allegations which would not affect the ongoing enquiry. It was important to let the police know this so that they had the opportunity to push the investigation forward and avoid any negative publicity.

After all we were all on the same side of the victim. The source told me that the allegations were being taken seriously and that Walsh was due to be arrested soon. The gardaí were also concerned that the pervert still had access to young children. The senior officer confided that they believed there had been many more victims.

A few weeks later Christy Dunne rang me and said Ruth felt she was ready to tell her story. Over a number of days I spent several hours with Ruth. As she related her horrific story I could see the terrified innocent nine-year-old looking back at me. There were many tears. She was also angry and apprehensive. Sexual predators do enormous psychological damage to their innocent victims, instilling a sense of fear and shame which never leaves them.

Ruth described how she and her sister used to play with Walsh's daughters at his home in Sandymount. He was a good friend of her dad and was a regular visitor to their home.

Walsh was known as someone who loved kids. He would take Ruth away on the pretence of bringing her for a drive in his car or down to see his daughters. It emerged that he had been grooming her for a long time before making his move. Everything she told me spoke of a serial, well-practised predator.

Walsh abused Ruth on three occasions in 1993 in the period before he was jailed. He raped her twice and sexually assaulted her once. She described in detail how during the first incident the Monkey committed a sex assault on her when he took her to the home of a prominent Dublin solicitor. I don't propose to go into the details here. The lawyer was not present when the incident took place and there was no evidence that he was aware it ever happened. As our investigation continued it became clear that no one apart from his victims knew the monster that hid in plain view.

The rape attacks occurred at the East Wall of Dublin Bay near Sandymount beach in south Dublin around August 1993. It was the same spot where the psychopathic gangster posed for pictures when he gave his boastful interview to the *Sunday World* in 2005.

The first rape took place when she was alone with Walsh there. On the second occasion Walsh was playing hide and seek with the two sisters. It was a ruse to separate his victim from her older sibling. We established that Rossi had a preference for victims who were under the age of puberty. On that occasion, in broad daylight, the gangster raped Ruth. However, Jennifer witnessed it from where she was hiding as part of the sick game. Out of earshot of her sibling, Walsh had threatened to kill Ruth, her sister and parents if she ever spoke about what he had done. It is a tactic commonly used by paedophiles.

On the day that Walsh's conviction was being reported on the news in 1993 Jennifer told their mother what happened. With Walsh in prison there seemed little that the family could do, and it was allowed to fade into the background of their lives but never went away. The abuse had taken a terrible toll on Ruth's life. She had difficulties in school and then dropped out even though she was an extremely bright kid. She went on to work as a care assistant looking after elderly people and in a chocolate factory. She told me:

> I hate him for what he has done to me. He interfered with my childhood and adolescence. He had no right to do that. I was terrified when I heard that he would be back on the streets again. I am talking to the *Sunday World* because I want to tell people exactly what he is and to protect other people, other families that he might be close to.
>
> He terrorized me. After he raped me he threatened me a number of times that he would get me and my mam and dad if I ever told anyone what he did. I understood that he was going to harm us or get us. I remember him raping me. I remember the pain, and I screamed. I remember how scared and confused I was.
>
> After we saw him on the TV my sister blurted out what she had seen. I had begged her to say nothing. Then my mam questioned me about it, and I told her it was true. Then my dad was told and he hit the roof. He called Walsh all the names under the sun. He was a friend of my dad. My parents were very upset and angry.

> After that we never really mentioned it again. I suppose my family thought that there was nothing they could do against someone like Rossi Walsh with all his heavy connections. Anyway he was already in prison so I suppose they felt there was nothing more they could do to him.

Ruth told me she had also experienced difficulties in forming relationships but in 2004 her life took a positive turn when she met the love of her life, Clint Hamilton, a charming, hard-working gentleman who would become her future husband. Clint was the first person outside her family with whom she shared her secret.

In the same year the highly intelligent and articulate young woman began attending counselling which she paid for herself. She was diagnosed as suffering from PTSD, depression and feelings of shame and self-loathing. But Ruth Dunne was a fighter, and she eventually became stronger.

As a result of that process, she plucked up the courage and made a complaint against Walsh in 2005, making her a champion for other abuse victims. She told me:

> It was always there, the memory of what happened. I just wanted to do something to let him know that I wasn't forgetting. I had a number of relationships but I could never open up to anyone. Clint was the first person I told about it. But I finally decided to go for counselling a few years ago because it was always there in my mind and it affected my relationships.
>
> I had dropped out of school and my parents had split up. At first I found the counselling very hard but eventually I got stronger. I wanted to let him know that he has no control or

power over me. I then went to the police and made a statement about what happened to me. They took statements from the rest of the family but we didn't hear from the police for a long time.

When she read about Walsh's release from prison she was terrified.

> I was in work one day and during my break I saw a picture of him in *The Irish Times* saying that he had been released from prison. I got a fright because I didn't know he was out. No one had told me. I was very scared. I rang the garda involved in the case. She didn't know that Walsh was out either. I came home and went to the police station with my dad to see did anyone know anything. The garda we spoke to didn't seem to want to know. I am afraid of him but I am also angry that nothing has been done even though I reported this crime 18 months ago, just before he was due to get out of prison.
>
> I asked the police for protection. He had known that I had told people what he did to me back in 2004. But the police didn't give me any protection, just a few telephone numbers. He seems to be well in with the law.

Ruth also revealed that after her allegations became known locally she had been approached by another girl who had been abused by Walsh as a child. The abuse took place when she was ten years old. Ruth said she would contact the other victim to see would she also talk to me. I was now aware of three victims. The story of Rossi Walsh, the gangland paedophile, was beginning to take shape.

I then interviewed her sister Jennifer and Ruth's other family members. Jennifer had a very clear recollection of what she saw in 1993. I typed up the notes of the interviews and presented them to

MacGinty and Kelly. However, we still needed more corroboration from other victims before we could take the big step of naming and shaming Walsh.

In mid-October 2006 gardaí arrested Walsh for questioning about Ruth's claims. True to form the barrack room lawyer refused to answer any questions and denied the allegations. Sources told me that he had also denied them to associates. For us, the arrest was important corroboration to help the story stand up to legal scrutiny. Confirmation that he was under active criminal investigation added impetus to the story. Then luck intervened.

Quite by accident I discovered that a female colleague in the *Sunday World* advertising department happened to be a friend of the woman who had made allegations against him in 2003. I told the colleague about the interview with Ruth and she phoned her friend who agreed to meet with us.

The revelation that we were planning to expose Walsh came as a great relief to the woman. At last she too was now being believed. She confirmed everything that we had heard about her case on the grapevine. The woman was related to Walsh's wife and had regularly stayed in their home in Sandymount when she was a child. She gave me graphic details of how he had regularly abused her in the late 1970s and early 1980s. The abuse began when she was around eight years of age and continued until she began 'fighting back' at the age of eleven.

The victim told me that she had been shunned by members of her family after she first came forward with her allegations. The abuse and the overwhelming sense of injustice had blighted her life. She had made three attempts to take her own life over the years before she began attending counselling. What was particularly revealing was that one of the only people who had supported her was another close blood relative of Walsh's. She told me:

> I am determined not to allow this case to drop. I want to help others who may be in danger. He [Walsh] once told me, 'I have loads of little girls... you were always my favourite little girl.'
> I am living in fear of this man but I want some justice for what happened to me.

She later asked the police to reopen her case in light of Ruth Dunne's allegations. The gardaí did subsequently revisit the case but the lack of corroboration meant that the DPP would not proceed with charges.

However, Walsh's arrest and the second victim interview gave us everything that we needed to finally get the story over the line and into print. I remember Kelly phoning after he read the first draft: 'You have the story, let it run.'

On 5 November we published the story on the front page with four pages inside the paper. We held nothing back. In a centre spread we featured the picture Walsh had posed for on Sandymount beach with the headline: 'How evil Rossi Walsh raped me as a young child on this very beach. The victim of ruthless gangster breaks her silence for the first time.'

Neither Ruth nor the second victim was identified in the story as we gave them pseudonyms. We also reported how Walsh had been arrested. As part of the coverage we revealed how a major gangster who had been suspected of organizing gang-related killings was supporting the victims.

The source of that information told me:

> He [named gangster] might not be the most savoury character around but criminals don't like this kind of thing [sex abuse]. So, the word has been sent out that no one is to mess around with [victim] or her family. Let the police do their job.

For once all of us – the police, the criminals and the *Sunday World* – were on the one side.

Legally the publication did not interfere with the criminal justice process. Walsh had the right to sue the *Sunday World* but strangely the litigious self-styled lawyer didn't even send us a threatening letter. The publication of the story got the desired effect. Walsh found himself being isolated in gangland and in the neighbourhoods where he had once been a man of respect. There were serious concerns being expressed that the paedophile was living with a young woman and had access to her children. However, he did still have allies amongst some of his old associates and fools who thought it would give them street credibility to be on his side.

Over the weeks and months that followed various sources contacted me with the names of other victims. I made discreet approaches to some of them, with the help of local people and family members, but they were too scared to go on the record or to report the assaults to the police.

But in March 2007 I added to Walsh's woes when a third victim agreed to tell me her story. The then twenty-six-year-old was the same woman who had approached Ruth when she first heard of her allegations. When Ruth's story was published, it gave her the courage to also come forward. At the time of the abuse she was seven years old and was a friend of Walsh's daughters, regularly visiting their family home. It was obvious that the Monkey had cynically used his daughters' friendships as cover for his crimes. His daughters were too young to have any knowledge of what had been going on. In the interview the victim revealed how she had tried to blank out the sordid memories. She told me:

> I spotted him one day in 2005 in Pearse House flats carrying a child in his arms. It was the first time I had seen him since I was a child. When I saw him I was overcome with panic, and I ran into my friend's flat nearby and vomited. My friend was one of the few people I had confided in.
>
> I also heard around that time what had happened to Ruth and then I knew that I wasn't alone. One of the reasons I have come forward is that this man will no longer be allowed near any more little girls. I was so sick when I saw him with a child in the flats.
> I also want to appeal to anyone else out there who has been a victim or knows a victim of this man to come forward and talk to the police.

Giving the young woman a voice and publishing her story also gave her the confidence to make a formal complaint to the gardaí a month later. As part of that investigation Walsh was arrested and questioned in July 2007.

A week after the interview appeared I revealed that the disgraced ordinary decent criminal had fathered a child with the young drug addict he was living with. We referenced the fact that the woman had two other young children without pointedly saying that they were also vulnerable.

Later that year the DPP gave a direction that Walsh was to be charged for the attacks on Ruth. He was accused of two counts of rape and one count each of sexual assault and oral rape on dates between 1 January and 9 November 1993. He was arrested and formally charged before the Dublin District Court. He was held in custody for a period but later got bail on strict conditions that he stayed away from his victims and the entire south Dublin area.

Sometime later he was also charged with the sexual abuse of the second victim we had interviewed. The charges related to two counts of indecent assault on the then seven-year-old which took place on two occasions between 1 May 1988 and 30 September 1988.

Despite the mounting evidence against him Walsh still had friends who refused to believe that he was a paedophile. They preferred Rossi's preposterous theory that it was all a conspiracy concocted by the *Sunday World* and the police to destroy him because of how he had challenged the legal system. For years afterwards Rossi would tell anyone who listened that he was going to 'take millions' from us for defaming him.

As a result of his bail conditions, he was invited to live in the home of one of his more vocal supporters in County Kildare in 2008. That turned out to be a big mistake. The man discovered the awful truth about his pal in the worst possible way.

In January 2009 I was in the *Sunday World* newsroom when Rossi's supporter phoned in looking to speak with me. I had watched him at one of Walsh's remand hearings in Ruth's case where he openly sneered at Christy Dunne. But the sneering had disappeared when he revealed how he had just discovered that his 'innocent' friend had begun sexually abusing his fourteen-year-old daughter shortly after he moved into his home several months earlier. Within weeks of moving in Walsh had tried to rape the schoolgirl and just weeks later he succeeded in doing so. When the man confronted Rossi the feared criminal claimed that he and his victim were 'going out together'. At this point the man ordered Rossi to leave his home.

I still recall how I lost my temper and called him a 'fucking fool' who should have known the allegations against his pal had not been concocted. Even if they were never proven then he should have surely erred on the side of caution when he had a young daughter. I showed him no sympathy and bluntly said that he was just as responsible for what had happened to his child as Walsh was. I reminded him how he had verbally abused and sneered at Ruth's family and the victims.

When I calmed down I told him he had only one option and that was to go to the police with his daughter which he duly did. A month later the father of the girl and his associates drove to Dublin where they confronted Walsh in a pub in Rathmines. A mass brawl broke out when Walsh and his underworld pals beat up the group. Despite his advancing years the Monkey was extremely fit and a very capable street fighter.

The gardaí investigated the young girl's complaints and Walsh was subsequently charged with eleven more sex abuse offences – two for sexual assault and nine for the defilement of the child at her home on dates between 1 August 2008 and 6 January 2009.

In the meantime I remained in constant touch with Ruth and her family. I became a part of her support network and was honoured to say that she and her family became friends. As a journalist and a father I felt protective of her and the other victims I spoke to. But in the stressful period before the trial there were wobbles.

One day I recall Ruth phoning in a panic to say that she had just spotted Walsh leaning on a wall somewhere in south Dublin. She was very distressed and took several days off work. The officer in charge of the case, Detective Inspector Kevin Dolan, went to court seeking to have Walsh put back in custody. However, the court refused the application but did tighten the Monkey's bail conditions. By that stage charges had not yet been preferred in the two other abuse investigations. As a result, they could not be brought to the court's attention.

Walsh finally went on trial before a jury in the Central Criminal Court in December 2009. Pleas of not guilty were entered on his behalf by the presiding judge, Mr Justice Paul Carney, when the serial abuser refused to indicate whether he was pleading guilty or not guilty to the offences. It was a typical Rossi Walsh stunt which made no difference to his case.

Ruth showed enormous courage and fortitude when she took the witness stand in front of her abuser and told in graphic detail what he had done to her sixteen years earlier. Her sister Jennifer also bravely gave her evidence of what she had seen in 1993.

At one stage in the trial I was subpoenaed to appear before the judge on foot of an order sought by Walsh. I was served with the order on the evening of Tuesday 8 December informing me that I was to appear the following day. It declared:

> You are hereby commanded to attend at Court number 1 the Central Criminal Court at 2 p.m. at the Four Courts, Dublin, from day to day until the above case is tried and to give evidence and to bring with you and produce at the time and place aforesaid all notes memorandum and electronic recordings in respect of the interview you conducted with Ms Ruth Dunne in respect of allegations made by her against Mr Stephen Walsh that the said Mr Walsh sexually assaulted and raped Ms Dunne.

It was clear Walsh wanted to take possession of my notes in an effort to find something that might get him acquitted. It was bizarre to say the least. I went down that afternoon with Kieran Kelly, who was prepared to object to any material being handed over to the gangster. Walsh's lawyers had requested the court to be cleared of all witnesses and for me to be examined in the absence of the jury. I brought a file containing the typed notes of the interviews I had conducted with Ruth but none of my other notes. Kelly was going to claim privilege over those documents on the grounds that they contained sensitive information from other victims and sources. Mr Justice Carney, who had a reputation as an extremely capable judge who took no nonsense in his court, bluntly told Walsh that he would not be handing the notes over to him. He said that he and he alone would decide whether there was material of any relevance to the defence in my file.

I was called to the witness stand in the courtroom which was deserted apart from a few gardaí, the prosecution and defence teams, and Walsh. I handed Judge Carney my file of notes. After spending about fifteen minutes reading through the notes the no-nonsense judge handed me back the file and thanked me for my presence. He said that he could see nothing of benefit to the defence and I was excused.

Walsh's defence team then demanded that I be generally barred from attending the hearing so that the jury could not see me which was equally bizarre. As a journalist I was entitled by law to be present in court to report on proceedings. It appeared that Walsh felt my presence there might in some strange way influence the jury. To avoid a major legal argument, I agreed to leave.

On 18 December 2009, after deliberating for seven hours, the jury unanimously found Walsh guilty on three of the four charges before the court including the two counts of rape. Inspector Colm O'Malley was called to give evidence of Walsh's character and previous convictions because Mr Justice Carney said he wanted the jury to know 'who they had been dealing with and what had been kept from them' during the trial.

The judge then ordered Walsh to be registered as a sex offender and remanded him in custody for sentencing in February 2010. It was a stunning victory for Ruth and her family. It was also a triumph of good over evil. Since I'd first met her as a terrified victim three years earlier, Ruth had blossomed into a strong, confident survivor. It was a profound honour to have played a small role in that transformation. Ruth had decided that she was going to waive her anonymity at the sentencing hearing. She was determined to show other victims of abuse that they too would be heard.

The conviction of one of the most notorious gangland figures in the country was big news. That weekend I wrote another story about the case and how justice had finally been done, declaring:

> One of Dublin's most notorious aging criminals, who was once a key member of the General's gang, was behind bars last night after finally being exposed for what he really is – a twisted paedophile.

It was one of the last stories I wrote for the *Sunday World* before my move to the Irish edition of the *News of the World* as crime editor. I loved the paper and everyone I worked with but felt, either rightly or wrongly, that it was time to move on.

By the time the sentencing hearing came around on Friday 19 February 2010 I was unable to write a line about the case. The *Sunday World* had sought an injunction blocking my move to the *News of the World*. As a result I was placed on enforced gardening leave for three months before I could officially start with my new employer.

Sentencing Walsh to ten years Mr Justice Carney described the case as one of the most repulsive he had encountered in his eighteen years as a judge. He noted the 'inherent gravity' of the attacks, the young age of the victim and Walsh's threats to the victim's parents. He said he could find no mitigating factors to reduce the sentence.

Judge Carney imposed seven years of post-release supervision and warned Walsh he could be jailed again if he failed to abide by its terms. After that the once powerful godfather of organized crime was taken to prison where he was segregated with the other convicted sex offenders for the duration of his time inside. It was a stunning downfall for a thug who believed he was untouchable.

Outside the court Ruth Dunne stood confidently beside her family and the gardaí as she addressed the waiting media:

> I am pleased with the results and justice that has been done here today. I am glad that this man has been exposed to the public for what he really is. I would like to thank my family, partner and everyone who has supported me. I would especially like to thank the court support service, my counsel and Mr Justice Paul Carney.

Later that evening I joined Ruth, Clint and her family for a celebration of her long, traumatic journey to justice. A month later I had the honour of being invited with Ruth to discuss the case and gangland's most prolific paedophile on the *Late Late Show* with Ryan Tubridy. I was so immensely proud of her. She had become a beacon of light in the darkness for so many others. But the story of gangland's Jimmy Savile didn't end there.

Eight months later, in October of 2010, sixty-one-year-old Walsh was back in court to be tried for the indecent assault offences against the third victim I had interviewed. The notorious thug defended himself during the four-day trial after sacking his defence team.

Wearing faded jeans and a T shirt with the word 'corrupt' emblazoned on the back, Walsh refused to enter a plea in the case and gave his address as 'the Irish Republic'. As in the previous case Judge Pat McCartan entered a not guilty plea on his behalf.

The psychopath seemed to relish putting his innocent victim through the hell of his abuse again when he cross-examined her. It was a horrendous ordeal for his victim to endure and very hard to stomach as I watched the contemptuous shenanigans from the press bench. But there was nothing the court could do about it – Walsh had the right to defend himself.

But just as Ruth had done in her case, the young mother showed great courage and resolve in the face of such blatant intimidation. When Walsh asked her why it had taken her so long to come forward she replied:

> Because I was ashamed; you hurt me and when you tell people you have to deal with it. I was ashamed. I felt dirty and ashamed. You know, you were there. You don't know how upsetting it is, you don't know how this has affected my life and you can stand there and question me? You say you want your rights, what about the rights of a child?

When the despicable monster then asked her if she was in a position to verify any of her allegations she replied: 'Obviously not, it was just you and me there.'

Walsh's contemptuous attitude was not lost on the jury or the judge. After a three-day trial they convicted him on the two charges of indecent assault. A month later he was sentenced to three years which was to begin on the expiration of the ten-year stretch he was already serving.

Walsh told Judge McCartan that he was taking 'no hand, act, or part' in the sentence hearing after his application challenging the legality of procedures bringing him before the court, and his request to have the hearing adjourned while he appealed the conviction, was refused.

Describing Walsh as a 'serious criminal' the judge said he had taken advantage of a young girl, and the woman had been obliged to relive the experience again during the trial where she was cross-examined by him. 'I have a clear recollection of her stressed condition,' Judge McCartan remarked.

After the conviction Ruth and the other woman gave me an exclusive interview for the Irish *News of the World*. The two brave women spoke of their delight that the monster was now where he belonged. The woman told of the sense of dread that engulfed her when she realized Walsh was going to cross examine her in court. She told me:

> I felt terrified and when I got a call a few days before the trial telling me that he was going to represent himself. I was in bits because I knew I would have to face him and answer his questions.
>
> With his track record I am amazed that he was allowed to do that. The way he dressed for court every day – in old jeans and a T shirt – showed that he has no respect for the law. I know that people say it is the system, but it doesn't mean that it makes it right. He should not be allowed to examine his victims like that.

She then reflected the feelings of Walsh's victims everywhere, including the many who never came forward.

> I cannot believe that God would create a creature like that, he is the scum of the earth. He is a vile, twisted monster. Sexually abusing a little child is the worst thing that anyone can do to another human being. I was so happy to see him being led out of the court with his head held down.

In 2022, however, the conviction was overturned on a technicality when Walsh successfully argued that he could not get a fair trial due to adverse pre-trial media coverage outlining Ruth's case. The Court of Appeal ruled that the trial judge should have adjourned the trial for such a time to allow a fade factor in terms of any juror's memory of the news coverage. In any event it didn't change Walsh's situation.

In December 2011, a year after the second trial, Walsh was jailed for another ten years for the sexual abuse of the fourteen-year-old child in 2008 and 2009. As before Walsh sacked his defence team and defended himself. His victim was subjected to the same intimidating cross-examination. The sentence was to begin when the previous sentence expired.

A year later in August 2012 my wife and I were honoured to be amongst the guests at the wedding of Ruth and Clint. It was an incredibly happy occasion and a memory I will always cherish. I recall during the speeches being asked to say a few words about the bride. There were some tears shed when I mentioned that I had first met her in very different circumstances and how proud I was to see how she had blossomed into a remarkable woman.

In November 2024 Stephen 'Rossi' Walsh was released from prison after serving nearly fifteen years for his appalling crimes against children. But, now aged seventy-five, the pensioner was still demonstrating his contempt for the law.

He was returned to prison in January 2025 to serve a five-month sentence for refusing to notify the gardaí of his address. Under the terms of the Sex Offenders Act he is legally obliged to give gardaí his name, date of birth and home address within three days of his release.

Walsh was released again on 30 July 2025. If he continues to refuse to comply with the law, he faces more time behind bars. If he does comply then he will be monitored closely by the police for the rest of his life.

CHAPTER SEVEN

THE ACCIDENTAL HERO AND THE TERROR OF MURDER INC.

Gang wars, like all wars, create a rare category of victims who become reluctant, accidental heroes when they face down malevolent forces. They are anonymous, ordinary decent men and women who, through no fault of their own, find themselves trapped by the hidden hand of fate in a nightmare of tragedy, fear and loss they could not have imagined in their worst dreams. When pernicious evil arrives uninvited into their lives it awakens an almost superhuman reserve of courage that they never knew they possessed. Rather than run, they turn and fight back in the quest for justice. In the process they become a powerful voice for crime victims everywhere and spur the State into action.

As a crime reporter I have covered countless stories of the heartbreaking collateral damage suffered by the innocent, especially those who have seen their loved ones murdered or maimed by ruthless gangsters for whom life is as cheap as a bag of cocaine. I have never ceased to be amazed and humbled by their stoicism in the face of such overwhelming adversity.

In my career I have highlighted the horrendous experiences and inspiring courage of a lot of accidental heroes, all of whom left me with an abiding impression of respect and admiration. Media exposure brings them a degree of justice and recognition – and the public's support and appreciation.

In the hierarchy of heroes – and not to diminish any of the others – there is one man who stands out as the most courageous of them all. He became a voice for the silent majority whose lives had been blighted by the scourge of organized crime when he shone a light into the vile world of the most barbaric and depraved mafia in Irish criminal history – Limerick's Murder Inc. That person is my dear friend Steve Collins, whose innocent family was subjected to the terrifying maniacal rage of the psychopathic Dundon brothers who waged an unprecedented war against gangland rivals, the law and the ordinary citizens of Limerick City for over a decade. Leaders Wayne and John Dundon, along with their brothers Dessie and Ger, wreaked havoc in Limerick after their arrival from the UK in 2000.

For standing up to Murder Inc.'s leader Wayne Dundon and doing his civic duty after his adopted son, Ryan Lee, was shot and seriously injured, Steve paid an unimaginable price. His eldest boy, Roy, who ran the family's business with his dad, was murdered in revenge.

For several years Steve, his equally courageous wife Carmel and their children, Steve junior, Ryan, Paul and Leanne, were targeted by the Dundons in a sustained campaign of unrelenting intimidation that still defies belief. One business was burnt down, and others were closed when customers were too fearful they would be shot in the crossfire, plunging the family into near penury. Steve was targeted for execution numerous times, forcing the family to live with armed police protection. They suffered post-traumatic stress and when they could tolerate the situation no longer were eventually forced to very publicly emigrate as part of a witness relocation programme. I still find it hard to contemplate what Steve and his family went through.

Steve Collins emerged as a hero whose warm personality and articulate honesty about what had happened to his family endeared him to the Irish public, the media and the political establishment. He campaigned to bring an end to the mindless bloodshed unleashed by the sadistic Dundons whose ascent to gangland domination was part of Mikey Kelly's inglorious legacy.

Steve's campaign encouraged the Government to introduce tough anti-gang legislation which he regards as his son's legacy. The laws introduced in 2009 have proved highly effective and have given gardaí the tools to smash many gangs in the years since, including the Kinahan cartel.

His courage combined with the longest, most-sustained police investigation in Irish history, ultimately led to the downfall of Murder Inc. It is not an exaggeration to say that if it were not for him the murder and mayhem would have lasted longer and claimed more lives.

He became the embodiment of Irish political philosopher Edmund Burke's dictum: 'When bad men combine, the good must associate; else they will fall, one by one, in unpitied sacrifice in a contemptible struggle.'

But it was a long and bloody journey before that was achieved.

———

Ireland had never seen the likes of Murder Inc. The Dundon/McCarthy cousins formed a mafia-style organization with tentacles everywhere. They had connections with gangs all over the country supplying guns and killers to feuding mobs in Dublin and Cork. Everyone in gangland, even the most hardened criminals, feared their awesome propensity for extreme violence. Their sphere of influence through extended family members and the travelling community included connections in the UK and mainland Europe. Other gangsters were anxious to stay on their good side. A secret garda intelligence report drawn up in 2003 identified seventeen criminal gangs operating in the country which were described as being 'highly organized'. The Dundon/McCarthy mob was classified as the most dangerous in Ireland.

I spent fourteen years chronicling their unprecedented reign of terror. In just over ten years they were responsible for over twenty murders including those of five completely innocent people, including Roy Collins. They left scores of people scarred and maimed for life. Like paedophiles they groomed impressionable children from deprived backgrounds who they effectively enslaved and forced to kill, intimidate and sell drugs on their behalf. I also covered the stories of at least five young men who resorted to suicide as the only means of getting out of the gang's clutches.

Wayne Dundon, a highly volatile bully literally took over the local neighbourhood where they lived in Ballinacurra Weston, on Limerick's southside, by waging a campaign of intimidation to drive families from their homes. He and his clan conducted their own version of social engineering that was akin to the Nazi-style *Lebensraum*. He forced people to sell their homes for a fraction of the market value by giving them an offer they could not refuse. The Dundons wanted to house members of the gang whom the council had evicted from other estates because of anti-social behaviour.

Many of those driven out of their homes had been customers of pub owner Steve Collins. He told me:

> They offered people about €10,000 for a house that was worth about €80,000, and when the people wouldn't take it the gang burned them out. They took over whole blocks of houses, marking their territory, so they'd all be living in a square in what they called their stronghold. The area was already neglected but they finished off the destruction.

In the process Wayne Dundon created a lawless ghetto, a desolate hell that felt like an open prison for the unfortunate people who remained. Their reign of unrivalled terror and depravity was even worse than the Kinahan/Hutch feud.

Like the people who were either victimized by them or who investigated their crimes, I still find it difficult to describe these monsters. In some ways the evil that they exuded was almost supernatural, like something you would see in a horror movie or read in a John Connolly novel. They defied criminological explanation.

Unlike any other criminals I have ever encountered Wayne, John, Dessie and Ger Dundon's unrivalled capacity for savagery stemmed from the fact that they were untroubled by behavioural boundaries. They had no moral qualms about killing on a mere whim, either by accident or design. Their upbringing and family DNA provides a partial explanation.

Their father Kenneth Dundon was an alcoholic, a violent criminal and a monster at home who regularly dished out beatings to his wife and children. His wife, Anne McCarthy, was also an alcoholic. It was probably little wonder that his sons followed in his dysfunctional footsteps. They didn't attend school and began getting in trouble with the police from an early age.

As a young teenager Wayne, who didn't smoke, drink or take drugs, once beat his mother so badly that she was hospitalized for three weeks. When he was eighteen years old he was jailed for a series of robberies of elderly people in London. During one burglary he savagely beat up a wheelchair-bound pensioner. When his sentence was served the British Home Office considered him to be so dangerous that it issued a deportation order against him. That was when the family from hell arrived back in their native Limerick.

Devoid of any semblance of empathy or remorse, the brothers were textbook psychopaths. Emotions such as pity, shame or guilt were deleted from their human hard drives and they regarded people only as targets and exploitable opportunities. Their sense of empowerment and satisfaction was obtained by inflicting cruelty. They had a natural aptitude for terror-instilled blind loyalty and enforcing a code of *omerta* in their subordinates. Apart from the absence of humanity in their psyche the savages in Murder Inc. were notoriously perfidious. Behind their backs and well out of earshot their associates nicknamed them the Piranhas. In the travelling community Wayne was called 'Ditch Rat'.

Everything the treacherous monsters said or did was wrapped in a web of lies, deceit and duplicity. As one former associate bluntly put it, 'the fuckers couldn't even lie straight in their beds'.

The only time the leaders of the mob were in any way sincere was when they issued threats of the terminal kind. The Dundons' principal motivation in life, like all other criminals, was money where the end always justified the means – but their means were more outlandish than most.

The murder of Kieran Keane in 2003 was the spark that ignited the gangland firestorm that engulfed Limerick. At the height of the conflagration the city became Ireland's murder capital and had the highest rate of gun crime per capita in Western Europe. Keane's cold-blooded execution led to an urban war for control of the drug trade between the Dundon/McCarthys on one side and the Keane/Collopys on the other.

The perfidious clan had once been friends and customers of Kieran Keane who was the city's biggest drug dealer. They killed him in a spectacular double cross when they staged a gangland coup for control of his territory. Driven by blind tribal hatred, the two groups were responsible for an astonishing catalogue of attacks and counter-attacks.

The situation deteriorated so much in 2003 that for the first time in Ireland the gardaí deployed high-profile firepower on the streets as a deterrent against the criminal gangs. The Emergency Response Unit (ERU), the gardaí's elite specialist weapons and tactics unit, effectively placed Limerick City under curfew. Backed up by police helicopters, they patrolled the streets after dark to try to quell the raging violence. Dozens more armed detectives were also mobilized from Dublin and Cork to assist their local colleagues who were struggling to contain the mayhem. I was covering the astonishing spectacle as it unfolded.

The volume of incidents involving improvised explosive devices became so bad that an army bomb disposal squad was stationed in Limerick on a semi-permanent basis. In the working-class estates worst hit by the fighting, unarmed police patrols had to be escorted by armed colleagues. The city had the highest concentration of gardaí, including armed units, in the country.

In the period between 2000 and 2010 the gardaí recorded up to a thousand incidents of drive-by shootings, arson attacks, criminal damage, abductions, stabbings, bombings, attempted murders and executions. In the same period there were 556 shootings recorded in the city compared to just fifty-one in Cork, a city at least three times the size of Limerick. Most of the violence was initially driven by inter-family feuds. When gardaí moved against the Dundons and the other clans, Mikey Kelly stepped in with his so-called peace process. (See Chapter 5.) That seminal event allowed the Dundon brothers to thrive.

The combatants strutted through the streets, openly wearing bullet-proof vests. The Dundons drove around in two armour-plated four-litre BMW X5 jeeps, valued at €150,000 each, which they imported from Germany. The Criminal Assets Bureau (CAB) subsequently seized the jeeps which were put to much better use when they were confiscated by the Emergency Response Unit (ERU) for use in operations against the gangs.

In full view of the police and judiciary in the city's courts complex, the two sides threatened and intimidated each other. The courts became the scene of some of the biggest security operations ever mounted by the police when they became a flashpoint for violent clashes. The Dundons even tried to burn them down to prevent the Kieran Keane murder trial commencing. They also firebombed the home of one of the prosecuting lawyers in the case.

On another occasion they burnt the offices of State Solicitor Michael Murray who handled all criminal cases in the city. As a result of death threats Murray had to live with armed police protection to do his job safely. He was also one of the heroes in this story, as were so many gardaí on the frontline including Inspector Jim Browne. When the offices were rebuilt the mob tried to burn them a second time. There were also bomb and arson attacks at the homes of local gardaí and prison officers.

Gardaí in the city, despite being stretched to the limit, had the distinction of having the highest clear up rate for serious crime not only in Ireland but the entire EU. They successfully prosecuted hundreds of mobsters on charges of possession of drugs, firearms, making threats to kill, wounding, assault, criminal damage, false imprisonment, attempted murder, murder and manslaughter.

Between 2005 and 2009 Limerick accounted for a quarter of all convictions for firearms offences in the Irish Republic and had the highest number of prosecutions for gangland murders. In the same timeframe there were twenty-eight homicides recorded in Limerick, including gangland murders, of which twenty-three had been solved and convictions secured. The local detective units had seized huge quantities of drugs, guns and explosives. They had also prevented dozens of planned murders. In return the officers on the front line were openly threatened by the rabid thugs. But despite the valiant work of the police the violence continued.

The outbreak of violence blighted a positive period in the city's history. Limerick had emerged as a vibrant, cosmopolitan hub of culture, arts, education and industry. It was also the proud home of Munster Rugby. But the outside world mostly viewed the city through the prism of the warring clans, prompting the comment in an international travel guide, 'Limerick is best seen through the rear-view mirror!'

The corrosive conflict threatened to undermine the commercial and social cohesion of the city. The belligerents struck a terror into the citizenry not seen since the English armies of Oliver Cromwell, William of Orange and the Black and Tans descended on its ancient walls.

During those years I spent so much time working in Limerick that it almost became a second home. At one stage the *Sunday World* considered renting an apartment for my colleagues and me to save on hotel expenses. I also made a lot of good friends in the Treaty City and had a few local pubs that I frequented on my many visits.

Practically every week during that era of upheaval there were incidents and violence to report on. In a typical week in the *Sunday World*, the news editor prepared an early news list which was discussed at the editorial conference on Tuesday. John Donlon would draw up a list of stories that were being pursued. Every week his news list included 'Limerick?'. That meant that before the week's end there would likely be another crime story from the Treaty City. When I first became interested in journalism as a naïve teenager I wanted to be a war correspondent. Covering the gang wars in Limerick was as close as I ever got to achieving that ambition.

A detective who knew the Dundons best once gave me his unvarnished opinion of them.

> They are the most devious and dangerous bastards that we ever encountered in Limerick or anywhere else in Ireland. They are called the Piranhas because they would eat each other if they were hungry enough. They run with the hares and hunt with the hounds. Killing or maiming comes like second nature to all of them and they have absolutely no fear of the law. They are so dangerous that they would be shaking your hand one minute and then shoot you in the back as soon as you turned away from them.
>
> They don't care about doing time or being shot and injured, although they would prefer to avoid both if they could. They accept danger as part of everyday life, like it is an occupational hazard.

At the height of the violence and mayhem I interviewed Michael Murray as part of a three-part documentary for RTÉ called *Badfellas* which told the history of organized crime in Ireland.

The State Solicitor had no doubts about who was driving it all – the Dundons. He told me:

> I think I would put the blame for that on one particular grouping, who have displayed a savagery that I find to this day hard to fathom. They have set the benchmark and the others have followed and it has ratcheted up to the stage now where many killings involve not only murder but the maiming and torturing of somebody in the most horrific of circumstances.

When I asked what he thought drove Murder Inc. he bluntly explained: 'Evil, there is no other word for it. I can't believe that greed does it, it's just these people are pure evil, and they have no respect for life.'

Then there are the insights from those inside the mob. Ger Dundon's partner, April Collins (no relation to Steve Collins), whose brother and father were members of Murder Inc., eventually gave evidence against them in court. She knew their dark secrets and where the bodies were buried after spending eight years with Dundon. She suffered constant beatings at his hands and once had to be hospitalized as a result.

April Collins eventually reached the end of her tether when Wayne and John Dundon threatened to kill her and her family after she left their brutal brother. She did the unthinkable and went to the gardaí to tell them everything she knew, including about several gruesome murders. April gave detectives a firsthand description of life inside Murder Inc.

> The Dundons are unbelievable people... they're monsters. They're very violent people. They terrorize everyone into doing things for them. People are frightened to say no in case they'd be

> killed. It was no life because they were so controlling. They beat me before. They said they will kill me, and I know they will. I am terrified of them.

April Collins's sister Lisa also came forward to help break down Murder Inc.'s impenetrable wall of silence. She told gardaí.

> Ye have no idea what the Dundons are like – they are vicious and evil. We were just always afraid of them like, they were savages. Ye really have no idea what it was like being around them.

Then she sat back, shaking her head and pondered aloud, 'Jesus. . . when I think back.'

It was against this dystopian backdrop of chaos that Steve Collins and his family found themselves in the crosshairs of Murder Inc. and became the human faces of the mindless carnage. In the many interviews I did with Steve over the years to highlight his plight in newspapers and TV documentaries he always struggled to describe the people who turned his life into a living hell. He once told me:

> It is really hard to describe what you're dealing with here because nobody has ever encountered people like these before. There were already plenty of dangerous psychopaths in Limerick when the Dundons arrived but they were a totally different breed of animal altogether. They brought the guns in and the filth in and they brought crime to a new level by showing that they were prepared to slaughter anyone who got in their way.
>
> I've tried to think of some expression to describe them over the years and pond life is probably the best. Their behaviour is

just not normal – words cannot explain what they are like. They infested the area where they lived. They ruined the lives of so many kids and brought the city to its knees. And all the time they seemed to grow stronger on the back of it. They don't get much worse than the Dundons.

Steve and his family can still pinpoint the moment when evil in the person of Wayne Dundon came to turn their lives into a nightmare – 9.25 p.m. on the night of 19 December 2004. It was recorded on the CCTV cameras at Steve's pub, Brannigans. The horror story began when he refused to breach the licensing laws.

The time code in the corner of the footage will be forever etched in the minds of the Collins family. Up to that point Steve, Carmel and their children were a normal happy family unit. Originally from Ballyfermot in Dublin Steve had just qualified as a young electrician when he was sent to do a job in Limerick in 1973 – and never went home. The reason was that he met and fell in love with a local girl called Carmel Lee.

Less than a year later, in January 1974, they were married and settled in Limerick City. They had four children, Roy the eldest, Paul, Steve Junior and daughter Leanne who was the youngest. For several years he had a thriving electrical contracting business before moving into the pub trade.

In 1990 Steve bought the Steering Wheel pub at Roxboro Shopping Centre in the heart of the Southill working-class estate, a short distance from Ballinacurra Weston, the domain of the Dundon/McCarthys. Two years later the family moved to live in Blackpool in the UK where Steve ran a nightclub while continuing to own the pub in Limerick. As his sons came of age they followed their dad into the trade.

In 1999 the family adopted Carmel's thirteen-year-old nephew Ryan Lee, who was tragically orphaned after the death of his father. As a three-year-old he'd witnessed his mother dying from a sudden brain haemorrhage. In 1999 tragedy struck again when Ryan's father, who had been suffering from a long-term illness, fell sick during a holiday in Limerick and died. Steve told me:

> Ryan was very close to us and the poor lad had a huge amount of tragedy in his life so it was natural that we would rear him after his dad died. He was a fabulous kid, and we all loved him very much. He has always been my fifth child.

The same year Steve bought Brannigans Pub in Mulgrave Street, Limerick, and in 2000 the family moved back to live permanently in the city. Roy remained in Blackpool where he ran another nightclub before he too returned to Limerick in 2002.

The Collins were a model family – decent, happy and close – who worked hard and reared their children to be the good people they became. In happier times Steve would bring the boys to watch Manchester United playing at Old Trafford and summer breaks included cruising on Ireland's waterways. In business Steve had a reputation as an honest, hard-working entrepreneur. He and his family had no enemies – until that cold December night.

Brannigans, which had become one of the most popular watering holes in Limerick, was full in the build-up to Christmas week 2004. Eighteen-year-old Ryan Lee, who was an apprentice electrician, was helping his stepdad in the pub to earn some extra money. Around 9.20 p.m. he took a break from behind the bar and went to the front door for some air. As he stood outside a car driven by Wayne Dundon pulled up. His wife, Anne Casey, and Dundon's fourteen-year-old sister Annabel got out and walked to the door.

Steve and his family didn't know Wayne Dundon but like everyone else in Limerick, they were aware of his fearsome reputation as a particularly dangerous thug who relished inflicting pain and fear.

By December 2004 Dundon and his brothers, along with their cousins the McCarthys, were already at the centre of several murder investigations. A year earlier five members of the crime clan had been convicted of the murder of Kieran Keane and given life sentences. The group included his brother Dessie and his cousins Anthony 'Noddy' McCarthy and James McCarthy. The trial of the killers was held in Dublin amid tight security after the court was unable to empanel a jury of twelve people from a panel of 529 in Limerick. It was a stark example of how the fear instilled by the mob was undermining the rule of law.

I had covered part of the trial in November 2003. It coincided with a bomb scare at my home. For over two years afterwards I was accompanied everywhere I went by two armed bodyguards from the Special Detective Unit (SDU). There was also a permanent garda presence at my home which lasted for over a decade.

I recall being advised by the senior officer in charge of the protection detail not to go back to the court after the five accused began jeering and threw some abuse at me in the courtroom. The abuse had not bothered me in the slightest and I smiled back at them. The cops were fearful, however, that some of the gang or John Dundon himself might make a grand gesture and try to assault me. Dundon had already made loud death threats against members of Kieran Keane's family in the court for which he was subsequently charged.

As previously revealed in *Crooks*, at the time the police were investigating a number of plots to kill me. They had received intelligence that associates of Murder Inc. had offered to accept the murder contract. The Piranhas would do anything for money. Killing an interfering journalist would be a bonus. I reckoned I had nothing to fear from the Dundons when compared to my colleagues working in the Limerick newspapers. They had to walk a fine line in their coverage of the carnage because they lived there with their families.

After they were convicted for Keane's abduction and execution the killers sniggered and laughed in the dock as a senior detective, Superintendent Gerry Mahon, described the gang's business strategy.

> The motivation and objective was to murder Kieran Keane and Owen Treacy [his nephew] and to lure two other people into a trap from which I believe two other murders would occur. It [the murder] was to eliminate those who stood in their way and those perceived to be their enemies with the objective of totally dominating Limerick City.

Prior to the Keane murder, the Dundon/McCarthys had shot dead nightclub security manager Brian Fitzgerald in November 2002. The innocent and well-liked father of two young children had refused to allow the gang's dealers sell drugs in Doc's nightclub where he worked. He was then threatened by John Dundon and his cousin Larry McCarthy junior, who was an equally violent and volatile gangster. Fitzgerald made a statement to the police and McCarthy was arrested and held for a time on remand.

Despite the fact that Fitzgerald subsequently withdrew his statement Murder Inc. still had him murdered. As Steve Collins later discovered the evil clan harboured long grudges and their thirst for vengeance was hard to quench. The killing outraged the people of Limerick who held a candlelit vigil in protest at the appalling crime.

Just over a month later the mob were also the chief suspects for the murder of another innocent man, used car dealer Sean Poland. Shortly before midnight on New Year's Eve 2002 Dessie Dundon, Noddy McCarthy and Gary Campion burst into his home in County Clare. Campion was Murder Inc.'s most dangerous hitman who murdered four men and was behind several attempted murders. He is currently serving life sentences for two of those murders.

Sean Poland had sold a car to Campion a week earlier for €1,000. It was later used in a shooting, and they feared that it would be traced back to the car dealer and he would talk. The gangland vultures also wanted their cash back. When Sean Poland answered the door they immediately shot him at close range in the lower abdomen. The thugs calmly stepped across their fatally wounded victim and began ransacking the house. They beat up the victim's terrified girlfriend before tying her up. Then they left, leaving Sean Poland to bleed to death.

Wayne and John Dundon also illustrated their propensity for savagery when they lured Michael Campbell McNamara, a member of the Keane/Collopy mob, to a grisly death in October 2003. McNamara was a violent thug who had been involved in gun and arson attacks at the homes of Murder Inc. He was also a suspect in the murder of John Ryan, a brother of Eddie Ryan whose assassination in 2000 laid the foundations for the explosion of hostilities in 2003.

Together with Gary Campion, the Dundon brothers forced a friend of McNamara's to arrange a meeting on the pretence of selling him a gun. When McNamara walked into the trap they dragged him onto a patch of waste ground called Barry's Field and began torturing him. The following morning McNamara's horrifically mutilated body was found lying in the dirt. His hands and feet were bound, and he had been gagged to silence his screams.

A post-mortem showed that he been stabbed several times in the back and chest as well as being severely beaten. A shotgun had been fired into his pelvis and buttocks, mutilating his lower body. The killers finished him off when he was blasted in the back of the head with the shotgun at close range disfiguring him beyond recognition. It was one of the most gruesome acts of savagery ever witnessed in gangland. Investigating gardaí, shocked by the barbarity, described it as a medieval-style torture and death.

Given his track record to date, it was little wonder that Wayne Dundon had no regard for new licensing laws which made it illegal for children under eighteen to be in a pub after 9 p.m. As Ryan Lee stood at the front door of Brannigans he could see that Dundon's sister was underage. Doing his job, he asked her for ID to establish her age.

Annabel Dundon protested, claiming that she was over eighteen, but she could not produce any identification. Anne Casey demanded she be let in and the young barman apologized as he told her she was welcome but he had no other choice but to refuse the child. Ryan, who was an inoffensive young man, gently repeated that it was against the law and Steve could lose his license if the police arrived. As the argument continued, Wayne Dundon appeared at Ryan's side to find out what was wrong.

Ryan Lee would later tell me in an interview about the incident:

> Dundon came up to me and asked me in an aggressive tone:
> 'What's the problem?' I told him that it was late and that I would

need to see the young girl's ID before she could be let in because it was the law. Dundon got angrier and said: 'It's her first night out, give her a fucking break.' I replied that I couldn't because it was way too late for an underage person to be on the premises. I would need ID to prove that she was over eighteen years of age.

This was not what Wayne Dundon wanted to hear and his mood darkened. Ryan continued:

He stepped up close to my face and put his finger in the shape of a gun and said: 'Fuck you, you're dead.' He was really big and intimidating. Up close you can see the evil burning in his eyes. I thought that he was going to hit me there and then, but he didn't. He said to his wife: 'Are you staying?' Then he grabbed his sister by the hand and took her back to his car. He kept staring back at me, even when he got into the car. He watched me for a short while and turned the car on the road and sped off so hard that the tyres spun on the road.

Anne Casey went into the pub to join her friends. Exactly 24 minutes later, at 9.49 p.m., the pub's CCTV cameras recorded a motorbike arriving outside with two men on board. Wayne Dundon, the pillion passenger, was wearing a crash helmet when he got off the bike. He walked quickly through to the lounge and went inside the bar counter. As he stalked up the length of it, he looked closely at each startled staff member. Then he went into the front bar where he spotted the subject of his murderous rage, Ryan Lee, pulling pints for the locals.

Dundon stood behind his victim and produced a large handgun. He fired a single shot from close range, hitting the barman in the side of his left knee. The bullet travelled through the eighteen-year-old's kneecap and out the other side, shattering it in the process. The bullet lodged in the floor.

Ryan later recalled:

> I was standing at the taps about to pull a pint and, out of the corner of my eye, I noticed a guy standing behind the counter with a motorbike helmet. I half turned to look at him to find out what was going on. I could see that he was wearing a balaclava under the helmet. I could see his eyes... they were pure evil. I didn't see the gun at first. Then I heard the bang and felt a burning sensation in my left knee. I spun around and remember looking into this girl's eyes across the counter. She looked shocked. I grabbed my knee and then fell down. I knew I had been hit. It was a weird feeling.

Dundon tried to leave through the front door of the bar but it was locked. Then he turned to go back out the way he'd come in. As he stepped over his victim, who was lying on the ground in shock and pain, the crazed gangster fired another shot into him. This time the bullet hit Ryan's right hip, travelled through his groin and lodged in his left leg. In the confusion that followed Dundon lowered the weapon and walked quickly back out through the lounge.

Steve Collins heard the bangs and the screams of shocked customers. He chased the gunman outside as he ran to the waiting motorbike. Steve grabbed Dundon as he got on the bike and tried to pull him off. The killer turned and fired a single shot which missed the publican's head by millimetres. 'The blast from the gun was deafening but I heard the whistle of the bullet going past my ear. I felt the force of the bullet,' Steve recalled when I first met him.

The bike sped off into the night and disappeared as gardaí raced to the scene. In less than 90 seconds the incident was over – but the Collins' troubles were only beginning.

Ryan Lee underwent emergency surgery to save his knee. He remained in hospital for two weeks and had to spend Christmas away from his family. The teenager was unable to walk for several months and underwent further operations to rebuild the knee. The barbarous Wayne Dundon assumed that he would get away with it. But this time he had attacked people who refused to be intimidated and believed in the rule of law.

Steve Collins had known Brian Fitzgerald and the reason for his murder. He was all too aware of the fate that lay in store for those who incurred the wrath of the Dundons. He knew in his heart that once the mob had come into their lives they would never leave.

Steve was faced with an appalling dilemma. If he did nothing the Dundons would smell fear and make their lives a hell. If they made a complaint to the gardaí they would remain a target – but at least there was a chance of making Dundon pay for his indiscriminate savagery. The Collins were damned either way but Steve hoped that the police would protect his family.

The gardaí had identified Wayne Dundon from the security footage shortly after the shooting. Ryan was able to identify Dundon as the man who threatened him and there was CCTV footage to corroborate that. Ryan and Steve agreed to make an official complaint and were determined not to back down. It was a decision that had devastating consequences but one that the family never regretted. Steve told me:

> This sudden act of violence terrified the family because we had never known something like this before. It was something that

you read about in the papers. We took the decision together as a family, that we had no other choice but go all the way with this. And once a complaint was made against them they were going to come after us no matter, even if we withdrew the charge. They had done it to Brian Fitzgerald; he withdrew his complaint and they still murdered him. That is the type of animal you are dealing with, so we didn't really have a choice.

Ryan Lee shared his stepdad's beliefs:

Dundon wanted to kill me and there was no way I was going to let that go. I knew that these people were terrorists but I had to go ahead and give evidence against him in court or else he would get a lot worse. But I was scared. I have never been in trouble in my life.

The officers leading the investigation, Detective Inspector Jim Browne and Detective Sergeant Eamon O'Neill, were already involved in several investigations of Murder Inc.'s growing catalogue of crime. Browne was the officer in charge of investigating Brian Fitzgerald's allegations against Larry McCarthy junior and John Dundon. I was aware from talking to Browne that he and his colleagues had been deeply affected by the security manager's murder and felt in some way that they had let him down. They were determined that the cycle would not be repeated with the Collins family. Steve and Ryan were placed under round the clock armed police protection from then on.

Dundon's uncontrollable rage had given them an opportunity to put the most dangerous hoodlum in the city away for a long stretch behind bars. There wasn't sufficient evidence to charge the thug with the actual shooting because the bike and gun had not been recovered. Dundon, who was forensically aware, had also gone into hiding so the gardaí would be unlikely to find evidence linking him to the outrage. But there was ample evidence to sustain a charge of threatening to kill Ryan Lee which carried a maximum sentence of ten years.

Dundon was arrested two days later and taken in for questioning about the shooting and the threats to kill. While he was being questioned by two detectives Dundon flew into an uncontrollable rage and jumped across the table at them. Before they could react he pummelled the startled officers, breaking the jaw of Detective Garda Arthur Ryan.

The vicious assault was recorded on the garda cameras recording the interview. Dundon and his clan had plenty of form for attacking cops. Shortly after he arrived in Limerick the gang leader attacked and seriously injured another garda. His injuries were such that the detective was forced to retire.

Later the same day Dundon was brought before the local District Court where he was charged with threatening to kill Ryan Lee and assaulting the detectives. The police objected to bail on the grounds that Wayne Dundon had access to firearms and posed a serious threat to his victims. There was also a risk that the accused might abscond to the UK or the Continent where he had connections.

The gang boss spent Christmas behind bars. He joined his brothers John and Dessie, his father Kenneth and several of his cousins and associates who were either serving sentences or awaiting trials. John had been remanded in custody on a charge of threatening to kill the wife of Owen Treacy after he testified against the killers of his uncle Kieran Keane. John Dundon made the threats in the court building beside Cloverhill Prison in front of several police witnesses. He was also facing charges for threatening to burn down the home of a prison officer. Their father Kenneth was being held on foot of a European arrest warrant issued by the UK police after he had stabbed his ex-wife's partner to death in a drunken rage. Dessie was doing life for Kieran Keane's murder. With so many of the Dundons behind bars, Limerick enjoyed a peaceful festive season.

Wayne Dundon's trial was due for hearing in Limerick Circuit Criminal Court on 19 April 2005. A few months before it started Dundon appeared before the court to appeal an earlier decision turning down an application to give him back a bullet-proof vest which had been seized by the gardaí. He claimed he needed the body armour because people had shot at him.

The gangster became angry and excitable in the witness box as he was being quizzed about why he needed the vest by State Solicitor Michael Murray. The State was opposing his appeal. Such behaviour tended to signal an imminent emotional explosion. When Dundon was riled he tended to jabber incoherently.

When the judge refused the appeal the maniac sprang from the bench where he was flanked by prison warders and dropped his trousers. Before they could restrain him, Dundon bent over, slapped his bare buttocks and shouted: 'See that, your honour – that's what the Dundons think of you and the gardaí – fuck you, your honour.' Subtlety was alien to the Piranhas.

Wayne was doing everything he could to dissuade Steve and Ryan from giving evidence against him. Showing utter contempt for the police protection, the insidious mob were determined to get the message through to Steve. At first the warnings were not openly threatening.

People began approaching extended family members and friends to advise them of the dire consequences if Steve went ahead with the case. Larry McCarthy junior approached one of Steve's employees with a message offering him €30,000 to drop the case. Steve later told me: 'I knew that McCarthy would be coming back looking for the money plus interest if I ever stooped to take his dirty money – I sent him a message saying, no thanks.'

The pressure was soon ratcheted up when there was a failed arson attack on Brannigans. Then Steve told me he received a phone call in case he hadn't got the message:

> This voice on the phone told me: 'In the interests of your family don't go near the steps [of the courts] or there will be bloodshed.' Then there were cars pulling up outside the pub and revving their engines and all that sort of thing but we were determined to stick to our decision to proceed with the case.

The night before Wayne Dundon's trial a letter addressed to Steve was dropped through the door at the home of Ryan Lee's girlfriend. The chilling message it carried was unambiguous. It read:

> Steve, if you think it's over, think again. Look at all the people that are dead. Look, if you want to call it quits you know what to do. If not, we will attack you, your staff and your businesses... it's up to you.

Time would show that Wayne Dundon meant every word. The following morning Steve gave the letter to the gardaí who were escorting him and Ryan to court. The family remained undeterred.

The mob didn't stop there. Just as the case was about to start it emerged that one of the jurors had been recognized by the gang. His son had received a phone call that implied that if he did not deliver a not guilty verdict and convince the rest of the jury likewise they would be got at. When the matter was brought to the attention of the judge a new jury panel was sworn in.

As the trial began on 20 April 2005, Ryan Lee and Steve Collins were surprised to be told that they could not refer to the shooting incident at Brannigans in their direct testimony. This was because Dundon was appearing on a charge of threatening to kill or cause serious harm. Although there were ample grounds to suspect that Wayne Dundon was the actual shooter, there was no evidence to charge him with that offence. Any mention of the incident could prejudice the jury and the existing charge would be dropped.

My local sources in Limerick had alerted me to the case which was a major story. I covered the two-day hearing during which Dundon demonstrated his contempt by listening to music on headphones as if he were no more than a bored observer. He sneered across the courtroom at his victims whenever the jury wasn't watching. Steve Collins would tell me later how the hoodlum stared at him and tapped his watch 'indicating what I thought was your time will come'.

But undeterred Steve and Ryan, who was still using crutches because of his injuries, gave their evidence. With the CCTV footage it was pretty much an open and shut case. The jury returned a unanimous guilty verdict. He was remanded in custody to await sentencing. A week later the brute pleaded guilty to the attack on the two detectives.

On 12 May Dundon was brought again to the Circuit Criminal Court to hear his fate. In keeping with the mob's attitude to the judiciary again he listened to music on his headphones throughout. The court was told that Ryan Lee, Steve and their family were still under garda protection and were in fear of their lives.

Detective Sergeant Eamon O'Neill gave evidence of Dundon's

previous criminal record and read out the threatening letter that had been sent to Steve Collins before the commencement of the trial. The experienced detective described the gangster as 'one of the most violent criminals I have ever come across during my time in Limerick City.'

Judge Carroll Moran sentenced Dundon to the maximum ten years for the threat to kill. He also imposed two concurrent three-year sentences for the assaults on the detectives. Dundon appeared nonchalant as he was led away to a prison van.

The twenty-seven-year-old killer might have seemed unconcerned but he was anything but. His wife gave birth to their second child three days later. In his cell in Cork Prison, where a wing had been allocated to Murder Inc., Dundon showed his true feelings about the court result. He was sharing a cell with Gareth Collins (no relation to Steve's family), who was serving a five-year stretch for possession of a firearm.

Nine years later, when Collins broke the mob's code of *omerta* and spoke to the police, he described how Dundon was 'cracking up'. He said he overheard Dundon on the phone to his wife Anne shortly after he was sentenced, crying with rage and telling her: 'I swear, I swear, they're not getting away with it.' Dundon was fuming and wallowing in self-pity when he got off the phone. His wife was home alone looking after his two kids. In his warped mind the psychopath blamed his innocent victims for her plight.

Gareth Collins claimed that Dundon said Anne wanted him to 'make sure I kill one of them for this'. He quoted his boss as saying: 'Look what they [Steve Collins' family] are after doing to us, they're after tearing the family apart.' The remorseless psychopath did not have the cognitive capacity to realize that he had been author of his own destiny.

As Dundon was brought back to prison Steve Collins and Ryan Lee went for a few drinks to celebrate with the garda investigation team. Ryan later said:

> People who we never met before were coming up and shaking hands and congratulating us because they were delighted that Dundon was behind bars. For weeks we were getting messages of goodwill from people all over Limerick. It was incredible to think that one individual in particular could cause so much fear and anxiety among people.

The jailing of the gangland savage received extensive coverage in the national media, confirming his well-earned reputation as one of the most dangerous criminals in Ireland. The gang war in Limerick had become a staple of the daily and weekend newspapers by then. After the hearing Jim Browne contacted me to say that Steve and Ryan would happily do an exclusive interview with me. They wanted the public to know what had happened and the evil they had confronted. I travelled down from Dublin with my bodyguards to interview Ryan and Steve in Brannigans where the attack had taken place. It was the first time I met them.

I recall how we laughed about the fact that the three of us had bodyguards. After the interview Steve quietly pointed to Brian Collopy, who was sitting with a few guys having an afternoon pint in a corner of the large bar. Steve said that he wasn't a regular and as long as he had manners he would be served. It was the first time that I laid eyes on Collopy who had already featured in many of my stories.

By May 2005 an uneasy truce had existed between Collopy and Wayne Dundon for just over a year. Both sides had realized that the continuing violence was very bad for business. The police had seized huge quantities of drugs from both sides worth multiple millions of Euro and the CAB was moving to seize their cash and property. The police had arrested and convicted so many gang members that soon most of them would be behind bars.

Despite his reputation for treachery and deceit, not to mention the two attempts they made to kill him, Collopy had shaken hands with Dundon at a meeting in March 2004 chaired by Willie O'Dea, the local TD and junior minister for justice. Collopy was a pragmatist who didn't believe in the use of indiscriminate violence, avoiding it as much as possible.

The truce, however, had greatly angered Christy Keane, Kieran Keane's older brother and the overall head of the gang. Christy was in prison serving a sentence for drug trafficking. For a tense few months it caused a dangerous split between the two allies which threatened to mutate into another shooting feud. Gardaí had prevented one incident between the two sides and calm was later restored. I knew about the truce and had reported on the fallout in the *Sunday World*.

That day in Brannigans Collopy was minding his own business and wasn't there to threaten or annoy anyone. In any event the fact that Steve and Ryan had helped to put Dundon away meant Collopy didn't have to worry about him breaking the truce. In a way he was showing his respect for Dundon's victims.

The pub contained quite an eclectic mix of characters that afternoon. There were three people who were under threat from organized crime, including a hated crime reporter, a total of six armed detectives protecting them and the boss of the city's other major gang having a pint in the corner. Collopy drank up and left before I could approach him for a chat. It was surreal. In less than a year Murder Inc. would forget about the truce and resume their efforts to kill him.

The following Sunday we splashed the story across the front page under the heading, 'Face to Face with Evil', with four pages inside. It carried a picture of Ryan from the back because he didn't want to be easily recognized, a picture of his injured knee and a shot of Wayne Dundon which had been taken at the courts by one of our photographers. It was a unique opportunity to expose him to the world.

Over a two-page spread, I told the full story of 'Ireland's most vicious and evil criminal'. I held nothing back and named him as the person who had shot Ryan.

From the moment I met Steve and Ryan I took an instant liking to them. They were warm, gentle and honest people who certainly never deserved the outrage that was foisted on them.

When the article appeared, I got a call from Steve thanking me. But I recall feeling that this was not over, and it was obvious that the local police didn't think so either.

While the gang boss's incarceration brought relief to the lives of some, Wayne Dundon had no intention of forgetting the family who had stood up to him. A month later he sent a message to Steve Collins and Ryan Lee to remind them that Murder Inc. would never forgive or forget.

Around 4 a.m. on the morning of 16 June 2005, Brannigans Pub was extensively damaged in a fire which gutted the premises. Steve Collins was devastated and the insurance company refused to recoup his losses until the pub was rebuilt. He spent a considerable amount of money designing plans to construct shop units and apartments beside the new pub to help recoup their losses but planning permission was turned down. When the economic crash came in 2008 and the banks suddenly stopped lending it prevented Steve from rebuilding. The once thriving business would never re-open and it dealt a huge financial blow to Steve and his family from which they would never recover – and all because a psychopath's teenage sister wasn't allowed into a pub to have a drink. In the meantime Steve and his family struggled on.

Back on the streets of Limerick there was a huge sense of relief that the worst of Murder Inc.'s rabble was locked up. But it didn't mean an end to the violence. Within a week of Dundon's sentencing Murder Inc. carried out bomb attacks on two houses as part of the feuding. While they observed their truce with the Collopys they had escalated attacks on the Keanes. In one incident young children had a lucky escape when a live grenade exploded after it was thrown through the front window of their home.

However, by Limerick standards, there was a period of relative calm when it came to shooting incidents – which was short lived. For the first nine months of 2005 there were thirty-three shootings recorded. That suddenly changed towards the end of the year. Between October and December there were fifty such incidents, representing an increase of twenty-three on the previous year and over double the figure for 2003. The shooting rate would continue to rise. The following year it reached 97 and in 2007 it peaked at 103.

Apart from shootings, however, there hadn't been a gang murder in fourteen months, primarily because most of the killers were in prison. That came to an end in October when David Nunan, a member of Murder Inc., was lured into a trap and shot in the back. He had just been released from prison. While inside on a firearms charge he gave a severe beating to a member of a Dublin gang with whom the Dundons did business. From his prison cell

Wayne Dundon had no problem ordering the revenge slaying of his own soldier as a favour to their Dublin pals. The shooter had been a friend of Nunan's. There was no such thing as loyalty in Murder Inc. and Nunan was a dispensable asset.

On a national level the year 2005 was also one of the bloodiest on record since organized crime first emerged in Ireland. The names of nineteen people were added to the growing toll of gangland murders. All but two happened in Dublin.

The noughties would prove to be the most violent decade in Irish criminal history. There were so many gang related killings that it was often difficult to keep pace. By the end of the decade over 150 people were categorized as gangland killings including at least eight completely innocent people who were murdered either by design or in cases of mistaken identity.

Roy Collins's name would be added to the death toll when Murder Inc. finally took its revenge.

CHAPTER EIGHT

MURDERING THE INNOCENT, A HERO'S STAND AND THE MOB'S DOWNFALL

On 13 February 2008 Steve Collins received distressing news that brought back the trauma that he and his family were still struggling to put behind them. That morning the Court of Criminal Appeal in Dublin reduced Wayne Dundon's sentence for threatening to kill Ryan Lee from ten years to seven. Much to the shock and despair of Steve, Ryan Lee, the police and the people of Limerick, the court found that the sentence had been 'unduly severe'. It meant that the Ditch Rat would be released from prison two years earlier, in March 2010. That was bad news for everyone, including the gangster population.

In a supreme twist of irony, at the same time a court in Cork was sentencing two of Dundon's henchmen for their part in a conspiracy he had organized to buy an arsenal of military grade weapons. A year earlier Dundon had sent orders from his prison cell telling his gang to procure a cache of twenty-four weapons including two Russian-built RPG-7 rocket launchers, five AK47 assault rifles, five American AR-15 assault rifles, two Uzi submachine guns, ten semi-automatic pistols and a large quantity of high-velocity ammunition. The disparity could not have been more absurd.

The weapons were to be used to murder James Martin Cahill, the hitman they'd hired to murder nightclub manager Brian Fitzgerald in 2002. Cahill had come forward as a State witness against members of the gang involved in the shocking crime including John and Dessie Dundon. The mob's diabolical plan was to use the RPG-7 rocket launchers – weapons often used by terrorists – to blow up the prison van on the motorway as the supergrass was being ferried between court and Portlaoise Prison.

There was no concern for the fact that prison officers, police and innocent bystanders could also be killed or maimed in the attack. Wayne Dundon was also determined to use the extra firepower to escalate Murder Inc.'s violent campaign in Limerick. It was still raging even though the police were filling the prisons with their members.

Gang members Glen Geasley and Sean Callinan were dispatched to meet with members of a Turkish organized crime group based in London where Murder Inc. had extensive underworld contacts. On 22 February 2007 they met what they thought were two members of the Turkish gang in London. They didn't know that the arms dealers were actually two undercover officers from the UK's Serious Organised Crime Agency (SOCA) who had set up an elaborate sting operation, codenamed Operation Beam. Gardaí had received intelligence about the plot and, working in tandem with SOCA, had set a trap for the mob.

Geasley told the spooks that he was representing Wayne Dundon who was a 'major criminal godfather' in Ireland. He said Dundon was the 'decisions man' and that he wanted the weapons 'for a war in Limerick between Wayne's people and their enemies'. Before a deal was struck the undercover officers told Geasley they needed confirmation that he was in fact acting for Dundon.

In April Geasley told the undercover officer to visit an inmate called Thomas Flood in Wheatfield Prison Dublin, where Dundon and his gang members were being held. The violent criminals were practically running the prison. When the officer arrived for the visit Dundon was sitting in the next cubicle. The feared gangster wanted to see the arms dealer himself. The undercover officer handed over a copy of the *Irish Independent* which contained inserts from the *London Life* magazine, including an ad for mobile phones. The mobile number on the advert was the undercover agent's contact number for further discussions on the proposed deal. Dundon picked up the newspaper and nodded to the spook as he went back to his cell.

A few days later Geasley contacted the SOCA agents with the shopping list from his boss. They agreed to provide the cache of weapons in return for Stg£45,000 in cash, on the condition that it was handed over before the delivery. In April 2007 gardaí took weapons that had been seized over the years from the IRA to show Dundon's thugs.

As soon as they produced the money the pair was arrested and later charged. It marked another significant victory for the good guys against the worst mob in Ireland. But progress was slow and incremental. In 2008 the number of shootings dropped to forty-three, yet the war waged on with several people injured in drive-by shootings. It continued to be the top priority for the police as the Government pumped money and resources into the city. The Limerick gang had become a regular topic of discussion around the Cabinet table.

Steve later recalled how he felt when he heard the news from the court:

> When I read that Dundon's sentence had been reduced I just couldn't believe it. I couldn't understand how I was reading on one page that he was getting three years off his sentence in one court and on the opposite page he's linked to buying rocket launchers in another court. It just didn't make any sense to me.

It didn't make sense to anyone.

That following Sunday I wrote about the absurdity of it all, along with the rest of the media. It represented another extraordinary chapter in the story I was covering. Within twelve months Steve would bear the full brunt of the gang's capacity for pure evil. By that time I had written extensively about one of Murder Inc.'s most appalling atrocities yet.

In Wheatfield Prison John and Wayne Dundon focused on plotting the next moves in the war. Despite being locked up, they continued to direct their narco-terrorism issuing orders on smuggled mobile phones and to messengers on visiting day. The fact that he would be getting out a lot sooner than planned was a source of comfort for Wayne who celebrated his victory over the law. John Dundon, who was every bit as volatile and psychotic as his brother, was to be released in July 2008 to take the reins and ratchet up the mayhem.

Less than two years earlier Wayne showed that he had no compunction when it came to plumbing the depths of depravity. In November 2006 he organized the murder in Dublin of Baiba

Saulite, an innocent twenty-eight-year-old Latvian mother of two young children. It stands out as one of the most shocking gang murders I ever covered as a journalist. He did it as a favour for his cell mate, Baiba Saulite's husband Hassan Hassan, a Lebanese crime boss who was serving time for car theft and the abduction of his two sons.

Hassan was the leader of a gang from the Middle East and North Africa and controlled rackets in Ireland and the UK. He ran a sophisticated international multi-million-euro car 'ringing' scam in which high powered cars were stolen to order. Through his connections in Lebanon he was also involved in large scale drug importation and the sale of illegal firearms. Hassan had forged links with Irish gangsters, including Marlo Hyland from Cabra in Dublin, one of the biggest drug traffickers in the country at the time. Hyland was also closely associated with Murder Inc. I had been writing about Marlo for several years, ever since he took over the operation of his boss, PJ 'The Psycho' Judge, whose murder he organized in 1996.

In June 2006 John Dundon asked Hassan to supply a hitman to kill Brian Collopy by luring him into a trap. They thought Collopy would drop his guard because he was unaware of the connection between the Lebanese criminal and Murder Inc. and had done business with the thug in the past. Also Collopy naively believed his truce with the Dundons was still intact. Luckily for him the gardaí knew better, having received intelligence about the plot and saved the godfather's life. Hassan's hitman, thirty-six-year-old Egyptian national Ibrihme Hassan, was arrested with a loaded gun as he was about to carry out the attack.

The murder of Hassan's estranged wife was a return favour. The Lebanese gang boss had sworn revenge on Baiba and her solicitor,

John Hennessy. Hassan had abducted the couple's two sons, aged five and three, in December 2004 and taken them to live in Syria. From his newly opened law practice in Swords, County Dublin, Hennessy fought a year-long legal battle to help his client get her children returned to Ireland. He kept up the pressure on the gardaí to take action against the Lebanese car thief who was subsequently charged with abduction. When her children were initially taken Baiba won the public's sympathy when she spoke of her desperate situation to Joe Duffy on his *Liveline* radio show. With the help of the authorities the children were eventually returned to their mother.

In the early hours of 27 February 2006, there was an attempt to kill Hennessy when petrol was poured through the front letterbox of his home and then set alight. The hallway was engulfed in flames but the lawyer managed to escape. Despite the attack, Hennessy testified against Hassan in the Circuit Criminal Court in Naas. Convicted of running a car theft racket, as a mitigating factor against imprisonment, Hassan had deliberately misled the court, claiming he was the children's sole guardian. Hennessy's evidence exposed the lie and Hassan was jailed for four years. The violent bully developed a deep hatred for the solicitor and his ex-wife whom he had subjected to appalling physical abuse during their marriage.

But Hennessy's first case would almost cost him his life. On 11 October 2006 detectives from Swords Garda station called to see John Hennessy. They had just received detailed intelligence through the Garda Crime and Security branch and the gardaí in Limerick, that a Moroccan asylum seeker had been hired by Hassan Hassan to kill the lawyer. I later discovered through my sources that John Dundon had organized the handgun and a silencer to be used in the assassination. The hit was foiled when an informant in the gang tipped off his garda handlers. The asylum seeker was then arrested on a separate matter by officers from the Garda National Immigration Bureau (GNIB).

Hennessy was kept under observation by armed and uniformed garda units for two weeks until the Crime and Security Branch was satisfied the plot had been thwarted.

Baiba was also being threatened and intimidated by Hassan. In the same month her car was petrol bombed outside her home in Kinsealy, north Dublin. She moved to live in a house near Swords but the mobsters found her again. Baiba told her friends and gardaí that she was living in fear of her ex-husband and talked of leaving Ireland for good with her children and returning to Latvia.

Shortly after the security alert in October I got a call from a barrister friend who said she was looking for some advice. The barrister said John needed to talk to someone with experience of being threatened and having to receive police protection. Through the years I was asked for such advice on many occasions by individuals who had crossed swords with evil people. I was happy to oblige. I phoned John and we had a long conversation about the background to the threats.

I remember hearing the fear and anxiety in his voice. I shared my own experiences about being placed under full-time protection. It could be very intrusive and stressful but I explained you got used to it. If the cops recommended armed protection then I advised him to accept it. I knew that, given the cost and resources involved, such recommendations are only made if the police feel it is absolutely necessary. Gangland violence had reached epidemic levels by 2006 but I remember being astonished that the mobs were prepared to target an officer of the court.

The conversation was strictly off the record but I told John to ring me anytime if he needed to talk. John also asked me to make a few enquiries with my own sources. I contacted a senior garda I was friendly with in Swords who confirmed their concerns for the safety of the lawyer and his client. It was an active security operation. I relayed the information back to John and told him to take care.

I would later reveal in the *Sunday World* how Hassan had sent two more members of his Lebanese gang to kill Baiba. However, the non-nationals had refused to go ahead with it when they saw the mother with her children. Hassan again turned to his cell mate. This time Dundon called Marlo Hyland and asked him to source a handgun and a getaway car.

At the time the gardaí were in the process of tearing Marlo's empire apart and I was following closely. Over eighteen months the National Bureau of Criminal Investigation (NBCI) had seized over €20 million worth of his drugs, a large arsenal of weapons and arrested over forty members of his gang. They were also investigating a string of murders Marlo had ordered against rivals. The CAB was also on his case. The mob boss was under pressure to pay his main suppliers, the Kinahan Cartel. He also owed money to the Dundons. Hyland needed ruthless allies.

Marlo Hyland's people stole a getaway car. He then collected a firearm from fellow drug trafficker Troy Jordan. Three years earlier Jordan had been involved in a plot to attack me and my wife in revenge for exposing his criminal activities that included his links to the Limerick gangs.

Dundon had contacted Paddy Doyle, a notorious hitman for hire who had at least four murders under his belt. He was a sicario for the Thompson/Byrne gang in Crumlin which worked for the Kinahan Cartel. Doyle then recruited two killers from Cabra to do the job. They met with Dundon's sixteen-year-old sister Annabel. She handed them a map showing the location of Baiba's home along with her picture to one of his henchmen. John Dundon had sent it out during a prison visit.

Just before 9.45 p.m. on the evening of Sunday 19 November a lone gunman shot Baiba Saulite at close range as she stood at her front door smoking a cigarette. She died instantly. Her two boys were asleep in their beds. A garda friend later told me how he and his colleagues bundled Baiba's two boys in blankets and took them out of the house, protecting their innocent eyes from the horrific sight of their lifeless mother on the ground.

Within an hour armed cops had taken John Hennessy from his home fearing that he was next to be hit. Gardaí also raided the prison cell occupied by Dundon and Hassan but found no evidence. The two psychopaths had made sure of that. Early the next morning my garda source called me with the shocking news.

I then phoned John who was deeply distressed by Baiba's murder. The courageous lawyer found himself trapped in a nightmare similar to the one Steve Collins was experiencing. He was to spend the next seven years living under full-time armed police protection. John later decided to go public and gave me an exclusive interview to highlight the horrific case and how gangland violence was out of control. Like Steve, I had huge admiration and sympathy for John. He has remained a good friend ever since.

The execution of an innocent mother and an attempt to murder her lawyer horrified the entire nation and sent shockwaves through the legal profession. It illustrated just how dangerous the gang culture had become. The murder of innocent people was becoming all too regular. Earlier that year another young mother, Donna Cleary, was shot dead when a drugged-up thug indiscriminately fired shots into a house party in north Dublin, in revenge for not being invited. Baiba's death brought to twenty the number of gun murders to that point in 2006.

The level of public revulsion could be gauged through Joe Duffy's *Liveline*. Over the following days thousands of callers flooded the show's phone lines to express their anger, shock and disgust. Hundreds attended a memorial service in Baiba's memory after her remains were taken back to Latvia for burial. Her boys were placed in care. There were calls on the Government to get much tougher on organized crime. When Hassan Hassan applied for compassionate temporary release to attend the funeral the police strenuously objected.

In an unprecedented move the officer in charge of the murder investigation, Detective Inspector Walter O'Sullivan used the hearing to point the finger of suspicion at the thug and leave the public in no doubt who was responsible for the outrage. He said that he feared that John Hennessy would be the next victim. He told the hearing that if Hassan was released, 'he will commit more serious offences that, according to information I have, include murder, assault, intimidation and interference with witnesses.' Hassan was refused the temporary release.

Over the weeks that followed it was the only story I worked on. We gave it front-page coverage a number of weeks in a row, and I participated in TV and radio interviews to talk about the case.

Through John Hennessy and my sources in the gardaí and the underworld I was able to reveal how the murder was organized and named the prime suspects – John Dundon and Hassan Hassan. On another front page I also revealed the involvement of Marlo Hyland and Troy Jordan, both of whom I had a major interest in. Thanks to my sources I was able to exclusively disclose how secret garda phone intercepts had recorded Jordan angrily berating Hyland for indirectly involving him in the horror that had repulsed the entire nation and even elements of the underworld. Thugs killing thugs was one thing, the cold-blooded premeditated destruction of a defenceless mother was a whole different matter.

We were the only newspaper to go so far as to name the suspects, but we had solid information from reliable sources. In the *Sunday World* we always liked pushing out the parameters and this was a case where it was not only appropriate, but a damned important public service. Solving the crime had become the number one concern of the Irish public.

Then three weeks later there was yet another gangland horror story. On 12 December two members of Marlo's gang shot him as he slept in bed. They blamed him for the intensive police operation that had resulted in so many of them being arrested and facing long sentences behind bars. The assassins were working on the orders of Marlo's treacherous former lieutenant, Eamon Dunne, the Don.

There was little sympathy for Hyland's violent demise. The Piranhas were most likely impressed by Dunne's act of supreme betrayal. The shocking aspect of the crime was when Marlo's killers also shot dead Anthony Campbell, an innocent young trainee plumber who was fixing a radiator in the house. They were afraid that the nineteen-year-old might identify them to the police. Although they were never convicted of the crime six years later I got an opportunity to name the killers using court privilege when I was subpoenaed to appear as a witness in the trial of one of Dunne's associates. The disclosure gave the rest of the media an opportunity to identify the pair to the public.

The murder of another innocent soul reinforced the public's anger and revulsion. No one could accuse the media of hyperbolizing the crime situation, particularly the embattled Justice Minister Michael McDowell with whom I had many run-ins. As part of the coverage I was contacted by Anthony's brave mother Christine who wanted me to tell her story. She too became an accidental hero, as a brave voice for victims amidst the carnage.

Two weeks after Baiba's murder John Dundon was taken from his cell by Limerick gardaí and charged with the murder of Brian Fitzgerald. His brother Dessie, Gary Campion and gangster Anthony Kelly were also charged. Kelly, who was a major business partner of Murder Inc, was no relation to Mikey Kelly. Hitman James Martin Cahill testified against them. However, in 2007, Kelly and the Dundon brothers were acquitted by the court on the grounds that Cahill's evidence was unreliable. But Campion was convicted of the murder after Brian Fitzgerald's wife was able to identify him.

In the meantime the Dundons continued to direct their war from prison, issuing orders for people to be killed. There was nothing pragmatic or businesslike about their strategy. It was simply to keep fighting until they had wiped out the opposition. It hadn't dawned on the Piranhas, as it had on the Collopys, that the feuding had descended into a monotonous war of attrition where the police were the only side winning.

Ireland's prisons were filling up with gang members who had been caught with drugs and guns in the implacable counter-offensive from the gardaí. The 'Dumdum' Dundons, as they were also known, were upset about losing the guns and drugs, which were expensive to buy, but they were untroubled by any concerns for the boy soldiers caught doing their dirty work. John Dundon dismissed them simply as 'fools'. There was an endless supply of disaffected kids in the sprawling estates they ruled for use as cannon fodder.

One of those fools was twenty-year-old James Cronin who relished the street cred he got for being a made guy in Murder Inc. Cronin was one of the gang's getaway drivers. Wayne and John Dundon sent orders around March 2008 that Cronin and another of the 'fools', cocaine-addled thug Stephen O'Sullivan, were to murder Mark Moloney. In January 2008 O'Sullivan had shot and critically injured Jonathan Fitzgerald, Mark Moloney's nephew and a hitman for the Keane/Collopy side. The attack was in revenge for Jonathan Fitzgerald killing Murder Inc.'s Noel Crawford in December 2006. The revenge scenario was typical of the tit-for-tat madness. Fitzgerald spent weeks on a life support machine and recovered. He was eventually convicted for the Crawford hit.

The fact that Jonathan Fitzgerald hadn't died annoyed the Dundons. To cause him as much grief as possible they ordered the death of Mark Moloney, his innocent uncle, a petty criminal who was not involved in the violence. On Saturday 5 April 2008, O'Sullivan shot Mark Moloney in the back as he walked along the street near his home in Garryowen, Limerick. Cronin drove the stolen car used in the attack. What happened next exemplified the mindset of the Dundons and the chilling extremes they were prepared to go to protect themselves.

Armed gardaí moved quickly in the aftermath of the killing and O'Sullivan was arrested within a few hours. He later admitted his role in the murder and subsequently pleaded guilty. But the gang was more concerned about James Cronin. After the murder the wannabe gangster was overcome with remorse and broke down crying when he realized that he wasn't a natural born killer. That was a fatal weakness in the feral eyes of his malevolent bosses.

When I subsequently wrote the book *Murder Inc.* I obtained a statement that Ger Dundon's ex-partner April Collins made to gardaí about what happened to Cronin. The evidence was never used in court.

She was present when Ger got a call that evening from Wayne in prison. The call concerned James Cronin. During the conversation Ger Dundon confirmed to his brother that Cronin had cried after the murder and asked Wayne if he could trust him. April said in her statement: 'Wayne said, "I'll ask someone and ring you back." Wayne rang back in ten minutes and said, "Don't trust him. . . do what you have to."' Ger Dundon curtly responded, 'alright' and threw away the phone.

James Cronin's fate was sealed.

Murder Inc. had a zero tolerance approach – it was part of their survival strategy. They were paranoid about leaving 'loose ends'. Gang members who had shown weakness and talked in the past had caused too much unnecessary grief. Cronin had to be disposed of. It wasn't personal, it was just business.

April Collins later heard Ger Dundon giving instructions to seventeen-year-old Nathan Killeen to deal with the problem. Killeen was the younger brother of Ciara Killeen, John Dundon's wife. Ciara was a central participant in her husband's business including organizing logistics and cleaning up after various murders. Nathan lived with his sister and her husband from an early age. John Dundon had moulded him into a cold-blooded killer.

A few hours later Killeen returned to Ger Dundon's house laughing. His runners were covered in blood. He announced to his sister, Ger and April, 'Ya, that job is done.' Collins later described how Nathan, Ciara and Ger were 'laughing about what had happened between themselves'. Despite being inured to the violence I had been covering for so long I found the murder of Cronin truly shocking.

Killeen had lured his friend to an area of waste ground at Caledonian Park on the city's southside, on the pretence of burying guns. He gave Cronin a shovel to dig a hole for the weapons but he was really digging his own grave. April Collins recounted in chilling detail how Nathan Killeen was laughing as he described the murder. Collins said that Killeen mimicked how his victim begged for mercy pleading with him, 'please don't'.

The killer went down on his knees to show the position of Cronin just before he killed him. He said Cronin had tried to run away but he hit him with a shovel. The twenty-year-old was on his knees crying for mercy when Killeen shot him in the head. What April Collins was describing could have been a scene from a Martin Scorsese gangster movie.

Less than 48 hours later gardaí found Cronin's partially buried body. It was yet another horrific chapter in the story of Murder Inc. And they had not forgotten about Steve Collins.

———

John Dundon was released from prison in July 2008 and began throwing his weight around. Amongst the people to suffer his wrath were his own gang members, including his cousins the McCarthys, who lived in constant fear of him and his brothers. They were regularly threatened, beaten and bullied by the evil monsters. The abuse sowed the seeds of dissent within the gang which would eventually contribute to the downfall of Murder Inc. But there was a much more sinister development before that could happen.

In October 2008 Wayne Dundon sent a handwritten note to John from prison. The gang boss wasn't prepared to relay the message on a mobile phone or to a visitor in case the police had everything bugged. They'd already scuppered some of his more ambitious plans, and this was too important to screw up. I was later shown the note. The combination of squiggly letters and figures was scrawled in pen on a small, crumpled piece of paper. To the uninformed eye it was no more than an absent-minded doodle scribbled in a moment of boredom.

It read: '75 Pitchfork 75 SC blk jp pref morn.'

The deceptively innocuous permutation of twenty-eight characters carried a dark message. It was the catalyst for a chain of tragic events that would result in the murders of two innocent men. But it would also have unexpected, drastic consequences for its brutal author.

The reference to '75 Pitchfork' was code for a contract worth €75,000 to murder their most hated foe, Johnny McNamara. They'd nicknamed McNamara 'Pitchfork' after Larry McCarthy junior had stabbed him with one nine years earlier. McNamara had testified in court against McCarthy junior which had not been forgotten. The drug dealer, a close associate of the Keane/Collopy mob, was top of their list for eradication. But the rest of the note contained an even more sinister message.

The reference to '75 SC blk jp pref morn' was another €75,000 contract to murder Steve Collins. Dundon's message informed his lackeys that Steve drove a black jeep and the best time to hit him was in the morning when he would most likely be without police protection. It was a measure of Dundon's resolve that the notorious miser was prepared to invest €150,000 to kill the two men.

The coded message came to light when an associate of the gang tipped off Steve that his life was in danger. The gangster respected Steve and his family. He wanted no part in such an atrocity. Steve told me:

> I couldn't believe it and it was like a bolt out of the blue when I was handed that note. We had been trying to get our lives back on some sort of track and we had put Dundon out of our minds. I had already lost two businesses over him, and we were facing bankruptcy. I knew that we would have to look over our shoulders for standing up to this animal but realising that he was now trying to have me murdered was terrifying.

When Steve was given the note he contacted the gardaí who took the coded message seriously.

Detective Superintendent Jim Browne, who had been promoted as the head of the city's detective branch was leading the charge against Murder Inc. Browne was not surprised that the mob wanted to murder McNamara. They had already made numerous attempts to kill him. In 2006 he narrowly escaped when Murder Inc. opened fire on him with a machine gun as he walked into his house. But the violent gangster wasn't exactly innocent. He was responsible for several retaliatory gun and arson attacks on his enemies.

Targeting Steve Collins was a very different proposition. Detectives were divided as to whether Wayne Dundon would dare to cross the line so far and murder an innocent businessman who had testified against him in court. However, those most familiar with the Dundon mindset had no such doubts.

Sources tipped me off that behind the scenes feverous efforts were made by the police, using their network of informants and the Crime and Security Branch in Dublin, to get to the bottom of the plot and stop it. Physical and electronic surveillance on the gang were stepped up. The protection on Steve and Ryan

Lee had been stood down a few years earlier. Armed gardaí were re-assigned to escort Steve to and from his last remaining pub, the Steering Wheel in Roxboro.

McNamara was informed by the gardaí that his life was in danger – again. Pitchfork, who had been spending most of his time in his Spanish villa since the last gun attack, laughed at the officers when they offered him personal security advice. After so many attempts on his life he joked that he was an expert on such matters.

The plot to murder both men bore testimony to the long, unforgiving memories and the blind, irrational hatred at the core of the Dundon psyche. The Ditch Rat and his Piranhas were hell bent on revenge and murder. There was no place in the world for their enemies; no matter how long it took to eviscerate them. Unknown to the police Dundon had vowed to kill Steve Collins when he was in the cell with his henchman, Gareth Collins, in 2005. And promises to kill were the only ones he ever kept.

What happened over the following six months would confirm the mob's credentials as a narco-terrorist organization on a par with cartels in Mexico and Colombia. The murders created a reluctant hero, who in turn galvanized the State into a final showdown with Ireland's most pernicious gang. Ultimately this coded prison message heralded the beginning of the end for Murder Inc.

A month before Dundon issued his murder contract I covered what we in the media business refer to as a good news story. On 3 September 2008 a new squad appeared on the streets of Limerick which dramatically bolstered the firepower of the local force in their war on the gangs. Over the previous years, garda units had come under gunfire as they patrolled the worst hit areas of the city. When the Regional Support Unit (RSU) appeared, the highly trained and heavily armed specialist weapons and tactics (SWAT) unit quickly proved to be an invaluable physical and psychological weapon against the mobs.

Garda HQ decided to deploy the RSU on a trial basis, with a view to establishing similar units in other garda regions. Most importantly it would be based in Limerick City on a permanent basis and was comprised of twelve officers handpicked from the local divisions. The unit members underwent a rigorous training programme in firearms and tactics supervised by the Emergency Response Unit (ERU) and military instructors.

The RSU wore combat-style uniforms with ballistic vests. They were armed with the same sophisticated lethal and non-lethal weapons as the ERU. The arsenal included Heckler and Koch MP7 machine guns, Sig automatic pistols and non-lethal Taser guns to stun armed and dangerous suspects.

Each RSU was equipped with two custom-built, high-powered, armour-plated Volvo XC70 station wagons and were deliberately decked out in bright insignias with banks of flashing lights for maximum visibility. When they first appeared the criminals didn't know what to make of them. But they would soon find out.

The first criminals targeted by the RSU were the Dundon/McCarthys, especially John and Ger Dundon. A member of the RSU told me at the time that the squad was sent out with one mission: 'To break their balls, make them look small and show the public that these people were no longer untouchable. A lot of local gardaí who took on the Dundons and their henchmen were often followed to their homes and subjected to intimidation. But all that was about to change.

The specialist officers took on the role of getting in the faces of the most dangerous gangsters on the streets. The cops wore balaclavas and baseball caps to protect their identities. I was granted access to follow the unit with a photographer on a number of occasions as it went about its job. Public awareness was an important part of the operation. It was great fun. One member of the unit smiled as he told me of their first confrontation with the Dundons:

> When we arrived John and Ger were running riot around the place and our first encounter with them came very soon after that. John Dundon was trying to be a hard man one day, so he was pulled over on a street in the city centre and ordered at gun point to lay spreadeagled on the ground while he was searched in full view of the public. Then Ger got the same treatment just so as everyone understood that the game had changed.
>
> We patrolled the areas where they lived and did checkpoints at all hours of the day and night. The gangsters and their friends were stopped on the streets and searched at gun point. It made these feared hard men look small in the eyes of the younger kids who looked up to them.
>
> For the first time the public in the worst affected areas of this city could see that there was a new force in play that would put manners on these boys and not stand back. We got a lot of people coming up and wishing us well and thanking us for being there. I think that was a very important psychological victory for the gardaí and the decent people.
>
> From the time the RSU was established we were the first through the doors of their homes during search and arrest operations. All searches were dynamic breech entry in full ballistic protective gear which normally meant taking the jambs off the door and going in hard. We took no chances, and all operations were done on the assumption that we would be met

by armed and dangerous criminals. The gangs didn't know what to make of us and it was freaking them out.

They thought we were from Dublin, and they would complain bitterly to other gardaí that they weren't getting fair play. The funny thing was that the likes of the Dundons never made any official complaints. After a while they all got the message and whenever we arrived through the door or pulled them over, they would put their hands up and lie down on the ground without a quibble.

There was also a sense of renewed optimism in Limerick in the autumn and early winter of 2008. The magnificent new Thomond Park rugby stadium, which dominated the skyline, had become the symbol for that new hope. On 18 November it would be officially opened with an historic match between Munster and the New Zealand All Blacks. Munster hoped to repeat its legendary victory over the formidable Kiwis thirty years earlier. It would be a huge day. But the mob would cast their long dark shadow over the event. Despite the presence of the potent new police unit, Murder Inc. was still determined to satisfy their urge for revenge.

On Saturday 8 November cold winds and heavy rain from the Atlantic lashed the Treaty City. That afternoon twenty-eight-year-old Shane Geoghegan captained the Garryowen thirds in a rugby match against Shannon RFC. Shane, an aeronautical engineer, lived for his sport and family. He was a popular young man, described as a 'gentle giant'. He lived with his partner Jenna Barry in a terraced house in Clonmore across the road from his beloved Garryowen club grounds. His home was four doors away from Pitchfork McNamara. The rugby player didn't know the drug dealer. The only thing common to both men was that they had similar beards.

Shane was walking home from a friend's house around 11 p.m. when disaster struck. He pulled a beanie over his head as he braced against the cold. Hitman Barry Doyle, a brother of Paddy Doyle, was lying in wait. In the dim glow of the streetlight the killer saw Shane's beard and the stocky physique matching the description he had been given of McNamara by John Dundon who had sent him out to kill.

Doyle opened fire on Shane hitting him in the shoulder, back, upper arm and abdomen. The terrified rugby player ran to get away and tried to vault a six-foot wall but couldn't get across. As he lay against the wall Doyle caught up and stood over his victim who pleaded: 'Please, don't.' The cold-blooded killer finished off his victim with a fatal shot to the back of Shane's head.

Lisa Collins, the sister of April Collins, who also turned against the Dundons and became a State witness later told gardaí how John Dundon was delighted Doyle had whacked McNamara.

A few hours after the murder Dundon phoned Brian Collopy's brother, Philip to gloat about it. Collopy then rang Johnny McNamara who was very much alive. He called Dundon back to inform him he got 'a pizza man' – his slang for an innocent civilian. Now Collopy was laughing at Dundon.

Lisa later revealed that John Dundon flew into a violent rage, ranting at Doyle for getting the wrong man. He was not upset over the death of an innocent man. Shane Geoghegan's life was of little consequence to the psychopath. It just meant that Dundon and his clan looked stupid and were going to be the laughing stock of the underworld.

The murder of Shane Geoghegan came as a depressing bombshell to the people of Limerick. 'Scum killing scum' was tolerable but killing yet another innocent victim was an outrage. Whenever the city had something positive to celebrate a small group of vile criminals cast a cloud over it. It reaffirmed the belief that Limerick City was in the grip of evil men.

The sense of revulsion reverberated throughout the country and the wider rugby confraternity across the world. For the second time in six years the Munster rugby family was united in grief to mourn an innocent brother who had fallen to merciless thugs. They'd last gathered to bury Brian Fitzgerald in November 2002. City Mayor John Gilligan, who had been outspoken in condemning the gangs and later stood by Steve Collins's side, summed up the feeling of the demoralized people: 'We were so looking forward to the visit of the All Blacks next week and the opening of Thomond Park, but all that seems so inconsequential now.'

Thousands turned out for Shane Geoghegan's funeral to support his distraught mother Mary, his brother Anthony and his girlfriend Jenna Barry. A special pressroom was set up, complete with an audio/video link to the church, to facilitate the large media presence. The huge crowd applauded and cried as Shane's coffin – draped in the sky-blue and white of Garryowen RFC – was placed in the hearse to be taken for burial.

Very quickly the feeling of shock and despair turned to intense anger. I wrote a front-page story about the murder which was accompanied by pictures of Shane, alongside the intended victim to illustrate how the killer had made a grave mistake.

The murder prompted a special debate in the Dáil, the Irish parliament, during which then Justice Minister Dermot Ahern described the perpetrators as 'scum'. He promised new laws to crack down on organized crime.

Fachtna Murphy, the Garda Commissioner, travelled to Limerick where he appealed for the public's help in finally ridding the city of the cancer of the gun gangs. The mood was changing from fear to anger among the law-abiding citizenry. A group of people planned to stage a silent candlelit procession through the Dundon/McCarthy enclaves in a public act of moral defiance. However, it was cancelled at the request of the Geoghegan family who didn't want to see any more decent people suffer.

The murder came as a profound shock for Steve Collins. Shane Geoghegan had been killed in mistake for McNamara. The scribbled note had become a terrifying reality. The gardaí increased their protection around Steve and his family. He later told me:

> I was stunned when I realized that Shane had been murdered in mistake for McNamara – I could not believe that they had killed an innocent man in such a way. I went to the funeral and paid my respects to his family, decent people who never did anything wrong in their lives. I couldn't even begin to think what they were going through. I also knew that I was the second name on that list, and it was likely they would come after me now. It had a dreadful effect on the family.

The latest atrocity by Murder Inc. coincided with the publication of my eighth book, *Crime Wars*. While covering the ongoing gangland mayhem across the country I was also engaged in an obligatory round of interviews as part of the publicity campaign for the book, including the *Late Late Show*. However, it turned out to be a very emotional time in my personal life. Patricia, my mum, had been suffering for some years with a terminal condition called cerebral vasculitis which causes inflammation of the blood vessels in the brain.

It caused a series of mini-brain haemorrhages in the frontal lobe which meant that my mum couldn't deliver coherently the words she wanted to say. That was a cruel infliction on a strong-willed woman who was never found wanting when it came to articulating herself. While she looked physically fine it was very upsetting to witness her gradual cognitive decline who at the age of sixty-six was still relatively young. She taught all three of her children to be independent and never be afraid to stand up for ourselves. In many ways my mum instilled the attributes and passion which drove me in my career including the ability to stand up to threats and intimidation. It was that passion that made me despise the injustices being inflicted on innocent victims by the likes of the Dundon monsters.

The last time my mum enjoyed a gathering with her family and friends took place a few weeks after Shane Geoghegan's murder when I was immensely honoured to receive the *Leitrim Guardian* Person of the Year award.

I was deeply humbled to even be considered worthy of the award from the people and county that I love so dearly. My colleagues and friends from Dublin came to party that night in Lough Rynn castle in Mohill. Patricia Williams was a very proud mother that night. It conjures bittersweet memories. A week later she lapsed into a coma and was rushed to Sligo Hospital. Twelve days later, on 16 December 2008, my mum passed away. It came seven years after we lost my dad.

In the time that I was preoccupied with personal grief the Garda Commissioner and his top brass began investigating innovative ways of piling more pressure on Murder Inc., now the nation's undisputed Public Enemy Number One.

In addition to the RSU the gardaí in Limerick needed to deploy more psychological pressure, or what the US Army term 'PSYOP' – psychological operations – to gain the upper hand. The idea brought them back in time to resurrect a concept from the days of the General. A new squad of dedicated cops was formed to use the template of the famous Tango Squad which twenty years earlier had mounted an intensive overt surveillance and harassment operation against Martin Cahill and his mob. The operation ultimately broke the General's gang. (See *Crooks*.)

Assistant Commissioner Derek Byrne, the head of the Garda National Support Services (NSS) hand-picked six Dublin-based gardaí to specifically target Murder Inc. A particular type of cop was required to make the operation a success. The officers selected had to be level-headed, patient, tough and resilient under pressure. They also required plenty of experience dealing up close with hardened, dangerous criminals. This would not be an easy job. In Limerick they were joined by two local gardaí selected by Det. Supt. Jim Browne.

The ad-hoc unit was equipped with high-powered jeeps and cars fitted with surveillance cameras and blacked out windows. They were armed with SIG automatics and Uzi submachine guns fitted with laser sights. They had one priority target – Murder Inc. – in an operation codenamed 'Weston' after the geographical area that was their stronghold. The new version of the Tango Squad was told:

> Wherever they go, you follow. Stop them, search them, and question them at gun point. Do the same to anyone they meet.
> There are no rules for this game - just don't break the law.

The officers were to wear bullet-proof vests, balaclavas and baseball caps to protect their identities. On 1 January 2009 they headed to Limerick, and the game began.

Over the next two years or so photographer Padraig O'Reilly and I were given regular exclusive access to ride along with the new

Tango unit and record the action as it openly harassed the most dangerous criminals in Ireland. We also went on patrols with the RSU, one member of which had by happenstance previously been my bodyguard. Garda Commissioner Fachtna Murphy gave the permission, with the blessing of the local garda chiefs, because it was important to show the public the efforts being made to smash the Dundon/McCarthys. They wanted to show that these guys were not glamorous or untouchable.

Wherever the thugs went the masked cops followed. If the thugs walked, the officers walked behind them as the jeeps drove alongside on the road and up on the footpath. No words were exchanged during these interactions – making for bizarre spectacles. When a target went into a shop the cops stood inside with him and then left with him. Some of the thugs tried to make light of it by laughing that they were being protected from their enemies. But, just like in the General's mob, the strain soon began to show.

Anyone who met the Murder Inc. bosses on the street or visited their homes was pulled aside, questioned and searched. It led to the arrests of individuals who were wanted on warrants and provided a huge amount of high-grade intelligence for the local detective branch. The Dundons and their rabble were being humiliated and defenestrated in full public view. They could no longer swagger as if they owned the city. It became a relentless daily ritual. It wasn't unusual for thugs to be stopped and searched several times in quick succession in the same day –sometimes in the space of an hour. Further down the road the RSU would also be waiting for them to do the same thing. And week after week I was reporting from the frontline on the action. It drove the bastards mad.

The ride-alongs provided me with several exclusive spreads in both the *Sunday World* and then in the Irish *News of the World*. We published spectacular pictures of the action as cops smashed in the doors of Murder Inc. and searched the Dundons and their killers at the point of Uzi submachine guns in the streets. It was the first time that I had gotten up so close to the action. It was fascinating, exciting and very dramatic. I dubbed the unit the 'Dublin Squad'.

I remember on one occasion sitting in the back of one of the jeeps behind the blacked-out windows as the officers drove slowly behind Nathan Killeen as he walked in the city centre. At one stage the young murderer shouted over to his tormentors: 'Have ye Paul with ye in there?' The officers got out and spreadeagled him on the ground for the fourth time that day. His suspicions were confirmed the following Sunday when pictures of the search appeared on the front page with a report under my byline.

The pressure was soon getting to the mob membership. They fell back on the old Mikey Kelly tactic of setting up a 'peace process'. Gang member Jimmy Collins gave an interview to *The Times* in London and German TV to claim that the 'Dublin guards' were there to ensure that a peace pact didn't succeed. Like all criminals the rationale was that it was always someone else's fault.

Collins complained bitterly that the squad was the source of all the trouble in the city and demanded that they be 'reined in' and brought back to Dublin. The nasty gangster even went so far as to praise the local gardaí who had been on his case for most of his life. 'The Limerick guards are great,' he said, without a hint of irony.

By March 2009 after three relentless months Operation Weston was wound down by Garda HQ. It had succeeded in seriously disrupting the gang's operations. Several more members of the mob were charged with serious offences including Barry Doyle for the murder of Shane Geoghegan. John and Ger Dundon were forced to flee to hide out in the UK, leaving Nathan Killeen in temporary charge.

Operation Weston was a success but such a high-intensity operation was expensive and draining on the officers involved. It could not be sustained indefinitely. When the cops left Murder Inc. came back on the streets. A few weeks later the Dundons made their strike against Steve Collins.

On Holy Thursday 9 April 2009 Steve Collins was escorted as usual by armed gardaí from his home to the pub, arriving there at 7.50 a.m. Roy arrived at 11 a.m. to open up the family's adjoining amusement arcade which he managed. His father was very proud of his eldest boy. Roy was in the final stages of completing his dream home in picturesque Killaloe along the banks of the Shannon in County Clare. He was engaged to be married to fiancée Melissa in June and he lived for his two daughters, Shannon, 12, and Charlie, 8. Steve told me:

> Roy and I were more friends and buddies than father and son. He came to see me as he always did before opening. The next day was Good Friday and he was going to go to IKEA in Belfast where he had spotted a bargain kitchen. He left me in good form and went in next door.

Around noon a stolen Mercedes driven by Nathan Killeen pulled up outside the arcade and twenty-four-year-old James Dillon went inside. Dillon was a cousin of the Dundons. He was also a heroin addict, just another of the young 'fools' Murder Inc. enslaved and exploited. Nathan Killeen and Wayne Dundon had coerced him into taking on the job.

Wayne Dundon gave him no choice when he threatened him on the phone from prison. It later emerged that the Ditch Rat told Dillon:

> You'd better do this, you never do nothing for our family, you'd better do this or you'll be sorry. If you don't do it then you and your mother are going to be sorry.

Roy Collins was standing inside when the Murder Inc. foot soldier spotted him. He pulled an automatic pistol and fired one shot which hit Roy in the chest at close range. Dillon turned and ran to the getaway car.

Steve Collins didn't hear the shot. The first he knew that something was wrong was when a member of staff ran in to say someone was bleeding next door. When he ran into the arcade he found his son in the corner. He was bent down on his hunkers and gasping for breath. Steve later recalled:

> I went over to comfort him and he said: 'Dad, I've been shot.' I could see the bullet on the ground and he kept saying that he couldn't breathe. I tried to move him to the side, and he couldn't move and every time I moved him it was making it worse, so I jumped up and I called the ambulance.
>
> I held Roy and he just held on to me. He told me he loved me and he loved his mother and then Steven junior came and we were both comforting him. When the paramedics came they gave him a shot of adrenaline and he bucked up a bit. Roy gave me a thumbs up when we got him onto the gurney and into the ambulance.
>
> Steven went with him and I went back in to get the CCTV for the gardaí to see exactly what was after happening. Steven rang

me and said it wasn't looking good and that Roy had taken a bad turn. As they got to the hospital, he had a heart attack. I dropped everything and I rushed out to the hospital.

I could see the doctors working on Roy inside and we were told to wait in a family room and that they would tell us when he was ok. I thought he was going to be ok. I couldn't believe when the doctor came and told me that Roy had had another heart attack and they couldn't bring him back... so we lost him... we lost our beautiful boy.

Within minutes of the shooting being reported local gardaí and the RSU converged on the Murder Inc. stronghold. Before the cordite had cleared no one was in any doubt who the culprits were.

Meanwhile in Wheatfield Prison, Noddy McCarthy read that a man had been shot in a pub in Limerick. McCarthy would later tell the Special Criminal Court that sometime after 2 p.m. that afternoon he met Wayne Dundon on the prison landing and told him about a shooting in Limerick. He said that his cousin then tapped on his watch and told him: 'Steve Collins didn't believe me when I did that in court.'

Dundon was referring to a gesture he made to Steve during his trial in 2005. McCarthy said he asked his cousin if the man was shot in the leg, to which Dundon malevolently replied, 'as for him being shot in the leg, he's dead... I warned James Dillon to kill him.'

The rapid response of the local gardaí quickly paid dividends. Dillon and Killeen were arrested within an hour. James Dillon didn't have a chance to clean up after the horrific crime. Forensic examination found firearms residue on his clothes and a glove he was wearing. After being questioned for a number of days, and after a visit from his grandfather Bart, who had reared him, Dillon finally admitted: 'I shot Roy Collins.' He was charged with murder and remanded in custody.

The Dundons later tried to murder their cousin in prison in case he had a change of heart and decided to talk. They ensured that some of their associates doing time in Limerick prison supplied him with heroin laced with poison. They had no compunction about killing their own kin.

Eight years earlier I'd exposed how John Dundon used a machine gun in an attempt to murder another cousin, John Creamer. Despite being hit fourteen times, leaving twenty-eight entry and exit wounds in his body, Creamer survived. He had the distinction of having the most bullet wounds of any gangster who had survived a hit. Creamer even outdid the record of my old foe, Martin Foley, the Viper, who had been shot in four separate attempted hits.

After a spell in intensive care Dillon survived to plead guilty and do his time. Just like Barry Doyle and the other young 'fools' who did Murder Inc.'s bidding, he was too terrified for the rest of his family to implicate Killeen or Dundon. Instead, he sacrificed his life for the sadistic thugs.

Steve Collins also knew his family:

> Dillon was just another example of the disposable muppets the Dundons used. He had been well-reared and did his Leaving Cert. His grandfather, Bart Dillon, was a great community man and his uncle was an international weightlifter. But when he got in with those evil animals they dragged the kid down with them and he murdered my son and destroyed our family.

On Holy Thursday evening a garda contact in Limerick phoned to tell me the shocking news that Roy had been shot. He hadn't yet been publicly identified. I was in RTÉ and about to record a slot for the Saturday night Ryan Tubridy TV show which was being taped early because of the Easter weekend. I was there to talk about crime, including what was going on in Limerick. I couldn't believe it, but straight away I knew who had been responsible. By then everyone in Limerick knew.

I hung up and immediately phoned Steve. I had only spoken to him a few times since interviewing him and Ryan four years earlier. I still hear Steve's trembling voice in my ear:

> They killed my boy, Paul. Dundon told me he would kill me but now they have taken my beautiful innocent son... I can't believe it... I can't believe it. Our world has been blown apart today... we are broken.

I remember being lost for words: what do you say to someone who has experienced such mind-numbing tragedy? I was angry and upset for the poor man and his family. The only thing I could do was offer to help him in any way I could in my limited capacity as a journalist.

The next day I again spoke at length with Steve who wanted me to put his words in print. He told me:

> This is the Dundon family getting revenge because I stood up to them. They shot my nephew in the legs, my pub was burned down – and now my son's been shot dead. I cradled my son in my arms as he lay dying. Roy was a wonderful father and son – he was my best friend. I'm heartbroken – how could this happen? Everyone has to stand up now and put an end to this.

On Easter Sunday I did the only thing that I could do in the circumstances: leave the reading public in no doubt about who was responsible for the latest gangland atrocity. The *Sunday World* front page carried a picture of Wayne Dundon's face under the headline: 'He Had Roy Killed – Dundon ordered Dad's Death'. Over four pages inside under the strap head: 'Slaughter of the innocent – Killed by Murder Inc.', I wrote everything I knew about the mob and detailed the obvious motive for the murder.

In keeping with our culture of print and be damned, I bluntly stated that Wayne Dundon had ordered the killing from prison and ran all the quotes from Steve. There was no room for words such as 'alleged' in the copy. I also spoke to Det. Supt. Jim Browne who had no problem confirming that Dundon was the prime suspect. We were the only newspaper to bluntly accuse Dundon of being responsible. If the scumbag tried to sue us then our editor Colm MacGinty was quite happy to take him on in court.

The murder attracted unprecedented publicity which reflected the public's outrage and anger. Thousands of people in Limerick signed books of condolences. The public began demanding action. The Dublin Squad and the ERU were sent back to Limerick. Together with the RSU they turned over gangland. A large contingent of detectives from the National Bureau of Criminal Investigation (NBCI) were also deployed to work with the local detective branch on the murder investigation. Every specialist garda unit was mobilized for the battle.

Roy's killing, coming so soon after that of Shane, was a murder too far. This time the Government was determined that there would be no let up in the counter-offensive. The full resources of the State would be thrown into the fight back, with no concern for budgets.

Murder Inc. had declared war on an innocent family and by extension, the rest of our civilized society. All the organs of the

State – the political establishment, police, the media and the public were united. The primeval scumbags wanted war and war was what the bastards were going to get.

From that day on Steve Collins had my full support and that of the newspaper I worked for. I vowed to shame and scandalize Murder Inc. in every way I could. It was a sentiment shared by the rest of the Irish media. There was no room for impartiality – this was personal.

On 13 April the Collins family were joined by thousands of mourners for the funeral mass of their beloved Roy. For the second time in five months a family was bidding farewell to a loved one, cruelly taken from them by atavistic, soulless monsters who loved killing. There were impassioned pleas from the altar for an end to the madness. The Bishop of Limerick, Dr Donal Murray, told the congregation: 'We all appeal and pray that this madness, this utter madness, will stop.'

Predictably the 'pond life' that inhabited Murder Inc. showed no hint of remorse or regret. Wayne Dundon was just annoyed that his cousin hadn't killed Steve who was still a target. Despite the intense public outcry, his lackeys in Limerick continued to intimidate Steve Collins. A week after burying Roy, Steve was parked along Childers Road near Weston talking to his son Steve junior, who was in another car. They were spotted by members of the Dundon/McCarthys. The gangsters pulled alongside the father and son and began making threats and gesturing with their hands in the form of guns.

Steve told me: 'They were shouting abuse at my son, saying that he was next to get it. . . It was crazy.' Steve then followed the car to confront them but a red van blocked his way.

> This was intimidation, and it was all well-planned. As I did that... they came over the walls like a tribe of wild Apaches from an estate in Weston, twenty-five of them with sticks, chains, bottles and attacked the car. I had to get away in a hurry and barely made it through the gates of the level-crossing. I don't know what would have happened if I had been stopped there... they probably would have killed me.

Later Steve junior went back to the Weston area with gardaí to see if he could identify the men. When they arrived there was a group of about thirty standing around laughing and joking. They seemed to think it was funny. The mindless, insane hatred of the Murder Inc. lackeys stiffened Steve Collins' resolve to stand up against the scourge of organized crime in Limerick.

That day Steve phoned me. He said he wanted me to help him start a campaign to encourage the State and the people to face down organized crime. I readily agreed and promised to do whatever I could. The next day I travelled to Limerick and spent several hours interviewing Steve and Carmel. They spoke candidly that the spectre of Murder Inc. would never leave their lives.

In the often heart-wrenching interview Steve told me: 'I wish it was me they had taken. I was the intended target and not my son. Then maybe this nightmare would be over for my family.'

I was awestruck by how stoic and dignified they were in the face of such soul-destroying adversity. I had never witnessed such fortitude before. I would not have been able to cope if similar violence had infected my own life.

Carmel came up with the idea of organizing a march through the streets of Limerick to send an unequivocal message to Murder Inc. and crime gangs everywhere. By asking people to wear red, the Munster colours, she believed it would be a potent symbol of defiance and solidarity. They wanted the ordinary citizens to join them in demanding justice for the innocent victims and make politicians listen to their message that 'enough was enough'.

That weekend I told their story on the front page under the heading: 'Save My Family'. I ran the interview over two pages inside which the editor flagged as the 'interview the nation must read'. The story detailed the recent chilling incident Steve and his son had experienced. And the biggest selling paper in the country appealed to the readers, on the family's behalf, to march with them in defiance of the terror gangs.

From then on the media and the nation took Steve and his family to their hearts. He had a natural ability to speak in public which the accidental hero didn't know he possessed. Steve always came across as warm, eloquent and sincere. He quickly became a potent voice against the dark forces which had destroyed so many lives. In particular he demanded that the Minister for Justice, Dermot Ahern, go ahead with tough anti-gang legislation that his department was drafting. At the time there was so much opposition being voiced by the noisy liberal lobby both inside and outside the Dáil – I prefer to call them gobshites – that there was a real risk of the legislation being watered down. Steve Collins single handedly changed that.

He became a popular hero in the process. Whenever he was about to do interviews Steve would ring me beforehand for advice. I always told him he didn't need advice: his honest, articulate delivery got the message across. As I had been so involved in the case, becoming Steve's ad-hoc mentor I regularly appeared with him on TV and radio shows. He wanted me there as his support act in case he lost his words which, of course, he never did.

The late, still sadly missed, Marian Finucane also took Steve to her heart and gave him a platform on her radio show at every opportunity. One time I remember being in the studio for her weekend show to discuss the ongoing case with Steve on the line from Limerick. I remember Marian's eyes filling with tears of sympathy as she listened to him tell his story. During that period I had experienced the same thing. That was the effect this incredible hero had on people. Even all these years later, as I exhume the memories and write them down here, my eyes are welling up again.

Within the space of ten days Steve and Carmel Collins organized the biggest public demonstration against organized crime ever seen in Ireland. It was held on Sunday 10 May which marked the month's mind of Roy's death. Observers estimated that 5,000 people turned up wearing red in solidarity with the family.

I travelled to Limerick that day with solicitor John Hennessy and his bodyguards. As a result of his own harrowing experiences, John wanted to stand with the family. That day I introduced him to Steve and they have remained friends ever since. John is now the family's legal representative. People are bonded together through shared traumas.

We walked the journey from Perry Square to City Hall on Merchant's Quay in bright sunshine. The huge crowd who came from far and wide to stand in solidarity made their way in solemn silence, without slogans, chants or placards. I remember thinking that we were witnessing a thing of beauty, an emphatic stand of good against evil. Despite the conservative estimates of the crowd it looked more like 7000. As far as the eye could see there was a sea of red.

Steve and his family locked arms as they took the lead alongside Mayor John Gilligan and the incoming Mayor Kevin Kiely. Over the years John and Kevin had often put themselves in harm's way by bravely declaiming the crime gangs' grip on the city. Emissaries of the mob had attempted to intimidate them into silence. In his role as chairman of the city's joint policing committee, Kevin Kiely publicly demanded that the Government introduce emergency legislation, including internment, for the likes of the Dundons. Other politicians had called for troops to be deployed in the worst hit estates.

Limerick TD Willie O'Dea, who was the Defence Minister, was also there, as were politicians from every party. Willie made no secret of the fact that he was prepared to resign if the legislation was not enacted. I knew him long enough to know that he wasn't bluffing. Willie told me that many more people would have attended but they were afraid of the rabid Dundon/McCarthys. They had even sent their lackeys to observe and try to intimidate but when they saw the sheer size of the crowd, they slithered back to Weston.

Also at the front of the march was Brian Fitzgerald's father Martin and Tony Geoghegan, the uncle of Shane Geoghegan – two more innocent victims of Murder Inc. Even some criminals turned up to show their solidarity and send a message that the mindless butchery was not done in their name. It was an emotional and heart-warming day that I will never forget – the day the ordinary decent people demanded freedom from the grip of anarchic nihilists. The march received blanket coverage in the media.

Later that evening we joined the family and their friends in a local bar. Over a few pints Mayor John Gilligan confided that he had been worried that people would be afraid to turn up. When he was writing his opening address for the end of the march he had initially included the words 'irrespective of the size of the crowd'. Happily he didn't need them when it came to delivering his fiercely passionate speech on the steps of City Hall. He said the people of Limerick were not prepared to allow those who 'introduced the death penalty to our streets' to continue their terror. He said:

> This will have ended when Steve Collins and his family no longer have to look over their shoulder in fear, and the people who have inflicted these dreadful wrongs on them are no longer in a position to do so any more.

John spoke for everyone there when he described the mobs as 'cruel, heartless monsters'. His words were greeted by prolonged applause and cheers of agreement. Gardaí who were watching the monsters told me they could hear it back in Murder Inc.'s lair in Weston.

When Steve stepped up to the podium, he had to wait for some time before the crowd's warm applause ended. He said:

> This has been a traumatic time for our family, which we felt should not have gone without some kind of message to the thugs who have destroyed our lives and have let us down and have let the good name of Limerick down.
>
> By your actions here today you have spoken and said we have had enough of the low-life mutants that have eaten into the fabric of our society like a cancer that must be cut out. Let's hope that this action yields some kind of reward going forward because, believe me, nobody wants to go through what my family has had to endure. From the bottom of my broken heart, thank you all.

As he finished he embraced his wife and children. The applause from the crowd continued for what seemed like an eternity. In that memorable moment it appeared that all of Ireland supported the Collins family.

The huge sea of red which filled the square in front of the courts complex and city hall in Merchant's Quay then observed a minute's silence. In the background the Tricolour fluttered, and the afternoon sun struck the shimmering water of the mighty Shannon. Then a lone uilleann piper played 'Limerick's Lament'. In that electrifying, emotion-charged moment I knew in my heart that no matter how long it took, Murder Inc. was finished.

The following week Justice Minister Dermot Ahern introduced a raft of tough new anti-gang legislation not seen since the murder of Veronica Guerin. It effectively put organized crime gangs on a par with terrorists. It made membership of a gang an offence and allowed for the non-jury Special Criminal Court to hear gangland trials. A new surveillance bill also gave gardaí powers to plant bugs in cars and properties used by gangsters. The bill allowed the covertly gathered evidence to be used in the courts which was a huge game changer. The legislation has helped gardaí smash several crime gangs in the years since. The use of secret recordings resulted in several of Daniel Kinahan's drug dealers and killers convicting themselves with their own words.

The new laws appeared draconian but the need for a proportionate response meant they were absolutely necessary. A letter signed by 133 criminal solicitors published in *The Irish Times* said it was 'astounding' that society would 'jettison ancient rights' under the new legislation. An illustration of how powerful Steve's voice had become was in evidence when the Irish Council for Civil Liberties sent representatives to Limerick in a bid to dissuade him from supporting the new laws.

I was more than happy to publish his comments about the meeting the following week:

> These people didn't come to see me when my son's civil rights were taken away with his life. I have always seen the introduction of these laws as my son's legacy... it helps me to think that he didn't die in vain.

In the meantime I continued to pummel Dundon and his savages every week in the newspaper. In June Wayne Dundon's lawyers sent the *Sunday World* a strongly worded letter threatening legal action for accusing him of orchestrating Roy's murder and so many others. The sensitive gangster also threatened to make a complaint to the Press Council of Ireland concerning my coverage of his criminal activities. The depraved thug complained that my stories about him were lacking in truth and accuracy. It was proof of the old adage: you only get flak over the target. 'We must be doing something right,' Colm MacGinty remarked when it arrived. We gave Dundon his reply by publishing his complaint on the front page. We didn't hear from him again.

In early September the new mayor of Limerick Kevin Kiely hosted a civic reception for the Collins family which I attended. On 12 September Steve's outstanding bravery was acknowledged when he received a Rehab People of the Year Award. I was honoured to be asked to provide a recorded testimonial and I spoke of why he deserved the prestigious recognition. I said that he was a hero.

Less than a week after the glittering televised ceremony in Dublin, John Dundon was remanded in custody for a string of road traffic offences. He had returned to Limerick after fleeing to the UK to escape the garda pressure a month before Roy's murder. He was subsequently sentenced to a year in prison.

When the initial euphoria receded, the family had to face the grim reality of trying to rebuild their lives. As they grieved for their son they were still living in fear despite the police protection. Since Roy's murder, business had dropped dramatically in their last remaining pub the Steering Wheel. Financially Steve was on his knees. He had huge borrowings on businesses which were burned down, closed or undermined because he stood up to evil. Carmel had become a prisoner in her own home, too afraid to face the outside world. The children's lives had also been seriously restricted. They could not go out for a night without being constantly vigilant against attack.

In the wake of Roy's murder the State had offered Steve and his family a place in the witness protection programme. He confided this to me but it was not something that we ever publicized. Apart from my role as a crime reporter I was also his friend and confidante. The family's welfare superseded front page stories.

He told me:

> The programme they had was designed for criminals. Most of them are on the dole anyway, so you whisk them away and give them a few bob, a place to live and a job maybe. I asked what happens to us. They said, 'We'll get you over maybe to Austria, and your parents and sisters and brothers can meet you once a year, maybe down in Marseilles.'
>
> I was mystified and asked for somewhere I could speak English and they came back with Canada. But pub work or electrical contracting would be ruled out, they said, as these would make me traceable. They said I could train as a carpenter. I asked them were they having a laugh expecting a fifty-five-year-old man to train as a carpenter, but they were serious.

When he asked the people in charge of the programme in Garda HQ how starting a business might work, they had no response for him. Steve commented:

> It was hard enough to get a loan from a bank manager here who knows your track record, so how in the hell could I walk into a bank in Canada, under a new name, and ask for money to start a new business? They couldn't answer.
>
> We would just be dumped there and left to get on with it. I could not believe that this was how the State treated innocent people who helped them put criminals behind bars.

In any event Carmel and Steve wanted to be near their son's grave which they visited every day. Steve continued to raise awareness of the gangs and regularly contributed to documentaries and news reports. I did everything I could to keep his campaign alive. When I wrote and narrated the *Badfellas* documentary in 2010 we dedicated one of the shows to Limerick and did an extensive interview with Steve.

But he and his family remained trapped in a hellish limbo.

In March 2010 the Collins family and the people of Limerick braced themselves when Wayne Dundon was released from prison. His release coincided with my appointment as Crime Editor to the Irish edition of the *News of the World*. Some of the first stories I wrote were about Murder Inc., which continued to provide copy over the following months. One of the first stories was an exposé of how the Dundons were terrorizing and bullying the rest of the inmates in Wheatfield Prison, west Dublin.

I was contacted by a relative of an inmate who wanted the world to know about the sadistic monsters' reign of terror on the landings which the Prison Service appeared to know nothing about. The source handed me pictures which proved that other prisoners were as much victims of the gang's savagery as anyone else. They showed a pathetic young criminal whom Dessie, John and Wayne Dundon had tortured and humiliated just for fun. It was their way of relieving the boredom of incarceration. The prisoner had been badly beaten, stripped and had part of his head shaved.

The mindless thugs then wrote 'fuck me' on their victim's forehead and backside. The unfortunate youth was chained to a bed and the Dundons ordered other inmates on their wing to take turns beating him. In the final act of degradation, John and Dessie laughed as they posed for pictures with their victim which were taken by Wayne on the mobile phone he wasn't supposed to own. The images were truly shocking.

On 21 March, three days after Wayne's release, I published the pictures along with testimony from the source which revealed how the Murder Inc. savages had inflicted a regime of intimidation and horror in Wheatfield Prison. The stories were corroborated by prison staff I spoke to. They were equally sickened by the way the mobsters could get away with flouting the rules. They told me the senior managers of the Irish Prison Service didn't want to know. They didn't have to work in what was a brutal zoo.

The sources described Wayne Dundon as being particularly deranged and dangerous. In the same edition I also had an exclusive story about Hassan Hassan who was taken from his prison cell and immediately deported having completed his sentence. We even had pictures of him being escorted through Dublin airport.

The revelations in the Irish *News of the World* had the desired effect. It was seriously embarrassing for the Irish Prison Service which was supposed to protect the civil rights of its inmates. The day after the story appeared, prison authorities ordered a massive search on the landings controlled by Murder Inc. The operation was similar to the one prompted after killer John Daly phoned *Liveline* to berate me in 2007 (see *Crooks*). Several mobile phones were seized and John Dundon was put in solitary confinement.

The prison service separated the Murder Inc. members and moved them to different prisons much to the huge relief of the rest of the inmates. Their poor unfortunate victim was quietly granted immediate temporary release to make up for his horrendous ordeal. I found it very satisfying to have caused the mob so much grief. For once the underworld's most hated crime reporter had come to the rescue of a cohort of villains. As soon as he got out Wayne launched an investigation to identify the source who'd supplied the damning images. He found nothing. I had made sure that the trail was well covered.

As soon as Wayne Dundon arrived in Limerick the gardaí launched yet another major surveillance operation. The Dublin Squad, which had again been stood down after several months, returned once more. The cops made sure Dundon got the message that life on the outside was not going to be easy. Just minutes after being picked up in an armour-plated jeep at the prison gates, Dundon and his driver were stopped and searched by armed officers.

A week later I humiliated Dundon with another exclusive front page. Padraig O'Reilly got pictures of the Ditch Rat and his wife in Dublin airport as they were about to jet off for a holiday in Mexico. I revealed that he was planning to have liposuction to reduce the size of his flabby belly. The vain psychopath had a hang-up about his weight.

The pictures were published across two pages inside, under the headline: 'Run Fat Boy, Run'. They showed Dundon glowering as a uniformed garda stopped him to check his passport before he went through check-in.

Through my network of sources, I was receiving ongoing live updates about the movements of the gang members so that we could have photographers there to snap them. I was more than happy to play a part in the PSYOPs being deployed against the monsters.

In other stories we revealed how the Ditch Rat was intimidating several other criminals and members of the travelling community, demanding donations for his 'coming home' fund.

Steve and his family were understandably deeply distressed at Dundon's return. Across the media there were stories about renewed fears for him now that his nemesis was back on the streets. The accidental hero hoped the criminal would move away from Limerick. He told me:

> I think it is time for him to move his wagons. I hope he will see that there is nothing here for him anymore. I think he is finished in Limerick as far as I can see. There is no more damage that they can do; the guards are on top of them.

In other front pages over the months that followed we ran dramatic pictures of the Dundon brothers being stopped and searched at gun point by the Dublin Squad. We were also present on several occasions when the ARU smashed in their front doors in dawn swoops. In May we ran pictures of Wayne Dundon's daughter's First Communion day when the soulless monster hired a horse-drawn Cinderella carriage to take her to the church. The media coverage, which was also in other tabloids, drove him mad. He went to the *Limerick Leader* newspaper where he gave the editor an interview in which he ranted about the unfair treatment he was receiving. Like Mikey Kelly, the scumbag was playing the victim card.

Just over a week after Dundon's release Steve was invited to a meeting in the office of the Justice Minister Dermot Ahern. The meeting was organized by Defence Minister Willie O'Dea, the one politician who knew more than anyone about Murder Inc. Willie was Steve's steadfast supporter and told me:

> I have no doubt that despite all the garda activity Dundon will come back to kill again. Steve is still his top target. We have to do everything possible to protect the man and his family.

The meeting was attended by Willie O'Dea, the Garda Commissioner Fachtna Murphy and senior department officials. The only item on the agenda was Murder Inc. and keeping the Collins family safe. After all Steve had fulfilled his side of the social contract by doing his civic duty and testifying against the monster. The State had an obligation to protect him and his family. Steve later told me that the minister had expressed his concerns that Steve's regular appearance in the media denouncing mob violence was continuing to make him a target.

In an interview he gave me at the time Minister Ahern confirmed this:

> I told Steve I didn't want to silence him, but I was very worried that his commentary would provoke those thugs further because it was obvious to me that they were capable of anything. I made sure that I got daily briefings on what was happening in Limerick.

Commissioner Murphy informed Steve that he was immediately reinstating full-time armed protection for him and two of his surviving sons, Steve junior and Ryan Lee. Paul lived in the UK.

They were each assigned two armed bodyguards. He also assured Steve that the Dublin Squad would remain in Limerick for as long as it took to neutralize the Dundons. As part of the State's support package a uniformed garda was posted permanently outside the Steering Wheel pub and state-of-the-art security systems were installed in the premises and the family home.

Steve explained to the meeting why he had rejected the witness protection scheme. Then he asked exactly what the State was prepared to do to compensate him and his family. He detailed the financial stress he was under. He needed help from the State or else he would become bankrupt. Ahern promised to do what he could. A senior civil servant was assigned to investigate a suitable package for the family whereby the State would buy his properties and business. The wheels of bureaucracy turned painfully slow, and it would take almost two years before a solution was found.

In early May 2010 I travelled to Limerick to mark the first anniversary of Roy's murder. To commemorate the occasion Steve had a plaque erected at the arcade where it took place. Family, friends and well-wishers gathered for its unveiling by Steve. It had a simple message on it for all who passed by:

> *In memory of Roy Collins, 1974–2009.*
> *A wonderful son, father, brother and friend,*
> *taken from us here on April 9, 2009.*
> *The world is a dangerous place*
> *not because of those who do evil*
> *but because of those who look on and do nothing.*

Two weeks later the gardaí notched up a significant victory over Murder Inc. As part of a major investigation, Ger Dundon, his cousin Christopher McCarthy, Jimmy Collins and his son Gareth were among seven gang members arrested and charged with extortion, intimidation and the attempted abduction of a local nightclub owner, Mark Heffernan. Heffernan had been terrorized by the thugs for two years. After escaping an attempt by the mob to abduct and shoot him the businessman sought advice from Steve Collins for whom he had once worked.

Steve told him there was only one way to deal with the mob: go to the police and have them put behind bars. Murder Inc. had already shown that they never let up on their victims. Mark Heffernan later gave me an exclusive interview about his ordeal. His decision to go to the gardaí meant that in one fell swoop most of the gang's middle management had been taken out. Thanks to the new legislation the gang members were sent for trial to the Special Criminal Court. In 2011 they all pleaded guilty and were jailed for between five and seven years each.

In the meantime Wayne Dundon made a bizarre attempt to turn the tables when he made several complaints to incredulous gardaí that he believed Steve Collins was going to have him killed. I exposed that ludicrous claim on the front page of the Irish *News of the World*.

On 5 May 2010 James Dillon pleaded guilty to Roy's murder and was sentenced to life imprisonment. It was a pyrrhic victory because everyone realized that he was merely a slave doing the bidding of Murder Inc.'s demented boss. Steve asked me to help him write his victim impact statement which he read to the court.

As tears streamed down his cheeks he said:

Evil came into our lives on that fateful day and took the love of our lives in a callous act, a cowardly act, an unforgivable act, a total waste of a good life.

Now, every day, we have to look at Roy's two beautiful daughters lost in confusion as to where their daddy has gone, their little hearts broken beyond repair, too young to understand, too afraid to contemplate what's gone on and why.

Behind the scenes Murder Inc. was about to implode. It began when April Collins split up with Ger Dundon, who was in prison. She'd had enough of living in constant dread of him and his demonic clan. But the Dundons had no intention of allowing her to leave.

April and her mother made the momentous decision to break the code of *omerta* by making a complaint to the police after they were attacked in the street by the Dundon's other women, including Ciara Killeen. The assault was revenge after Gareth Collins had beaten Nathan Killeen in a fist fight in Limerick Prison. Killeen was on remand after he was charged with breaking into a house and demanding money. The Dundons and Killeen had a grievance with Gareth because he had refused to participate in the murder of Roy Collins.

The beginning of the end for Murder Inc.'s citadel of evil came into sight when April Collins and her mother reported that John and Wayne had threatened to kill them. Wayne also threatened to have April's gangster brother Gareth and another sibling, Jimmy junior, murdered as well.

For the first time someone inside Murder Inc. had decided to break the code of silence. From my vantage point as one of the gang's closest media observers it was a stunning development. In public April Collins had always appeared to be loyal to the mob. I had witnessed several of the foul-mouthed tirades she directed at the Dublin Squad whenever they stopped and searched her and Ger.

When it emerged that she had turned on the gang I referred to her in a story as a 'dead woman walking'.

The women were subsequently convicted of the assault and each received ten-month suspended sentences. In April 2011 Wayne and John Dundon were both formally charged with making the threats to kill and were remanded in custody. Although they didn't know it at the time, they would never be free men again.

Around the same time April Collins and her mother sought a meeting with Detective Superintendent Jim Browne. This time she had decided to share Murder Inc.'s darkest secrets and tell everything she knew about the murders of Shane Geoghegan and Roy Collins. She had been present when John Dundon and Barry Doyle plotted the murder of Shane. She then implicated Wayne and Nathan Killeen in the murder of Roy. She also told about the involvement of Nathan Killeen, his sister Ciara and Ger Dundon in the murder of James Cronin. April Collins was determined to smash a hole in the gang's wall of silence. She was also prepared to testify in court against the mobsters.

The astonishing development prompted a top secret garda investigation. Browne's detectives compiled files on the cases for the DPP in which they recommended murder charges be preferred against the leadership of Murder Inc. That started a domino effect over the next year. Gareth Collins contacted the cops from Limerick Prison and told them everything he knew about Roy's murder as did his girlfriend. They too were prepared to testify.

As the supergrass floodgates opened April's sister Lisa also came forward with more damning evidence. She was then joined by her boyfriend Christopher McCarthy, the Dundon' first cousin. It spelled the end of the once powerful alliance between the two sides of the family crime machine.

Having covered the horror show for over a decade I was witnessing the downfall of Murder Inc. A year later another relation broke ranks to join the growing queue of *pentitos*. Anthony 'Noddy' McCarthy, Christopher's brother, who was serving life for the Kieran Keane murder, also sent word to the cops in Limerick that he wanted to tell everything he knew about Wayne Dundon's involvement in the murder of Roy Collins.

Despite the fact that their world was imploding, the mob reminded Steve Collins that they had not forgotten him. On Monday 4 July a three-bedroom cottage he owned was extensively damaged in an arson attack just hours after a 'for let' sign was erected on the property. The building was a few doors from his former pub Brannigans, which had been gutted in 2005.

That same week the *News of the World*, the biggest selling newspaper in the world at that time, closed down after the hacking scandal in the UK. It followed the shocking revelations that for several years the newspaper's senior executives and journalists in London had engaged in egregious criminal activity by spying on the private phone messages of celebrities and crime victims. Even after all these years I am still shocked to think that a newspaper I worked for closed down because some of its bosses were every bit as bad as the thugs I wrote about. The last story I wrote for the

Irish edition of the paper was an interview with Steve about the arson attack. He told me:

> This is the most sickening part of this whole thing. These scum have no concern for the well-being of anyone. I'm more upset about the neighbours than I am about the damage they caused. The fire brigade saved us from having two deaths on our hands. They shot Ryan, they murdered Roy, they burned down our pub, now this. When will it ever stop?

The incident finally convinced Steve that he had no choice but to move his family out of Ireland. Over the next several months in total secrecy, the State started to put together a financial package, while the Departments of Justice and Foreign Affairs agreed to help them obtain visas for the family members so that they could move to Florida.

While that process was ongoing, in January 2012 April Collins made her debut as a prosecution witness in the trial of Barry Doyle. Despite being pummelled by defense lawyers who tried to undermine her credibility, she proved to be a very convincing witness. Her allegations were corroborated with independent evidence. A jury convicted Doyle of Shane Geoghegan's murder. A week later April Collins and her mother each took the witness stand in the Special Criminal Court to testify against Wayne and John Dundon for threatening to kill them. Fittingly their trial in the non-jury court was a consequence of the new anti-gang legislation.

The psychotic brothers had offered over €100,000 to have their former in-laws killed but by then no one was prepared to kill for Murder Inc. The women were under full-time police protection anyway. On 16 March 2012 the court convicted the brothers. The dangerous psychopaths were sentenced to a total of eleven-and-a-half years: Wayne for six and John for five-and-a-half years. It was another major victory.

Behind closed doors the State Solicitor's office in Limerick was preparing a case to charge John with Shane Geoghegan's murder. They were also preparing murder charges for Nathan Killeen and Wayne Dundon for Roy's murder. Meanwhile Steve and his family were in the final stages of leaving their home.

Steve had told me about his plans which for obvious reasons I kept a closely guarded secret that I shared with no one. Steve, Carmel, Steve junior and Leanne were going to try and start a new life in Florida. Ryan Lee, who was building an electrical business, had decided to remain in Limerick and Paul has lived for many years in the UK. In 2012 the State had finally agreed to buy the family's remaining assets and attempt to compensate them for their mammoth ordeal. Senior gardaí brought Steve to a meeting with officials in the US embassy in Dublin to discuss the family's application for residency visas.

Just over a week after the convictions of the Dundon brothers, on Sunday 25 March 2012, the family were escorted by gardaí to Shannon airport for their flight to the US. Steve Collins had asked me to break the news of his family's heavy-hearted departure. He wanted to thank the public and the State for their support and explain why they were going. The week before the departure I interviewed Steve for the story which appeared that morning in the new Sunday edition of the *Irish Sun* where I had been working since the closure of the *News of the World*. The night before they left I met Steve and Carmel to say an emotional goodbye. It was heartbreaking to see these good people being forced to leave.

The front page of the paper carried the headline: 'We can't live in fear anymore – Collins family flee mob for secret life abroad'. It was accompanied by a poignant picture of Steve visiting Roy's grave for a final time.

In the story Steve said:

> We don't have a life worth talking about anymore and it is having a serious effect on our mental and physical health. We had decided never to leave Ireland, especially where our Roy is buried, but it has just become unbearable, and we decided to try and start somewhere else afresh. Saying goodbye to our boy is heartbreaking and the hardest part of leaving Ireland. I never dreamt we would be doing this.
>
> It is very satisfying to see them [Dundons] being convicted and having the prospect of yet another long stretch behind bars – and all because they think they can threaten and kill who they like. That is why I would like to ask them one question today: How do you feel now, lads? And what have you achieved? Nothing.
>
> The truth is that they have been brought to their knees and their so-called empire is imploding around them. The State and the gardaí have proved they have the power to pursue these savages who are nothing more than mutant pond life. When they are sitting looking at their cell wall I hope they reflect on why they lost their liberty.

Then Steve summed up the reason for the beginning of Murder Inc.'s spectacular downfall:

> In return for the couple of weeks of pleasure they got from terrorizing my family they will be spending years, maybe even the rest of their lives, behind bars. My family were never a threat

to them but they were incapable of rational thought – they were too arrogant and stupid to realise what was coming to them.

I am happy that I have done my bit to damage them. Now they have been reduced to killing each other like the animals they are.

Steve also used the coverage to thank the public for its support over the years. Padraig O'Reilly took a final picture of Steve waving goodbye as he walked through the departure gates which was published in the following morning's newspaper. Such was the response from the public that we set up a special email address for readers to safely send their messages of support to the family.

That Sunday morning, as the family were checking in for their flight, Marian Finucane interviewed me about the dramatic news. Like everyone else in Ireland she was shocked and saddened that the family had been forced to leave. It was a major story over the following week. We told the public that the family was leaving as part of a relocation programme for protected witnesses. However, for the first time in over thirteen years, I can now admit that this was untrue but necessary in the circumstances.

The truth was that the US didn't have an agreement with the Irish State to accommodate witnesses. The American authorities told Steve this when he met them in the embassy. They would get residency visas and nothing else. In fact Steve had to apply for the visas himself like any other citizen. Publicly declaring that the family were in a witness relocation programme – which was also the line put out by the Irish authorities – was to give the impression that they were still being protected and thus dissuade anyone from trying to find them. When anyone asked me quietly where they had gone I told them to Australia.

The family's departure did not run smoothly either. When they checked in with US immigration in Shannon the officials knew nothing of any arrangement with their authorities. The family's passports aroused suspicion, and they were taken to a room and questioned by Homeland Security. The Americans thought they were in some way involved in crime. A few frantic phone calls to the Department of Justice and gardaí cleared up the misunderstanding and they were allowed to board the flight for Florida at the last minute. Their baggage had to be sent on a later flight.

Over the following weeks Steve phoned me most days so I could brief him on the reaction which had made front page news everywhere. Most of the commentary lamented the fact that despite the family's brave stand the mobs had succeeded in forcing them to flee Ireland. It was seen as a victory for organized crime.

In the weeks that followed the US authorities informed Steve that as part of the conditions for being granted the residency visas he had to immediately invest at least $1 million in a local business and employ up to a dozen US citizens. To fulfil the condition Steve hurriedly bought a large diner and bar which proved to be a financial disaster. I have always believed that it was tantamount to a shake-down by the US authorities. It was yet another blow to the beleaguered family. None of this could be revealed at the time for obvious reasons. Instead we all conspired in a white lie. The way they were treated still makes my blood boil. Steve later told me:

> I had always intended getting back into business but we didn't have a chance to familiarize ourselves with the local economy and properly investigate the prospects of a venture working out. It was a disaster actually because the business didn't take off. It felt like we would never get a break.

In early June the family secretly returned to Limerick for a happy occasion – Steve junior's wedding. It had been planned many months before the family left and they were determined to have it in Ireland. None of the media covered the event out of respect for their privacy and safety. Armed gardaí were assigned to protect the family and keep watch at the event. I was honoured to be invited as a guest. A week later they left Ireland again.

Over the following year Murder Inc., and their rivals continued to be hammered by the gardaí. I covered dozens of trials as a succession of the city's gangsters were charged and convicted for murder, drug trafficking and firearms offences. In 2012 the number of shootings in Limerick had dwindled to just seven. The murder rate had also dropped dramatically. There was one murder in each of 2012 and 2013, neither of which was gang related. The efforts of the gardaí, combined with Steve's campaign, had turned Limerick from one of Europe's most violent cities to being one of its most peaceful.

In August 2012 John Dundon was charged with the murder of Shane Geoghegan. The following February 2013 Steve and Carmel came back to Limerick to see relatives and visit their son's grave. While in Ireland Wayne Dundon and Nathan Killeen were formally charged with Roy's murder. The couple had an emotional meeting with senior gardaí in Limerick two days before their tormentors were charged. I also met them while they were home. The day after the accused appeared in court the couple returned to Florida. I wrote a story for the *Irish Independent* reporting that they were delighted by the development.

The trial of John Dundon lasted a month in the summer of 2013. Lisa and April Collins testified, along with his cousin Christopher McCarthy. They were undeterred by Dundon's feeble attempts to intimidate them across the courtroom and proved to be credible witnesses. Most days I rang Steve to update him on how it was going. On 13 August, Dundon was convicted of the murder of Shane Geoghegan.

The trial of Wayne Dundon and Killeen for Roy's murder began on 1 May 2014. That morning the family had returned to Ireland. Ostensibly they were there for Steve to give his evidence about the killing. In reality they had decided to come home for good. Carmel could no longer bear being so far away from Roy's grave. Steve had decided to cut his losses and sell the business in Florida

In all six former members of Murder Inc. testified during the most dramatic supergrass trial in Irish criminal history. Steve and Carmel, who received armed protection, attended every day of the emotionally draining twenty-nine-day trial which was spread over two months. I was in court for most of the proceedings. At the time I was writing the eponymous book about Murder Inc. and its impending downfall. Steve and Carmel were regular guests in our home during that period. They were extremely worried that the killers might get off. I assured them that, based on what I had seen in court, they would be convicted. It was an immensely stressful time for them.

In July their fears evaporated when the three female judges of the non-jury court convicted Dundon and Killeen. One piece of evidence that damned the Ditch Rat was the gesture he'd made to Steve almost ten years earlier when he tapped his watch to indicate that he would have his revenge. His cousin Noddy McCarthy testified that Wayne Dundon had made the same gesture to him in Wheatfield Prison after news of Roy's murder broke. It was a stunning victory and spelled the end of Murder Inc. It took the presiding judge two hours to deliver the court's analysis of the case and its verdict. Realizing that they had finally reached the end of the horror story Steve and Carmel broke down in tears as they embraced each other at the back of the court. Gardaí, reporters and even one of the judges had tears in their eyes. Shortly after the verdict I joined the family and members of the gardaí as we all celebrated the wonderful news.

When it was over Steve and his family quietly resumed their lives in Limerick. The good people of the city and the media gave them space to do so. Over the following years the local and national media respected the family's privacy. It was the honourable and decent thing to do. But just when it appeared that life was finally returning to some semblance of normality for them, fate again intervened to cause more heartache.

Carmel, who had always been Steve's rock, fell ill and was later diagnosed with cancer. No one doubts that it was the years of intense stress that caused it. I still recall meeting Steve one day when he told me of the diagnosis. 'Jesus Christ, will we ever get a break,' I remember him saying before breaking down in floods of tears. I held the big man in my arms for what seemed like an age as he wept. I cried with him. We were in a pub in Stillorgan, south Dublin, at the time and when we both regained our composure there was a long silence. To break the silence, I looked around at the other customers and wondered aloud: 'Everyone knows us here. . . I hope they don't think we're gay.' Steve replied: 'Jesus, they'll think I have very poor taste.' At that we both cracked up laughing and ordered another round.

In autumn 2014 I launched *Murder Inc.* in Dublin. Several members of the gardaí who had triumphed over the mob attended the occasion. The book was a comprehensive account of their battle against evil. It was also about the Collins family's brave stand. Steve marked the occasion by speaking about his experience over the previous decade of pure living hell.

A year later we all got together in Limerick to celebrate Detective Superintendent Jim Browne's retirement after an outstanding career as the city's most respected detective. He remains a dear friend of the Collins family.

In April 2019, almost ten years to the day that her eldest boy was murdered, Carmel Collins passed away. She had fought her illness with the same extraordinary courage she had shown against the monsters who infested the lives of her wonderful family. On an overcast Spring day, we joined Steve and his family in Limerick to say a final farewell as Carmel was laid to rest next to Roy.

Two weeks earlier, on the tenth anniversary of the heinous crime, Steve asked me to mark the event with a story in the *Irish Independent*. He wanted to publicly announce that the family were no longer living in fear and were rebuilding their lives in the city that they loved. Steve reflected:

> We are trying to rebuild our lives. We were comfortable and then we were destroyed and devastated. Now is a time for rebuilding things. Limerick is a safe place now. It took what we did. It took people to stand up and say, 'we're sick of this.' It took all of that. I'm just so happy it did happen.

Between the time that Murder Inc. first emerged until their downfall I had spent fourteen years covering the longest, most intensive gang war and police investigation in the history of Irish criminal justice. It has been said that if journalism is the first rough draft of history then crime journalism has a habit of being rougher than most. The Limerick wars will always stand out as the roughest draft of all. That is why this particular chapter of my history has been so long in the telling.

But there is a happy ending to the story. In 2023 my wife and I were honoured to be amongst the guests at Steve's wedding to a wonderful lady called Deborah who brought the light back into his life. He was joined that day by some of the other heroes of this incredible story including former Limerick mayor John Gilligan, TD Willie O'Dea and super cop Jim Browne. We celebrated in grand style.

It marked the end of the darkest of days. In the eighteen years since we first met, it was the happiest I had ever seen the accidental hero and friend for whom I have immeasurable love and admiration. No one deserved to be happy more than Steve. I often say to him that our friendship was one that should never have been. We would never have met if it had not been for the ordeal he and his family had endured.

That was the day that we buried the ghosts of the past. I pray that the Dundons remain in prison for the rest of their miserable lives.

CHAPTER NINE

THE ANGLO TAPES AND THE CRIME OF THE CENTURY

The single sheet of paper was pushed across the table for me to read as we sat drinking coffee in the lobby of a Dublin hotel. The people on the other side reckoned that it would explain things better than they could. The page contained less than 500 words of a transcript from a taped conversation between two individuals I'd never heard of.

This was the undramatic moment which marked the beginning of a story that eventually caused an unprecedented expression of shock, anger and disbelief among the public and the political establishment not only in Ireland but across the rest of Europe.

It was early February 2013 and I had been handed explosive inside information on the crime of the century. But the words on the A4 page were not those of a top international drug trafficker or gangland murderer. This was much more than that – it was potentially the single biggest story I had ever come across in my time as a journalist.

I was astonished as I read the short transcript. If what was on the page could be corroborated this was evidence of a conspiracy that had had catastrophic consequences for every citizen in the country when five years earlier the Irish banking system had imploded, the economy collapsed and the Celtic Tiger died a sudden death.

That momentous event left the Irish taxpayers footing the bill for the notorious €64 billion bailout of the banks and the loss of our nation's economic sovereignty. It resulted in punitive tax increases, high unemployment, economic stagnation and renewed emigration. The public had been living in a constant state of dread since 2008: dread of losing their jobs, their homes and vital public services. No one apart from the very rich had been spared.

The words provided the first tantalizing glimpse of what had caused the economic meltdown, bankruptcy and financial misery. I was informed that the transcript was an excerpt from hundreds of hours of taped conversations that had been routinely recorded in a particular bank in the lead up to the bailout. 'Wow' was the only word that I could utter.

This was my introduction to the premier league of white-collar crime. The subsequent series of stories I produced based on the recordings that ultimately flowed from that meeting would make front page news across the globe and expose the rotten heart of the Irish banking system. In particular they revealed a cynical, ruthless and contemptuous culture in the maverick Anglo Irish Bank that did the most damage and accounted for €30 billion of the taxpayer funded bailouts. This was a crime story like no other I had ever experienced where the entire population had become victims, including me and my family. This was a story that every citizen in the country could relate to. It will be forever remembered as the Anglo Tapes investigation.

That fateful February day in 2013 I had no inkling of the journey that we were about to embark upon. At the time I had been working as a freelance contractor with the *Irish Independent* for six months which coincided with Stephen Rae's appointment as editor in September 2012. My first big scoop with the *Indo* had been tracking down the suspected serial killer Larry Murphy in November 2012. (See *Crooks*.)

When we eventually broke the story in the *Irish Independent* it led to threats that were different to what I had grown used to over the years. This time they didn't come from shadowy figures in organized crime – the threats came from the State. The main concern of the Government and the liquidator who had been appointed when Anglo collapsed was to find out where we got the explosive tapes. They asked the gardaí to launch an investigation.

But there was a lot of work to do before we got to that stage. The meeting in the Castleknock Hotel was the latest in a number of contacts with the sources. A few months earlier I had been approached by another individual on behalf of people who had access to the Anglo Tapes. No one, apart from the Garda Bureau of Fraud Investigation, the Anglo liquidators, financial regulators and the bank's executives, knew they existed.

The source said that they may have evidence which could expose the truth about how Anglo Irish bank's senior executives had laughed and joked as they devised a mendacious strategy to pull the Irish State into the financial abyss with them. At first I thought that it was all pie in the sky: sources have a habit of exaggerating the importance of the information they have.

Experience has taught me that there is no point in getting too excited about a story until it is on the front page.

After much back and forth and assurances of confidentiality the sources, who were understandably very nervous, met me in the hotel and handed me the sheet of paper. It was then that I knew that they were deadly serious. They agreed to supply me with the first of the Anglo Tapes. However, they were extremely concerned that given the potency of what the tapes contained, and the fact that there were a number of sensitive investigations under way, their identities needed to be protected.

That was also my concern. Protecting sources is always sacrosanct especially for a crime reporter: sources for gangland stories can lose their livelihoods and their lives if they are caught talking. In hindsight I suspect that I was chosen as the conduit for the Anglo story because I was a crime writer. The logical suspicion would be that my police sources gave them to me.

At the top of the single page there was a brief explanatory note which placed the transcript in context. The conversation took place on 8 September 2008, between Anglo's then Director of Treasury, John Bowe, and the bank's Director of Retail Banking, Peter Fitzgerald. The call was recorded twenty-two days before the Government issued the infamous bank guarantee which eventually led to a full bailout of all the banks on a scale never seen before in Ireland.

In January 2009 the then Government took Anglo Irish Bank into public ownership and it subsequently became the Irish Bank Resolution Corporation (IBRC) which was placed in liquidation. In November 2010 Ireland lost effective control of its economic independence when the EU and the International Monetary Fund (IMF) bailed out the country that had beggared itself bailing out the banks.

My source explained that all calls made to and from Bowe's treasury phone line were automatically recorded, as they are in all banks, in keeping with Central Bank regulations. Ironically one of the few regulations observed by Anglo's sneering, arrogant top brass provided us with the unvarnished truth – in their own unguarded words. These internal recordings constituted the Anglo Tapes.

Fitzgerald and Bowe were discussing a meeting that had taken place the previous day between Central Bank officials, John Bowe and his boss, Anglo's CEO David Drumm. At the time the bank was within days of complete meltdown. It revealed how Anglo pursued a dual strategy of deception and scare tactics to lure the State into a financial trap that eventually cost us billions.

Bowe told his colleague how the Central Bank officials were astonished on hearing that Anglo needed a loan of €7 billion.

When Fitzgerald asked him how they arrived at the loan figure Bowe explained the perfidious strategy the bankers were pursuing. The transcript read:

> Bowe: As Drummer would say, picked it out of my arse, you know. . . and that number is seven [€7bn] but the reality is that actually we need more than that. But you know the strategy here is that you pull them in, you get them to write a big cheque and they have to support their money, you know.
>
> Fitzgerald: Yeah, yeah. They've got skin in the game and that is the key.
>
> Bowe: And they have invested a lot. If they saw the enormity of it up front, they might decide that they have a choice. You know what I mean? They might say the cost to the taxpayer is too high.

> But if it doesn't look too big at the outset... if it looks big enough to be important, but not too big that it kind of spoils everything, then, then I think you have a chance... it can creep up.

In the same recording the two men laughed when Bowe revealed that Anglo had no realistic prospect of repaying the taxpayer-funded loan.

History has shown that their strategy to lure the State into paying for the mess worked to perfection.

Needless to say the source didn't have the tape with them. Before I took possession of any tape I had to ensure that all the tracks were covered. We were going to upset a much more powerful entity than a mere crime gang. I knew it was important to establish a secure line of communication with the sources and to leave no traces. Before I left the meeting I suggested that they buy a burner phone with cash so that it could not be traced. Given the sensitivity, I would also get a burner. The phones would only be used for contact between us. I had decided that to protect the sources we would need to leave a few months between receiving the tapes and publishing their contents.

That afternoon I phoned Stephen Rae. We were old friends going back to journalism school in Rathmines. Steve had also been a crime reporter for many years. (See *Crooks*.)

I remember excitedly informing him: 'I may have the story that will define your editorship of the *Indo*.' When I explained what I had read in the transcript he was astonished.

Stephen had cut his journalistic teeth with the *Garda Review* magazine and as a crime correspondent for the *Indo* and *Herald* newspapers. Working the crime beat meant that we both knew how to keep secrets and this one in particular.

We weren't in a hurry to publish. A lot of work would have to be done before such an explosive story made it into print. We would be accusing bank executives of committing fraud, lies and deceit in the biggest scandal in Irish corporate history. Apart from the protection of sources we had to establish that the tapes weren't a hoax and be sure that the people who were speaking were truly directors of Anglo Irish bank. There were also serious legal issues to be resolved to avoid libelling the innocent.

The criminal investigation into Anglo was ongoing and its former chairman, Seanie Fitzpatrick, was facing prosecution. We would have to tread very carefully not to wander into contempt of court territory. Any references to Fitzpatrick would have to be expunged from the final published version to avoid that.

When the burner phones were connected I told the source to arrange to drop the first tape into reception at the *Irish Independent*. I deliberately organized for it to be dropped in mid-April when I was away for a few days in France with friends. It was in a sealed envelope with my name on it.

I got a call from the *Irish Independent's* news editor at the time, Cormac Burke, telling me that an envelope marked important had been dropped in. Cormac was the first broadsheet news editor I had worked with. He was conscientious, erudite and calm under pressure which was a must for the point person on a daily news desk. He is the current Editor-in-Chief of Mediahuis Irl., the company that now owns the former Independent group. I asked Cormac to keep the envelope safe for me until I got back but didn't reveal that I knew what it was.

I was preparing the ground. I knew the envelope was safe and decided not to pick up the tape for a few days following my return from France. As an extra precaution I wanted to allow time for the company CCTV system in the office lobby to be recorded over.

The prime motivation was to protect the sources. When the shit hit the fan and the cops came asking questions then the truth would be that the first tape was handed in anonymously for my attention. There would be no record of who had dropped it. When I drove in to collect the tape I phoned the assistant news editor at the time, Gareth Morgan, and asked if he could drop the envelope to me outside the building.

I parked my car at the rear of the *Indo* and Gareth came down. It was the first time I met the amicable Welsh gentleman and consummate professional in person. I don't think he ever raised his voice in his life – apart from cheering on the Welsh rugby team. He is the *Irish Independent*'s chief news editor whom I have worked closely with ever since. I didn't tell him at the time that he was also part of my plan, so that he wouldn't be have to be disingenuous. I opened the envelope in front of Gareth. It contained a single disk and nothing else.

I asked him to keep a mental note of me opening it. I didn't say what it was. In the event that the authorities came after us there would be a chain of evidence to corroborate that it came from an anonymous source. Cormac and Gareth would be amongst the first to know the truth when the time was right.

When I got home I played it. It was astonishing to actually hear the two voices laughing and joking about the biggest bank heist in Irish history. The two executives, Bowe and Fitzgerald, were discussing the prospect of the bank being nationalized. Bowe said that the other Irish banks didn't have the money to buy Anglo – and the best-case scenario was to be taken over by the State.

His prediction was correct. After the bank was taken over by the State and renamed IBRC Bowe was appointed Director of Corporate Development. He continued to work with IBRC until March 2012, a year before his taped conversations found their way to me.

> Bowe: I don't think we're an easy sell to anybody and the home interest should be there except that they don't have the financial standing themselves.
>
> So, do I think it's going to be possible to offload it [Anglo]? No, I don't. What will it end up being? It could be breaking it up and selling it in individual books, it could be nationalization, you know. That would be fantastic; if it was nationalization we'd keep our jobs.
>
> Fitzgerald: It would be fantastic, wouldn't it?
>
> Bowe: Yeah... civil servants. Yeah it is, it is... but once you do that then it's a very slow process, you know what I mean? It's five years now, it will be five years then.

Bowe also revealed how the bank's CEO David Drumm was planning a series of meetings with government ministers. Fitzgerald worried that the media might get to hear of the meetings. 'That will get out,' he cautioned.

> Fitzgerald: Well, it's in the hands of the gods now isn't it?
>
> Bowe: I'm going to say to people look, we have got to keep going here; don't worry about things... the bank has liquidity, and we are using our liquidity now and, you know, we are in contact with the regulators at the highest levels so don't worry about it, you know.

After small talk and some more jocularity Bowe ended the call. Unfortunately for the Director of Treasury, because the calls to his phone were recorded, his voice would appear in every single Anglo tape.

The tape ended with a piece of supreme irony when Bowe phoned his wife. In the short call she complained bitterly about the ongoing debate about the impending bank crisis on Joe Duffy's *Liveline* radio show. She thought it was very irresponsible to be talking down the country's financial system. Her husband sighed and agreed.

A few days later I went to a meeting in Stephen's office where we listened to the inaugural tape with his two deputy editors, Ian Mallon and Fionnula O'Leary. I remember how they were left flabbergasted by what they heard. They instantly agreed that this story was out of the ballpark. They began formulating a plan of how best to project the story.

By the beginning of June Stephen Rae had called a meeting of his top executive team; his two deputy editors, political editor Fionnan Sheehan and news editor Cormac Burke. I again played the tape. I recall the look of amazement on the faces of those hearing it for the first time. Never one to mince his words, Sheehan addressed the elephant in the room and voiced his concern that the tape was almost too good to be true. It could be a hoax.

That sparked a brief row when I argued that of course the tape was the 'real fucking deal'. The point Sheehan was making was perfectly reasonable. Like most journalists with a big story I was emotionally involved and took it personally. I knew that I was out of my depth when it came to the world of banking and the politics that went with it. This story was too big for one person, and it would require a designated team to contextualize the financial and political ramifications of what we had. Apart from that every word had to be transcribed meticulously before being legally reviewed. And I had a difficulty. Despite the fact that the voices were sharp and candid, I didn't understand some of the terminology they were using. Banking was foreign, uncharted territory for a crime hack. I also needed to be fully briefed on what was happening in the banking world at the time.

A few days later I met Donal O'Donovan, the *Indo*'s respected business correspondent at the time. Stephen Rae suggested I touch base with Donal because he had an encyclopaedic knowledge of the markets, banks and the economy. A former reporter and editor at Reuters, Donal joined the *Indo* group in 2010 as the full effects of the global and domestic financial crisis was taking hold. Donal has been the Group Business Editor of the *Irish Independent* since 2016.

We arranged to meet in a pub in Sandymount, south Dublin, where I played the tape on my laptop. I told him I thought that I was missing something. Donal looked astonished as he listened on headphones over a pint. He recognized the voices and confirmed this was actually senior Anglo executives talking about how they were lying about the events that led up to the crash. What's more, it was being said in a digestible form that the ordinary punter would understand.

I recall to my eternal embarrassment that I got very excited that his analysis confirmed everything Bowe and Fitzgerald were laughing about. So excited in fact that as we left the pub, heavy in conversation, I almost walked out without the laptop and the hugely important tape. From that point on Donal was intricately involved in the Anglo Tapes investigation.

The indefatigable Fionnan Sheehan was the leader and third member of the crew. Fionnan later became editor of the *Irish Independent* and is now the newspaper's Ireland editor and top political commentator. Stephen Rae told Fionnan to drop everything and co-ordinate the coverage. It was a perfect choice. His organizational and analytical abilities greatly impressed me over the weeks ahead. I learned a lot from the big fiery Tipperary man. In the media he is head and shoulders over his peers when it comes to cutting through the bullshit of Irish politics and life in general.

My ongoing role was to continue gathering the tapes, transcribe some of them and write up the main stories from each one. Donal was to analyse what was being discussed on the tapes in the context of what was happening in the discombobulated banking world at the time and explain the details for the readers.

This was all completely new territory for me as the only team I had worked with in the past was with the photographers covering much more straightforward crime stories. I had spent my entire career in tabloids. The dichotomy between broadsheets and tabloids can be best summed up as the following: broadsheet reporters tend to tap gently on a door, while in tabloids we kicked it in. I was extremely honoured to work with such professionals. The three of us became known as the 'Anglo Team'. The first thing Sheehan did was to go out and buy top-of-the-range headphones and portable speakers to aid with the transcription as new tapes came into our possession.

Rae set the publication date for Monday, 24 June 2013. Over several weeks, and without alerting anyone that we had the first tape, we established beyond all doubt that it was authentic. In the meantime Ian Mallon and I had a meeting with Kieran Kelly to get his initial legal opinion on what we had. Kieran was still the in-house lawyer for the *Sunday World*, and he also did some work for the *Irish Independent*. From our years working together Kieran had become a master at finding ways of getting edge-of-the-seat stories across the line that other legal teams would run a mile from. We all trusted and respected the advice of the *Consigliore*.

I would have to seek comment from the two stars of the Anglo tapes but left that task as close as possible to publication date to avoid anyone lawyering up and seeking an injunction to stop the presses.

On the Friday before 24 June, I approached John Bowe and Peter Fitzgerald. During the previous week Padraig O'Reilly had been recruited to get photographs of the two men in the street, just like we had done in criminal exposés so many times in the past. I made numerous efforts to speak to Fitzgerald including calling to his home but was unsuccessful. On the Friday morning I caught up with John Bowe outside his home in Glasnevin, south Dublin. He looked stunned when I approached him and told him why I was there.

Bowe brought me into the back garden and we sat in the sunshine at a table to discuss the matter. I think he was in a state of shock. At the time he was under investigation by the Garda Fraud Bureau which was looking into the Anglo Tapes. He said that he could not remember all the details of his meetings with the Central Bank officials because it was five years before. He confirmed that it was 'likely' that his boss, David Drumm, was with him at the soon to be famous meeting where they took the €7 billion loan figure out of his arse. By this time Drumm had left Ireland and was living in the US. I helped refresh his memory by reading some of his comments from the transcript I'd brought with me.

As I read Bowe's face grimaced with mortification. I left him no doubt that I did have the tapes. He described the conversation with Fitzgerald as 'off-the-cuff comments' and 'probably gallows humour'. But he refused to explain what he meant in his telephone comments about the strategy to mislead the Central Bank. He told me:

> If we had worked out that we needed €15 billion and asked for €7 billion to pull them in, then that would be misleading. We had no idea how much money we needed because we were in a funding crisis; funding had dried up – it was like going into a bank branch and seeing the blinds coming down at all the teller's positions. We were going to the bank of last resort, and I didn't know if the €7 billion would be enough... I should have told them I didn't know.

In the meantime a team of subeditors and designers were called in on a Saturday, when the *Irish Independent* is closed, to secretly lay out the pages. Lawyers had pored over the copy and the transcripts to ensure that they were legally safe.

I went into the *Indo* office on the Sunday afternoon as we prepared to go to print. It was extremely exciting. We were about to set the world on fire.

Arrangements had been made by deputy editor Ian Mallon that evening to provide edited excerpts of the tapes and the first story to RTÉ for the *Morning Ireland* programme that Monday. There was no point in having such a huge story and not sharing it with the biggest radio programme in the country. The first news the listening public would hear about that morning was the 'Anglo Tapes'.

That Sunday evening John Bowe's lawyers sent us a formal statement, stating:

> For the record, I categorically deny the allegation that I was, whether directly or indirectly, a participant in misleading the Central Bank in September 2008. I utterly refute the unfounded inference and allegation that I was a participant in any wrongdoing.

Around the same time we received a statement from Peter Fitzgerald's solicitors:

> I was not a member of the executive management board of Anglo Irish Bank in 2008 and therefore was not involved in the discussions that were conducted by senior executive management of Anglo Irish Bank with the authorities in 2008 in relation to the funding position of Anglo Irish Bank.
>
> I am not nor have I ever been aware of a strategy or intention on the part of Anglo Irish Bank to mislead the authorities in relation to the forecasted funding position of Anglo Irish Bank.

I was relieved that they hadn't told their legal teams to injunct us at the eleventh hour. We added the responses in full into the existing story.

However, our main concern at that stage was that the story might be a one-hit wonder because we didn't have any other tapes yet in our possession. What we did have was merely an appetizer and it was obvious that there was a lot more to hear. I had maintained contact with the sources of the tapes throughout the months and weeks since we first met. I told them everything that was contained in the story due to hit the shelves the following morning. They were extremely happy. More importantly the sources said that they would provide me with more tapes the following day. They promised that they would be much more explosive than the first.

By then we had a secure arrangement set up for the hand over and the sources would not be compromised.

That evening I went with Stephen Rae and Ian Mallon to a pub in Rathfarnham for a few well-deserved pints – and to prepare for the firestorm we were about to start. I was due to appear on *Morning Ireland* and the other morning radio chat shows that Mallon had tipped off. But there was concern that the Anglo Tapes story might not be the only big story over the next 24 hours.

The former South African President, Nelson Mandela, was seriously ill at the time and there were fears that he might die over night. Stephen rang the Irish editor of one of the South African newspapers then owned by the INM group to get an update. We were happy to hear that Mandela was responding to treatment. The most revered political leader in the world didn't pass away until December of that year.

We had a clear run. The headline on the front page the next morning declared: 'Inside Anglo: the Secret Recordings'. The strap head was: 'Exclusive: Tapes reveal the lies and deception that led to the bank bailout'. The story, accompanying transcript graphics and comment pieces ran over ten pages.

The digital revolution, the migration from print to online, had begun in earnest at the time. Deputy editor Fionnuala O'Leary had correctly reckoned the tapes would provide a perfect opportunity to fully utilize that platform. By putting the legally edited recordings online the public could hear the bankers in their own words and finally understand how and why the Irish economy had collapsed. It was the first time that an Irish newspaper had an opportunity to do that.

From first thing the next morning, and subsequent weeks, the Anglo Tapes dominated the media and public discourse. The reaction was extraordinary and unprecedented. The fact that the public had direct access to the recordings on the Independent.ie website made the story more tangible for a nation that was still paying the price for the reckless behaviour of the bankers. The furore convulsed political debate.

From 7 a.m. up to noon that Monday morning I gave interviews to national and local radio stations. Then I slipped away and picked up the second batch of tapes.

Later that day Stephen Rae was appointed as the Group's first ever Editor in Chief which was obviously intended to coincide with the scoop of the century. In the meantime it was decided to move the Anglo Team to a hotel suite in the Dublin Docklands. The story was so explosive we all agreed it was prudent that we set up a new base at a secret location. I remember arriving with Fionnan Sheehan in the hotel lobby, however, to find an electronic sign announcing: 'Irish Independent – meeting room, first floor' flashing across it. 'Fuck sake, so much for secrecy, James Bond it isn't,' Sheehan remarked. The sign was quickly switched off after that.

We worked at a frenetic pace in our 'hideout'. Fionnan and I transcribed the tapes as soon as we got them. Donal listened in and began mapping out his analysis of the latest tape. When that was done the transcripts were sent to the editor and the lawyers as we worked out the best news angle. I wrote the main story from each tape, checking Donal's overview to ensure I had captured the context correctly. Copy was filed, graphics designed and headlines written. Columnists wrote analysis pieces and commentary. An average of ten pages was devoted to the coverage each day. It was the busiest, most exhilarating time in my career.

The new tapes were also edited for use online and so that clips could be shared with radio and TV outlets. By that Monday afternoon several international media organizations were pounding on the door. The story had gone global.

Over the following days I did dozens of interviews for domestic and foreign TV channels. The revelations on the second tape proved to be even more incendiary than the first. It was the first time that we heard David Drumm's voice. By the time we were finished everyone recognized his sneering and cynical tones.

The second recording was made on 2 October 2008, two days after the Fianna Fáil led Government was effectively hoodwinked into rushing the bank guarantee through the Dáil on 30 September. The blanket guarantee covered all deposits and borrowings, including bond holders, at the six Irish-owned banks for a period of two years. At the time the Irish Financial Regulator and European leaders had expressed concern that the guarantee would be abused.

German Chancellor Angela Merkel and Alistair Darling, the British Chancellor of the Exchequer, expressed their anger to the Irish Government that the guarantee was encouraging Eurozone banks to move huge deposits into Irish banks – leaving their own banks vulnerable to collapse.

But Drumm and Bowe were in celebratory mood, laughing off the concerns that the movement of money was causing a rift between Ireland and its EU partners. The reputation of their country was the last thing on their minds.

In the recording David Drumm could be heard joking to Bowe: 'Ah, you're abusing that guarantee. Paying too much in Germany I heard now as well. Fucking ridiculous, John.'

Drumm then cackled with laughter as John Bowe sang a verse of '*Deutschland, Deutschland, Uber Alles*' the former German national anthem, often associated with the Nazis. They sneered and mocked the senior Central Bank regulatory official they were dealing with.

> Drumm: I had [regulatory official] on this morning. I should be recording these calls for the fucking craic – or at least making notes. [Mimicking official] 'It's fucking awful what's going on out there. I mean the fucking Germans are on to us now, David, you know.'

Bowe continued mimicking the official who they clearly had no respect for:

> Bowe: He's saying: 'Look, eh, have you seen any, eh, kind of strange money, market money coming through on the term?' And I said: 'I'm not sure what you mean.' He says: 'Ya know, two year money.' [laughs] He says: 'Ya know, ya have to be careful here... that people are setting us up.' And I said: 'Is it a bit of, eh, beware of strangers bearing gifts?' 'Exactly, exactly.'
>
> Drumm: Setting us up by giving us money? I don't mind being set up that way.
>
> Bowe: What he's suggesting is that UK banks are setting us up by pointing money in our direction and then saying: 'There ya go. That's something that was ours that they've got.'
>
> Drumm: So fuckin' what. Just take it anyway... stick the fingers up. I had a pop at him [the regulator] this morning about Northern Rock [UK bank that had also collapsed]. I said, 'Look, they went around with the fucking Union Jack wrapped tightly around them like a jumpsuit and grabbed all the deposits and where was our fucking Minister for Finance then? [Mimicking regulator] 'I know, I know – I'm

> getting it from all sides here, David.' So, I'm playing a little bit of a game of 'Oh Jesus [regulatory official], look we don't want you to be under pressure, we're going to do the best we can... We won't do anything blatant, but we have to get the money in.'
>
> Bowe: So I'm saying to the guys [senior staff] 'Look, just be smart... don't be stupid, get it [cash] in, don't be overtly pumping it so that somebody can quote you... but we want to get the liquidity ratios up.'
>
> Drumm: Correct and right. So ok, so just keep nursing along... jack the [interest] rates up. That's what I really meant... get the fuckin' money in, get it in.

As each tape was dropped they exposed even more unconscionable arrogance and excessive amounts of testosterone and machismo. It was telling that there were no women involved in any of the tapes. A constant theme was the contempt the bankers had for the financial regulator, the Central Bank, the Department of Finance, the finance minister, the rest of the EU and, of course, the people of Ireland.

In another recording Drumm dismissed the financial regulator as 'fucking Freddie fucking Fly'.

The Anglo Tapes effectively became the black box recorder of what was really happening in the cockpit of the rogue bank as it plunged to destruction, costing €30 billion in the crash. They also revealed how the management of Anglo Irish Bank had been cooking the books to make them look profitable as they teetered on the edge of collapse for over a year before the crash.

The publication of the Anglo transcripts succeeded in punching a hole through the veil of obfuscation and defensiveness that had built up around the bailouts. The voices on the tapes blew apart the narratives being used by the bankers which had been carefully written by PR and crisis management professionals. The public had been told at the start of the crash that there was no alternative. Now, through the unfiltered conversations inside the country's most toxic bank, they were learning how its executives had taken them for a ride.

One of the consequences of the exposé was that it was embarrassing for Ireland's international reputation, especially because the bankers had led the Government around by the nose. Our publication coincided with a visit by the then leader, Taoiseach Enda Kenny, to Brussels for a summit on banking supervision. This was seen as essential if Ireland was to convince other countries to continue to help share the cost of bailing out our busted banks.

Kenny's Fine Gael party was not in Government at the time of the bank crash yet his administration was resisting calls for a public inquiry around the bank guarantee and the bailouts. They had been elected on the back of the economic crash and the fact that Fianna Fáil had been almost wiped out as a result of their handling of the crisis. The Anglo Tapes eventually forced Fine Gael's hand, and they had to set up an inquiry.

In a statement at the time Kenny said: 'These tapes are a thunderbolt. They show the contempt and the arrogance and the insolence of senior personnel working in that bank towards everybody.'

The story made news headlines worldwide: in the first few days alone the Anglo Tapes story featured in 1600 articles over 450 publications in 48 countries. German Chancellor Angela Merkel was among the millions enraged and quickly spotted the impact the tapes would have on public willingness to keep carrying the banking burden — saying the conversations were 'damaging democracy, the social market and everything we strive for'. She said: 'I have nothing but contempt for this. The tone seems to be similar across all the banks.'

One German newspaper headline suggested that Irish bankers be put in a sack and beaten with sticks! For us the phenomenal domestic and international reaction was just noise in the background as new material had to be verified, transcribed, analysed, made into a video and graphics, checked by lawyers at every stage, and finally published.

But as the first week of the Anglo Tapes investigation roared on the main concern for the Government, and indeed Sinn Féin, the opposition party, was to find out who leaked the tapes to us. Finance minister Michael Noonan issued a thinly veiled warning towards the *Irish Independent* and urged other banks to lock down any similar evidence lest it reach the tender ears of the public. He warned:

> The gardaí are the people who investigate these things and other people shouldn't be mucking around in garda business because there is the risk of contaminating evidence and that is not admissible in court.

But by then, five years had elapsed since the banks collapsed, during which no banker had faced trial, so his words rang hollow. We were well justified in 'mucking around'.

We were warned that we could be arrested and the tapes seized. There was talk that the DPP was considering an injunction to prevent any further publication of the tapes. For the first time in my career I found myself on the wrong side of the law. It was being reported that the special liquidator at IBRC asked the gardaí to investigate how the *Irish Independent* obtained the tapes and the publication of their contents. They wanted the truth silenced, claiming that it was interfering in a major investigation.

I was warned by a source that I faced the prospect of having my home searched and of being arrested by the gardaí who in the past had protected me and my family from harm. There was nervousness that the police might also raid the offices of the *Irish Independent* in pursuit of the tapes and other material we possessed.

Anger that the unpalatable truth had been exposed meant that my colleagues and I were being treated as criminals with the prospect that we could be charged with criminal contempt of court. I originated the earth-shattering stories which made me the primary target of an angry State. I was warned that my phones could be bugged to discover my sources and then target them for arrest. However, I suspected that that would not happen as the Minister for Justice, Alan Shatter, would have to sign an order permitting such an operation. Shatter was not the kind of person who would interfere with press freedom. Also, bugging journalists' phones had brought down Charlie Haughey back in the early 1990s and no one in the Government would want to revisit that scandal. In any event I was too long in the game to say anything incriminating or revelatory on my own phone.

On the second day of the story, I got a call from a senior officer I knew who was attached to the Fraud Squad who had been investigating the Anglo scandal for a number of years. I suspected that he was taping the conversation when he pointedly asked me if the tapes had come from police sources. Being a crime reporter, this was the inevitable suspicion. It was probably the reason I was given the tapes in the first place – to divert attention from the financial world and the real sources. It was a febrile time.

But in the *Indo* we knew we had right on our side – not to mention the Irish public who were apoplectic with rage. If they wanted to arrest me or my editor Stephen Rae then fuck them: what we were publishing was very much in the public interest. It exemplified the term: print and be damned. In any event I had ensured that the trail to the sources had been eviscerated.

By that Thursday evening, pressure was mounting. I discovered that a member of the *Indo* staff who claimed to be in the know was the one who had been warning Stephen Rae that the DPP was about to move against us. The same person had claimed that the DPP had been on the phone to them warning that action would be taken. We subsequently learned that this was false and the person concerned was simply jealous that they weren't involved in the story. If the DPP wants to communicate with a newspaper it is always done through legal channels.

Elsewhere some journalists focused more on how we'd got the tapes than on dealing with the material on them. I remember, two days into the Anglo Tapes coverage, Fionnan had a blazing row with Vincent Browne on his nightly TV show when the scowling contrarian went on the offensive demanding to know how long we had the tapes and where they came from. Fionnan put Browne in his place and the spat went viral on YouTube. Journalism can be a very jealous, nasty and begrudging business, especially on the part of those who miss out on a scoop.

On the Thursday evening Ian Mallon came to the hotel and told us to pull the plug for a day to calm the waters.

We hurriedly took away our laptops and the tapes to a safe location where they could not be found. But after 24 hours we went at it again. We were still running Anglo exposés weeks later. The public could not get enough of them. In the end political pragmatism dictated that the State had to leave us alone. Our 'mucking about' in June 2013 was all about public service journalism in a democracy where there is a free press. That year I was honoured to receive the Scoop of the Year award at the National Newspapers of Ireland media awards. The *Irish Independent* team also won the digital media award. I also received the award for Breaking Business Story of the Year from the Smurfit Business School.

The Anglo Tapes investigation resulted in the Government being forced to set up an Oireachtas inquiry. However, when it closed two-and-a-half years later it turned out to be everything that the tapes were not. Despite all the political rhetoric the lengthy public hearings largely ran into the sand, lost amid an overly broad remit and a technocratic approach. Even if it had kept a tighter focus, the inquiry was hamstrung by the rules which prevent a political inquiry making findings against anyone who does not hold public office. It was further boxed in by the need to skirt potential criminal trials — a factor made worse because those trials had by then been subject to ludicrously long delays.

Inevitably, many of the lawyered-up bankers, developers and public officials who did appear were too defensive or taciturn to shed much light. In the end the inquiry found, more or less, that terrible things had happened and it should not be allowed to happen again. Many factors were to blame. It really was a waste of time and money.

In the end the *Irish Independent* threw more light on the scandal than any of the State's agencies, apart from the gardaí. We were all very proud of that.

In the intervening years some of the characters with leading roles in the Anglo Tapes, including John Bowe and David Drumm, were amongst nine former executives charged with fraud offences connected to the scandal. At the time of the Anglo Tapes publications the former chairman, Seanie Fitzpatrick, was already facing charges. Fitzpatrick and Peter Fitzgerald were separately tried and acquitted by a jury. Two others were convicted but the convictions were later overturned on appeal.

In 2016 John Bowe, Denis Casey and Willie McAteer went on trial for conspiracy to defraud. The case concerned a €7.2 billion loan to Irish Life and Permanent which placed the same sum back with Anglo to falsely inflate Anglo's balance sheet. The three bankers were convicted and sentenced to terms of between two and three-and-a-half years in prison.

Bowe received two years after the trial judge ruled that he was a 'lesser functionary' in the fraud and wasn't a board member. All these years later I have to admit to feeling sympathy for John Bowe in the publicity maelstrom we created around him. As I listened to hours of his conversations I felt that he was always trying to humour and placate his bosses, especially Drumm, who displayed the highest concentration of destructive testosterone of the whole cabal.

In 2016 David Drumm was extradited from the US to face trial in Ireland. He was subsequently convicted on two counts of deceiving depositors and investors into believing that Anglo was healthier than it actually was at the height of the crisis almost a decade earlier. In sentencing him to six years the trial judge concluded:

> This Court is not sentencing Mr Drumm for causing the financial crisis. Nor is this court sentencing Mr Drumm for the recession which occurred. This offending did not cause Anglo Irish Bank to collapse.

It was the longest jail term handed down to any of the dodgy bankers. He was released in 2021 and lives quietly in Skerries.

In June 2023 the *Irish Independent* marked the tenth anniversary of the Anglo Tapes investigation. Together with Donal and Fionnan we made a podcast for Independent.ie and also wrote a piece for the paper. I tried to make contact with Drumm but was unsuccessful. I called to see John Bowe at his home. I wondered if he would like to give us his side of the story now.

The last time we'd met was almost ten years to the day – just before we began publishing the Anglo Tapes. When he answered the door a decade later I smiled and said: 'Hello John, remember me?'

His eyes gradually opened wide when he realised who the unwelcome visitor was. Then he slowly retreated from the door with his head shaking from side to side and closed it gently.

John Bowe was saying nothing. But it was easy to work out what he was thinking.

CHAPTER TEN

AN ARMY RESERVIST, TRAINING A TERRORIST AND JOINING THE RANGERS

In September 1996 British police foiled a devastating bombing campaign in London when they swooped on a Provisional IRA active service unit. During the operation Scotland Yard's specialist firearms unit, SO19, shot dead IRA member Diarmuid O'Neill. The killing caused controversy when it emerged that O'Neill was unarmed. Three other members of the terror cell were arrested in what was one of the last major security operations against the Republican terror group before the peace process finally kicked in.

Working on intelligence from An Garda Síochána the UK security services seized over six tonnes of homemade explosives along with two pounds of Semtex, three AK47 rifles, two handguns, ammunition, bomb timers, detonators and two trucks that were intended to deliver the huge bombs.

Police said that the terrorists were plotting to launch at least three further massive bomb attacks similar to ones that had already devastated London's Canary Wharf and Manchester city centre in February and June of that year, killing two people and injuring over 250. The Manchester bomb was the single biggest explosion in Britain since World War II. The attacks had marked the end of the first IRA ceasefire when the leadership decided to vent their frustration with the embryonic peace process the way they knew best: killing and maiming innocent people.

The arrests in London that September spelled the end of the terror campaign. In July 1997 the Provos declared its second and lasting ceasefire which marked the official end of the Troubles.

The capture of the London terror cell was a massive blow to the IRA and made international news. I didn't pay much attention to the dramatic events in London because I was completely immersed covering events in Ireland. In June 1996 a Provo gang had murdered Detective Garda Jerry McCabe and critically injured his partner, Ben O'Sullivan, when the terrorists opened fire without warning during a post office robbery in Adare, Co. Limerick. That horrific crime shocked the Irish nation and set back Sinn Féin's electoral ambitions for years. When, nineteen days later, John Gilligan had Veronica Guerin assassinated it was clear the Irish State was under attack from terrorists and organized crime alike.

At the same time, on a personal level, I was under threat from the notorious killer, PJ Judge, the Psycho. (See *Crooks*.) On top of that I was also on the trail of international drug trafficker Mickey Green. (See Chapters 3 & 4.) It was a very hectic time to be a crime reporter.

However, the London arrests got my full attention a number of weeks later when it emerged that I had a tenuous link to one of the arrested IRA men. It came about because of my role as a part-time soldier with the Irish reserve defence forces, the FCA (Fórsa Cosanta Áitiúil), now called the RDF. I served for over fifteen years as a proud active member of the 'glorious' 17th Infantry

Battalion whose members came from Counties Longford, Leitrim and Roscommon and west Cavan. Those years of continuous active service with the unit were some of the best in my life.

It turned out that as a sergeant I had trained one of the bombers – Patrick Kelly from Ardagh in County Longford – in basic military skills including the use of weapons. During my time as an NCO (non-commissioned officer), I instructed at least 300 recruits as well as training existing privates from two-star to three-star grade. Although I didn't remember him, I had originally served alongside Kelly for eight years during the eighties after we joined the battalion at the same time.

Records later showed the IRA man left the unit in 1989 but then re-enlisted in 1994 which was where I came in. Despite background checks with gardaí, Kelly's involvement with the Provos did not come to light until his arrest in London. It appeared that the father of three had been drawn into militant republicanism somewhere between his early life growing up in Birmingham and returning to live in County Longford with his Irish parents. At the time of his arrest and subsequent trial Kelly was still officially on the books as an active member of the FCA. He was the most high-profile IRA man to infiltrate the reserves. It represented a very embarrassing security lapse for the Defence Forces.

I was reminded of all this in June 2025 when I had the immense honour of being asked to launch a fabulous book *The Glorious 17th Battalion* which chronicles in words and pictures the rich history of my old unit. 'The glorious' prefix was bestowed many years ago by a legendary company sergeant, Johnny Duignan. The book was researched and written by an old friend, local historian Hugh Farrell. He was a former member of the regular army's 4th Cavalry Squadron, an armoured unit which patrolled the Border throughout the Troubles. The Squadron shared its base, Sean Connolly Barracks in Longford, with the 17th Battalion HQ and A Company.

The book launch in Longford provided a rare opportunity for an unforgettable, heartwarming reunion with old friends and comrades, many of whom I hadn't met since I last served thirty years ago. Based on my length of service, which officially ended in December 2000 after twenty years, I was inducted as a member of the Organisation of National Ex-Service personnel. At the launch Hugh Farrell presented me with my ID card which officially describes me as a military veteran.

It was during the preparation for the event that I was reminded of my rather ironic and inadvertent contribution to the Provisional IRA, an organization that I have been an outspoken critic of throughout my career. Over the years I have exposed many IRA scandals, including its involvement in organized crime and its attempts to cover up numerous cases of child sexual abuse by so-called volunteers. Sinn Féin, its political wing, despises me as much as the gangsters do.

When it was discovered that Kelly had been a member of the FCA – a fact that was not publicly known at the time – Irish military intelligence launched an internal investigation. The regular army staff in the 17th was ordered to exhume every detail of Kelly's military service record, which included all the activities and training he had undergone. That was where I came in.

A few weeks later I got a call one day from Corporal Pat Donnelly, a member of the battalion's regular Permanent Defence Force (PDF) cadre that was responsible for the full-time administration and organization of the battalion. I had not been active with the unit for the previous two years and it was always great to hear from an old mate. It was a memorable call.

Pat Donnelly asked me:

> Have you heard the news about one of the Provos arrested in London... his name is Pat Kelly and he is a member of A Company in Longford. Do you remember him?

Initially I couldn't place the guy. I was in E Company and at any one time the battalion had over 500 members.

However, it wasn't that surprising to hear that we'd had a Provo in our midst. The battalion's catchment area included the border areas of south Leitrim, west Cavan and north Longford where there was support for the IRA amongst the population.

It was inevitable that over the years young lads who had trained with the reserves became radicalized and joined the IRA or they were deliberately incentivized by their Provo recruiters to join up. In such cases their allegiances would have been concealed so that they passed the police vetting procedures designed to prevent people with republican connections from getting in. Over the years more than a few former regular soldiers had also been exposed as IRA members.

Pat then told me about the search for Kelly's service record and wanted to refresh my memory. 'Do you know who was in charge of his recruit training and taught him how to shoot?' he asked mischievously.

I said I didn't and gingerly asked, 'Who?'

'You,' came the answer. I said something like, 'Oh fuck, are you serious?'

Pat continued: 'Not only that but do you know who was so impressed with Kelly that he was recommended for the best soldier prize at the end of the training camp?'

I suspected that I knew that answer, but again asked, 'Who?'

'It was you, Sergeant... Kelly was your star pupil,' Pat delivered the revelatory punchline with a long laugh.

At the book launch in June I shared the memory with the audience – before Pat got a chance to!

According to the battalion records when Kelly re-enlisted in 1994, the regulations stated that he had to undergo recruit training again. He was a member of a recruit platoon of thirty soldiers I was charged with training in that same year. The team of instructors under my command included four corporals. With my memory jogged I remembered Kelly because he had stood out from the other recruits. During his earlier service in the eighties Kelly was recorded as being an exceptional young soldier who regularly attended training camps and always turned out immaculately. He had impressed the officers and NCOs. Given his previous experience it was little wonder that in 1994 he stood out as the best recruit in the platoon.

We trained him in using and maintaining the FN semi-automatic assault rifle and the light machinegun. The FN had been introduced during the years he had been out of the unit. He mastered the weapon in record time. With hindsight he had probably been well trained in the use of IRA weapons. According to the records, I had coached him on the firing range when he fired the FN for the first time.

I remembered that he was also a good shot which the records of unit range practices confirmed. Given all of that it was little wonder that I had recommended Kelly for the best soldier prize. I could see that he was focused on his training and had potential for promotion in the reserves or as a candidate for the regular army. Most of the recruits to the PDF first acquire a taste for military service in the reserves. As it turned out his ambitions were oriented towards a very different type of army.

Kelly was well thought of in the battalion as a top-class soldier and a regular attendee for training days and camps. He was on the annual training camp in 1995, in Mullingar Barracks. A few months before his arrest in 1996 he had been due to take part in that summer's training camp. However, the PDF staff recalled that there was concern when he hadn't turned up. The regular army staff actually drove to his home to ask why. They were told by a family member that Kelly was 'away'. It later emerged that he had travelled to the UK with his Provo cell to unleash mayhem. A BBC *Panorama* documentary revealed video footage of Kelly and his cohorts which had been recorded by the security services who had them under surveillance over several weeks. After Kelly's initial arrest on 24 September the Irish army reviewed their vetting policies. Security around weapons and ammunition in Connolly Barracks was tightened up as well.

During the SO19 op, Kelly had suffered the trauma of witnessing his comrade O'Neill being shot dead beside him. In October 1997 Kelly and two other members of the Provo cell, Brian McHugh and James Murphy, were convicted by a jury after a trial in London's Old Bailey. They were sentenced to terms of between seventeen and twenty-five years for their roles in the bombing plot. Kelly was jailed for twenty years. His army record showed that his termination of service as a member of the FCA took place a month later, on 18 November 1997. He was released a few years later under the terms of the Good Friday Agreement. I'm told he has lived a peaceful, quiet life with his family in Longford ever since.

Training Kelly's recruit platoon also stood out because it was one of the last full-time duties I performed in the 17th. Although I didn't know it at the time 1994 was to be my last camp. A month later, Kelly's IRA comrades murdered Martin Cahill, the General, which prompted me to write his biography. After that my career in journalism swallowed up all my time and I could no longer commit to the unit. I remained on the books until my term of engagement officially ceased on 5 December 2000. I always regretted having to leave the unit. I missed the great camaraderie, the craic and the action. I had the privilege of serving with more than a few regular and part-time soldiers who were regarded as legends amongst our milieu. I remember them as being some of the most honourable and decent people I have ever met.

Like a lot of my comrades, I was underage when I signed up on 3 March 1981 at the tender age of sixteen with E Company HQ in Mohill, 16 kilometres from my home in Ballinamore, County Leitrim. The recruitment age was seventeen. That was not a problem. The regular army staff had a way around it: a copy of my birth cert and a touch of Tipp-ex smoothed the way and I was duly sworn in as a member of Ireland's weekend warriors.

The army reserve, which is now a mere tiny shadow of its former self, was a fantastic organization that played a major role in society which largely went unnoticed by the rest of the population. The training instilled confidence, discipline and pride in its personnel. The first time I ever spoke in front of a group of people was to demonstrate the workings of a weapon or drilling troops on the parade ground.

Throughout the Troubles the part-time soldiers provided a vital low-key support role for the regular army. Their troops were often stretched to the limit especially in the Border region. Reservists performed armed security duties at vital installations and military bases to free up regular troops who were supporting gardaí on patrols and checkpoints to counter the terrorist groups.

Such was the level of threat posed by the IRA and criminal robbery gangs that for almost three decades the Irish army provided armed escorts for the movement of cash between banks around the country. Regular troops also escorted subversive prisoners between prisons and the courts, and the movement of industrial explosives. Large numbers of full-time troops were also deployed to guard two of the country's maximum security prisons that housed republican paramilitaries. At the same time the Defence Forces had up to 900 troops deployed overseas on UN peacekeeping missions, especially in Lebanon.

The 17th Battalion fulfilled its support role by providing a full-time troop to perform barrack security duties in Connolly Barracks. Although I wasn't a member of the Security Troop I did some 24-hour guard duty shifts at weekends when personnel were scarce.

When I joined up the establishment strength of the FCA/RDF was 15,000 men. In 1994 women were admitted for the first time. In the preceding decade it was estimated that 45,000 men had served for varying periods in the FCA. The battalion had between 500 and 700 members on the books and was divided up between five company areas: A Company in Longford Town; B in Granard, Co. Longford; C in Strokestown, Co. Roscommon; D in Ballyconnell, Co. Cavan and E in Mohill, Co. Leitrim.

The distribution of units reflected the organization's geographical reach throughout Ireland. Before the force was inexplicably downgraded and then disbanded in the noughties by the Department of Defence, there were reservist companies based in many of the main towns in every county in the country. It was a community-based organization with friends and neighbours serving alongside each other in the same unit. The FCA had the same rank and Corps structure as the regular army, consisting of officers, NCOs and privates, who served in similar units such as the infantry, cavalry or artillery. One of the first things new recruits had to adjust to was addressing as 'Sir' a neighbour they had known all their lives who might happen to be a lieutenant or a captain.

The unique feature of the reserve force was that it attracted people from all walks of 'civvy' (civilian) life including business owners, factory workers, students, farmers, teachers, civil servants and even a few journalists. One characteristic that united the eclectic membership was the willingness to swap the comforts of civvy life for weekend exercises in all weathers that involved sleeping under the stars and existing on pack rations. There was also plenty of square bashing and shooting range practices which taught us to be team players.

One of the many positive features of being a reservist was that when we donned our uniforms for a field day or a camp we left our daily lives at the barrack gates. While on duty you were a soldier and servant of the State, defined only by the rank markings on your arm. I always considered it a wonderful respite from the cutthroat world of national journalism. When I was on a full-time camp there were no editors or sources or deadlines to worry about.

The annual training schedule consisted of weekly parade nights, field days, weekend camps and yearly full-time summer camps of one to two weeks' duration. Personnel had to accumulate a set number of training hours before qualifying to go on summer camps which were the highlight of the calendar year. It was also when we received our annual payment.

The pay consisted of a generous tax-free cash sum that covered the annual camp and included a gratuity to acknowledge the voluntary hours served in the rest of the twelve-month period. The money was particularly welcome during the economically grim 1980s when unemployment and emigration were at all-time highs. Several of my friends used their FCA pay to buy tickets abroad, particularly to the US, in search of work.

Recruits were introduced to all aspects of basic military life. We were trained in foot drill, arms drill and the handling of a variety of infantry weapons including pistols, rifles, machine guns, mortars and anti-tank weapons. We were taught map reading skills to ensure we could navigate our way across a mountain in the dark and not get lost.

We practised throwing live grenades, learned first aid and how to use field radios. There was also plenty of basic tactical training where we were shown how to mount attacks on enemy positions and not get our asses shot off. What we lacked in experience we compensated for with unbridled enthusiasm.

In 1986 I became an instructor following a punishing NCO course and was promoted to the rank of corporal. At the time I was working for the *Longford News* which was very convenient. After moving to the *Sunday World* in 1987 I remained with the unit even though I was living in Dublin, as were many of my comrades. It had been suggested that I transfer to a Dublin unit, but I wanted to stay with the 17th as it was more like a family to me. I served for another seven years after that and never missed an annual camp. In 1990 I was promoted to sergeant.

As a teenager I was never interested in sport, so the military became my primary hobby and passion. I was a decent shot with the rifle and the light machine gun which in recent years led to me needing hearing aids when the damage caught up with me. I was also introduced to the military sport of orienteering by Corporal

Mick Brennan, one of the many inspirational regular army leaders we had in E company and the battalion. It involves the use of maps and compasses to navigate challenging terrain in search of set points in the quickest time possible. Over the years I won a basket full of trophies – the only ones I ever got for sport.

The regular army staff, senior reserve officers and NCOs were brilliant role models who kept more than a few of us on the straight and narrow. Despite the fact that we inadvertently trained a terrorist the organization kept a lot of young lads out of the clutches of the IRA's recruiters. I was still in school for the first three years of my service. When I began to consider a career in journalism my army instructors were amongst the first people who encouraged me to follow my dreams.

I was also privileged to have served under several genuine military heroes in the battalion. When I first joined up the battalion's regular army commanding officer (CO) was Commandant Joe Leach. He was one of the heroic Irish UN soldiers who fought at the Siege of Jadotville during the Congo Crisis of 1961. Corporal Leo Boland, one of the PDF members in my company, and Quartermaster Michael Tighe were also veterans of that seminal episode in the history of the Irish Defence Forces.

The battle began when an Irish company of 150 troops, A Company of the 35th Battalion, were besieged and then attacked by a force of up to 3000 mercenaries and Katangese soldiers. Despite having no combat experience the Irish troops, most of them from the Midlands and the west, demonstrated outstanding bravery as they held out for five days against impossible odds. During the pitched battles they killed an estimated 300 opposing troops and injured a thousand more. The Irish suffered no fatalities with five soldiers injured but none of them seriously.

A relief force of Irish, Swedish and Indian UN troops tried to break through to support them but had been beaten back. During the battle they were strafed from above by a fighter jet. The company commander, the legendary Commandant Pat Quinlan, was finally forced to surrender after running out of ammunition and water. The leadership skills and tactical ability shown by him and his officers, including Joe Leach, were included in the training syllabi at military colleges in Britain and the US.

I don't recall ever hearing much talk about Jadotville over my many years in the battalion. The veteran I knew best was Corporal Leo Boland, a modest, soft-spoken gentleman who was originally from Donegal. Even though I knew Leo well and spent a lot of time with him he rarely if ever mentioned the incident. That was probably due to the fact that instead of being treated as the heroes they were, the Irish military authorities treated them – Leo, Commandant Leach, Michael Tighe and the other brave men – as cowards because they had been left with no choice but surrender. The veterans of Jadotville fought for decades before the Irish Government finally recognized their bravery and courage. It is one of the most shameful episodes in the history of the Defence Forces. Several other members of the PDF in the unit had also seen action in other battles in the Congo.

I first realized the full story of those extraordinary men when another regular army veteran, journalist and international security and defence expert Declan Power, published the definitive account of the battle in his superb bestselling book, *Siege at Jadotville*, in 2005. The story was also immortalized by the hugely successful Netflix film of the same name which was based on Declan's book.

They weren't the only military heroes I had the honour of knowing in the 17th. Corporal Peter Ward, who also hailed from south Leitrim, was attached as a member of the 17th Battalion's PDF cadre when I first befriended him. Peter was a consummate professional, an absolute gentleman and great fun out on the town. He was also a top martial arts expert.

In September 1992 Peter was shot and killed by the Iranian-backed militant Shia group Hezbollah in Lebanon. It has been responsible for the deaths of many Irish soldiers over the years. In 2022 Hezbollah extremists murdered Irish soldier Private Sean Rooney. Peter was the commander of an armoured personnel carrier which was going to the aid of other Irish troops who were being confronted by Hezbollah fighters at a checkpoint when the attack took place. He was twenty-nine years old and left a wife and four young children, who were aged between eight and three.

I remember attending Peter's funeral where he received full military honours. I went there as a friend, a comrade and a reporter. Peter Ward was the first person I knew in my life to die violently. Unfortunately, he would not be the last.

My relationship with the army left me with an abiding interest and deep respect for Ireland's Defence Forces. When I joined the *Sunday World* I had a unique opportunity to write features alongside dramatic pictures featuring the Army, Aer Corps and Navy.

Writing about the military became my journalistic hobby – a respite from the daily slog of crime reporting. I observed military training exercises and border patrols; spent time with the bomb squad; went flying in search and rescue helicopters and on patrols in the Atlantic with the navy. I visited Irish troops serving with the UN in Lebanon on numerous occasions where I witnessed firsthand the extraordinary, unsung humanitarian role they played in the lives of the people they were there to protect. I even gave the 17th Battalion a national profile when I wrote about one of our annual exercises which provided a great morale boost for the unit and attracted more recruits.

Needless to say the Defence Forces press office was delighted that it had a serving reservist who understood the military life and culture working in the biggest selling newspaper in the country. I had the distinction of being the only serving 'sandbag', the army's nickname for reservists, working in the national media at the time.

One of the stories on my wish list from the very beginning was to spend time with the Defence Force's elite special forces commando unit, the Army Ranger Wing (ARW). At the time the secretive Rangers were notoriously publicity shy. Eventually in 1999, after several years of persistence, and with the assistance of the then press officer, Captain Eoghan O'Neachtain, I finally got to fulfil my dream.

O'Neachtain, a charismatic giant of a man from the wilds of Connemara, was a superb communicator who understood the value of creating public awareness about our military forces. Despite the fact that he was a mid-ranking officer within the hierarchical military structure, he had the ears of the Chief of Staff and even the Defence Minister who came to rely on his judgment and advice. The former artillery officer's reputation followed him when he retired from the Army and he was later appointed as the Government Press Secretary reporting directly to the Taoiseach of the day, Bertie Ahern. O'Neachtain has the distinction of being the only press secretary ever to serve three Taoisigh during his time with Government. When he finally convinced the Rangers to allow me a glimpse behind the veil of secrecy I had no idea what I was letting myself in for. I had initially thought that they would give me exclusive access to observe some of their training exercises.

But O'Neachtain had decided to go much further than that. He arranged to literally throw me into the deep end by arranging for me to join the elite troops on a weeklong exercise in the wild, mountainous expanse of the Glen of Imaal, Co. Wicklow. It was a fascinating yet extremely challenging and exhausting adventure that I will never forget. I can still remember it in vivid detail.

Picture this: Easter Monday night, 1999.

Torrential rain is driven across the bleak mountainside by gale force winds as you strain your eyes to try to see ahead in total darkness. Add to that a backpack weighing around 50 pounds, a steep climb and boggy earth that sucks in your feet above the heel. In between are clumps of heather, rocks, mud banks and bog holes that you only discover when you stumble across them or into them. Several times all these elements conspire together, and you land face down in the mud. You scramble to get up only to flop down a few steps further on.

Each time it gets harder as the rain soaks into the backpack, making it heavier. Your only navigational aid in the midst of this nightmare is the big black silhouetted figure trudging ahead of you. Occasionally the shape disappears as it succumbs to the unsteady craggy surface leaving you feeling alone in this bleak nightmare. As soon as it disappears from the barely visible horizon between mountain and sky, the figure is back up and doggedly marching on to the objective.

For almost six hours between that Monday night and Tuesday morning this was my reality – the worst nightmare of my entire life. All I could think of was my cosy bed back in Dublin. The mountain probably had a name, but I called it HELL: the worst, most brutal, unforgiving, godforsaken place on earth. There was no point in complaining because there was no going back. After all this was what I had dreamt of doing for over a dozen years. I was finally on an exercise with the Army Ranger Wing. This was what the naive comfort-loving civvy and former FCA Sergeant had volunteered for – to experience at firsthand what life was like for our elite soldiers.

I will remember forever the reassuring voice of the Ranger behind me as he pulled me from a hole which had sucked me in up to my waist:

> This kind of thing is a real bastard especially when you're doing it for the first time but just remember it's only pain you are feeling. Don't let it rule your mind, it's all psychological. You can beat it.

Twelve hours earlier I had arrived at the ARW base at Plunkett Barracks in the Curragh military training camp, Co. Kildare, where only the fittest, brightest and bravest soldiers were bestowed with the honour of wearing the unit's coveted dark green beret. Like all Special Forces units their identities are kept secret. The small tightly-knit group of super-soldiers – a description they told me they hated – have earned an international reputation for being amongst the best special forces units in the world. The Rangers have always punched above their weight in international Special Forces competitions, beating the likes of the USA's SEALs and Britain's SAS. They are trained and proficient in every military skill and can operate on land, sea and air.

In September 2023 the Irish public got to see the secret soldiers in action for the first time in the Wing's forty-three-year history. The stunning TV footage showed Rangers risking their lives as they fast roped from a helicopter onto the deck of a huge freighter in treacherous weather in the Atlantic Ocean. The crew of the *MV Matthew* which was carrying 2.25 tonnes of cocaine – the largest single seizure of the drug in Ireland – was trying to evade capture as an Irish Navy warship gave chase, firing warning shots across its bow. The operation typified the skills and bravery handed down by the Rangers I found myself with in the Curragh in 1999.

The commanding officer greeted me with a smile when I arrived through the front gate. 'I hope this goes alright. You are the first civilian we have ever thrown in at the deep end like this. You'll love it,' he said.

I had been in training for almost two months to build up stamina and strength with the help of two instructors from the Eastern Brigade Physical Training School in Cathal Brugha Barracks in Dublin. Eoghan O'Neachtain had given an onerous mission to Captain Damian Siggins and Sergeant John Mulvaney in the training school whose job it was to ensure regular troops were battle fit.

They realized how hard the task would be when they brought me out for a short jog to assess my level of fitness which was as low as one could get at the time. With typical military eloquence they told me I was 'a bag of fucking ham'. But after the first hurdles Damian and John had me running up and down various places including Bray Head and the Wicklow Way. The plan was to get me just fit enough so that I wouldn't die on the first night of the exercise or make a holy show of myself. Everyone knew, including my colleagues, that I was preparing for the impossible. I was terrified before I even started.

When the Rangers gave the green light O'Neachtain decided that it would be a good idea for me to team up with Gerry Ryan to report my progress each day on his radio show. The legendary radio shock jock loved the military as much as I did. Getting access to the country's elite troops would make for a dramatic scoop and Gerry was always up for a bit of on-air drama which was why he was so successful. The plan was that at the end of the exercise on the fourth day, if I wasn't in hospital, I would fast rope into RTÉ along with three Rangers while Gerry was live on air. The Special Forces troopers would then give Gerry their first radio interview ever. The only problem was going to be getting me to that point.

In Plunkett Barracks the Rangers had formulated an elaborate training mission, which they appropriately codenamed Operation Scribe, for the benefit of the 'bag of ham' reporter. The scenario for the operation was that paramilitaries in a fictitious hostile region – Fantasia – had kidnapped an Irish UN Military Observer and an aid worker. The UN had uncovered evidence that the Fantasians were responsible for widespread atrocities against civilians with cultural and religious ties to their enemies, another fictitious country called Hibernia.

In response the Irish Government had recommended UN sanctions be imposed on the Fantasians. The hostile forces were threatening to shoot the hostages unless the Irish government forced the UN to rescind the sanctions. When they refused the Fantasians executed the military observer. If the Government had not given in to their demands by Thursday then the aid worker was also going to be shot. The ARW were ordered to mount an assault on the Fantasian base and rescue the hostage. A twenty-four strong contingent consisting of four teams was given less than 72 hours to achieve their mission.

Sitting in the briefing room it became immediately clear that while this was a training exercise it was being taken deadly seriously by the troops. Maps of County Wicklow, which for the purpose of the exercise represented Fantasia, were laid out on the walls behind the operations officer briefing the units. The officer assigned me to the six-man sniper team – Sierra team. I still remember feeling my gut tighten when six expressionless faces turned to look me over.

I could tell what they were thinking: 'Whose bright idea was it to give us the fucking civvy? We're not babysitters.' I gulped hard and gave them a nervous smile.

By 11.30 p.m. Operation Scribe was in full swing. The Sierra team had been wary at first but by then had begun to accept the civvy. The treacherous mountain route was the only one by which the team reckoned they could slip into Fantasia without being detected. The team leader, Danny, explained that we would have to hug the contours of the mountain, to avoid being silhouetted against the night sky. None of the unit used night vision goggles and had to rely on their own eyes. Every aspect of the mission was treated as if it were the real deal – the commandos were rehearsing for such an operation in the real world. I was warned that other members of the Wing, who were playing the part of the enemy, would be patrolling the area we were going into. If they spotted us then the mission would be aborted.

I had been given a combat uniform and a backpack which contained the basic requirements for a three-day operation – rations, sleeping bag, dry clothes, water, spare radio batteries and ammunition. I'd struggled to get the hefty bag on my back.

By 4.30 a.m. after what felt like an eternity, we had finally begun a precarious descent on the other side of the mountain. I was holding the team back from getting to their objective before dawn. I was shattered. They decided to crack on without me. I was assigned a buddy called Baldy, a senior sergeant, whose job it was to chaperone me during the ordeal. When the team went ahead he decided that we would kip down in our sleeping bags for the hour or so left before sunrise. I was delighted. As soon as I got into the bag I fell into a coma.

Baldy woke me at first light. I remember being stunned as I poked my head out. As far as the eye could see there were rolling mountains and wilderness. Off in the distance, between the mountain ridges, was the Army's main training grounds and artillery ranges in the Glen of Imaal. We had slept on the edge of the mountain, at a place which turned out to be Cavanagh's Gap. If I had veered too far to one side even by a few feet in the dark I could have fallen hundreds of feet into the valley below.

As I was officially still a member of the reserve Defence Forces I had the distinction of being the only one who had gone on exercise with the elite soldiers: I had gone from one extreme to the other. The ARW lads reminded me that they had a lot of respect for the reserves: many of them got their first taste of military life in the FCA.

I remember being so cold that I thought I was going to die. My combat trousers, socks and boots which I had taken off before bedding down were still sopping wet. The only thing that kept me going was the thermal gear I wore under the combats. I put on dry socks but Baldy told me to put the rest on again over my thermal gear. 'Once you start walking again with the pack your body will heat the moisture in the clothes and you'll be warm as wool,' he assured me. As a comfort-loving civvy it was excruciating putting on the wet gear but he proved to be right.

That morning I did my first live report for Gerry Ryan who lapped it up. I described in graphic detail the experience from the previous night and the scenario for Operation Scribe. To add to the drama I could only say we were at a location somewhere in Ireland. After that Baldy and I moved quietly through the forest to rendezvous with our sniper team. At one stage we almost ran into one of the 'enemy' patrols and crawled through a soggy ditch to avoid them. I was determined that I would not compromise the mission. O'Neachtain and Siggins would never let me live it down.

We eventually met up with the Sierra team deep in the woods. They had located the enemy camp and were monitoring it from dense undergrowth at the edge of a forest about a half mile away. Everything was incredibly realistic. The camp had been built in a field with makeshift tents and wooden framed buildings erected. There were sentry posts, defensive trenches and lines of barbed wire around the perimeter just like there would be in the real thing.

Through binoculars we could see the 'hostage' being taken between the buildings by the enemy who were armed with actual AK47 assault rifles. Two Scorpion tanks patrolled the area. At one stage we had to bury ourselves in the undergrowth when an Aer Corps helicopter and then a spotter plane posing as enemy aircraft swooped overhead searching for unwanted interlopers. I had to keep reminding myself that this was just an exercise.

Sleep was still a scarce luxury: between Monday and Thursday I got about three or four hours kip. After the first 24 hours I started to get used to the cold and the wet. I had no other choice. When darkness fell the Rangers brought me on close target reconnaissance patrols as they worked out the exact layout of the camp and the location of the hostage. Once I had acclimatized to the surroundings one of the most difficult aspects was getting used to finding my way through dense forests in the pitch dark. Like everything else, the Rangers made it look easy.

The attack on the enemy camp took place on Thursday morning of Easter Week. The other teams had gathered up and formulated a plan of attack based on the intelligence gathered by Sierra team. The night before everyone was given Kevlar helmets and body armour because the operation was going to be a live firing exercise meaning that real bullets, grenades and explosives were to be used just as they would be in the real thing. The Rangers announced that I was also going to take part in the actual attack. I was given a loaded Steyr rifle and a 16-pound radio to carry. At least they didn't have to show me how to operate the weapon.

Before daylight the Ranger force crept into position along a river bank out of sight of the camp. It rained incessantly. The 'enemy' had withdrawn for obvious reasons. The 'sentries' were represented by two small metal plate targets. A team crept up to cut a hole in the barbed wire fence for the rest of the force to enter. At the same time the sniper team lined up the plates in their sights. When we heard the ping of the two falling plates the order was given 'Go, go, go!' and all hell broke loose.

The breath rasped in my throat as I tried to keep pace with super fit soldiers as we moved through the mud on our bellies, under the wire fence into the camp. Explosions and gunfire broke the silence of the remote location as they stormed the objective. Ranger teams provided covering fire as others raced with incredible speed to clear bunkers using grenades followed by fusillades of bullets. I was given a target to lay down covering fire.

I was then brought in behind the rescue team to watch as they used explosives and stun grenades to blast their way into the 'building' where the hostage was being held. Inside life-size cutouts representing the bad guys were each dispatched at close range with handguns. The hostage represented by a life-size dummy was grabbed and taken from the building while the battle continued to rage outside.

After about twenty minutes of intense action the order was given to pull back. There were a series of much larger explosions which mimicked the effect of a supporting air strike. The whole exercise was carried out with precision accuracy. Despite the chaos of heavy gunfire everyone knew exactly what they had to do. It looked better than any movie. I came as close as possible to witnessing a real-life battle. It was a fascinating and unforgettable experience. The army later gave me a video recording of the exercise and presented me with a framed cartoon as a memento of Operation Scribe.

When the exercise was officially stood down an Aer Corps helicopter swooped in to pick me up along with the unit commander and two of his senior sergeants, including Baldy. The chopper took us to Baldonnel air base where I was given a crash course in the art of fast roping for the last part of the exercise, which was dropping in on the Gerry Ryan radio show in RTÉ, south Dublin.

Fast roping is a particular skill whereby a soldier grabs a rope with both arms and feet and slides down from the helicopter the same way that the Rangers boarded the *MV Matthew* in 2023. I am normally terrified of heights but the adrenalin coursing through my veins took care of that. The helicopter crew attached a safety wire to me in case I fell off the rope to my death. A civilian wouldn't be allowed to do something like that today.

In Baldonnel we rehearsed the fast-roping drill three times at the end of a runway before the Rangers and the heli crew were satisfied that I wouldn't kill myself. Then we took to the air and headed for RTÉ. At the precise prearranged time the Alouette chopper dropped into a hover over a car park at the rear of the radio centre. As we got ready to fast rope I could see Gerry Ryan and his roving reporter Brenda Donohoe below as they provided live commentary under the clattering noise of the helicopter. I also spotted my nine-year-old son Jake staring up at us. Liam O'Connor had brought him along to see his dad's dramatic return to reality.

As we dropped down one by one Gerry couldn't distinguish me from the elite soldiers: we all wore the same camouflaged helmets, mud-covered fatigues and our faces were blackened. Brenda Donohoe shrieked when one of the intimidating looking figures ran up to her – and I asked for a kiss. Later in studio we talked about the experience and the Rangers told Gerry what life was like for Special Forces troops. It made for scintillating action-packed radio. After the interview I said goodbye to my new friends as they flew back to base in the helicopter.

When Liam dropped Jake and I home my wife wouldn't let me into the house. The Loc said he had to fumigate his car. I was covered in dirt and stank to high heaven. I had to strip to my underwear at the front door and head straight for the shower.

A few months later it turned out that Operation Scribe was part of a strategic plan by O'Neachtain and the Army top brass. The publicity had bolstered their argument to deploy the Rangers to a war zone for the first time. An unfolding humanitarian tragedy on the other side of the world was about to present that opportunity – on part of a tiny island in Southeast Asia called East Timor.

Since 1975 Indonesia had occupied East Timor – now known as the Democratic Republic of Timor-Leste – after Portugal abandoned its former colony. The occupation was characterized by brutality and violence as the Indonesians sought to stamp out the people's desire for independence. Throughout that period it is estimated that as many as 200,000 East Timorese lost their lives out of a population of around a million.

In August 1999 the situation came to a head when the Indonesians, under pressure from the international community, agreed to a UN supervised referendum on independence. When the vast majority of the population voted for independence pro-Indonesian militias embarked on an orgy of brutality, murder and destruction.

The militias burned every building in the capital Dili and every town and village throughout the region. Hundreds were butchered, raped and beaten. Over 140,000 people in Dili alone fled to hide in the mountainous rainforests.

The international community decided to take action. In October 1999 the first squad of Rangers was sent on a four-month tour of duty to patrol the jungles of East Timor as part of a multinational UN force to restore peace to the lives of the inhabitants. In a short time they had forced the militias to flee across the border to West Timor.

In 2000 Eoghan O'Neachtain suggested that I should consider taking a trip to East Timor to go on patrol with the Rangers. The Army and the unit were willing to oblige in organizing the trip. It would provide a fitting sequel to Operation Scribe and I would be able to witness the commandos putting their training into practice.

O'Neachtain was about to retire from the army and wanted to have one last foreign jolly under his belt. Colm MacGinty gave the go-ahead for the exotic assignment and we booked our flights. We were sent to the military hospital in the Curragh for a dozen vaccine jabs to ward against an awesome array of nasty diseases. In May photographer Padraig O'Reilly, O'Neachtain and I headed to East Timor. We found ourselves in an alien world.

The distinctive thrum of the rotor blades of the Huey helicopter vibrated as the gunship flew fast and low over the dense jungle. As we sat with our feet dangling from the side, the gunship tactically hugged the contours of the deep gorges and mountain ridges to avoid hostile gunfire from the rain forest below. It was like being on a roller coaster ride. One moment I was looking into the dark rain clouds above and the next into the vast green canopy below.

Two crew men were perched on either side behind M60 machine guns, scanning the unforgiving terrain as the New Zealand Air Force chopper cut through the hot, humid air. Each time the chopper banked sideways the machine gunner beside me would stand on the skids and aim the weapon downwards ready to return fire if it came. I was living a scene that could have come straight out of a Vietnam war movie. The six member Ranger team seemed oblivious to the noise and the aerobatics as they sat inside: it was part of the daily routine of life in the jungle.

The three of us had arrived the previous day on a flight from Darwin in Northern Australia. When the military Hercules touched down in Dili we were hit by the intense 90 per cent humidity. For the three days that we were in East Timor our jungle fatigues were permanently soaked with sweat. The only respite came when we were drenched in biblical-level downpours as the monsoon season neared its end.

The Huey created a mini gale as it dropped down into an opening in the thick vegetation. Before the skids touched the soggy floor we jumped out with the Rangers who darted for cover in the undergrowth. In seconds the iconic big green aircraft lifted sluggishly into a hover, briefly bowing its nose before disappearing into the distance down along a deep gorge.

The Rangers were there to patrol the area around a village called Atoon in search of militia men who were reportedly seen in the area.

A few dozen local men, women and children suddenly appeared to watch the spectacle. They smiled and welcomed the camouflaged Irish soldiers who were there to protect them. Since the arrival of the UN forces eight months earlier the camouflaged commandos with their machine guns, rocket launchers and rifles had given these incredibly poor people their most cherished desire – peace and security.

By May 2000 a second contingent of thirty ARW soldiers was coming to the end of a four-month tour. From then on similar sized contingents from regular Irish army units took over. We had been flown from their tented camp in the village of Taroman, high up in the jungle-cloaked mountains, a kilometre above sea level on the border with West Timor. Apart from a two week break the soldiers had spent all of that time in the jungle where they lived in tents. Their only creature comforts were the excellent food supplied by two army cooks and a makeshift gym. A pump action shotgun was left standing by the entrance to the tent we were assigned to sleep in. The weapon was there to deal with another jungle enemy – deadly venomous snakes. A Ranger gave us a quick lesson in how to use it. Thankfully we didn't have to. The Rangers were one of three Special Forces units – along with the Australian and New Zealand SAS – deployed to what was known as Sector West along the border. It was the most dangerous flash point in the region. The unit's area of operations consisted of 170 square kilometres of the most inhospitable terrain in the world which made the Glen of Imaal look like a holiday park.

The three units had been involved in several confrontations with the militias as they attempted to mount attacks on the innocent inhabitants of isolated villages. The officer in charge of the patrol, Captain Colm Ó Luasa, who was recently promoted to the rank of Major General and Deputy Chief of Staff of the Defence Forces, told me:

> The threat here is very real. You don't know when you are going to come face-to-face with the militia as you patrol through the jungle. You only have a split second to judge whether the person is armed and a threat. You have to be alert every second. It is the difference between life and death.

A few days earlier an Australian unit had shot and wounded a militia member. In another contact, the New Zealanders shot one dead. The Rangers were clearly under orders not to discuss how many they had killed or captured but I had been assured, off the record, that they had seen 'plenty of action'.

The daily routine involved patrolling the war zone where the climate and terrain could be every bit as dangerous as the armed militia men they were fighting. During heavy monsoons the Rangers were effectively cut off from the outside world when the dirt tracks that passed as roads were washed away in treacherous mudslides and choppers couldn't get through the cloud cover. In the preceding months the primitive roads that snaked precariously around the edge of deep ravines had claimed the lives of a number of New Zealand and Australian soldiers.

The Rangers also conducted long range six-day patrols deep into the jungle along the border. They carried everything they needed to survive: water, rations, ammunition and other equipment in packs weighing 80 pounds. As the patrol commenced Ó Luasa explained:

> We set up special observation posts high up along the border near tracks which are used by the militia and wait for them. On an operation like that there is very little movement, and you have to stay dug in like that for most of the six days, no matter what the weather. It requires patience and stamina but this is what we signed up and trained for. It's hard but we enjoy it.

As we moved through the village it was as if we had stepped into an alien world where the living conditions were primitive beyond belief. The people had no material wealth or comforts of any kind. Their homes were galvanized, rusting sheds and mud huts. Any proper buildings they had were burned by the militias. Most of the island's population was living under tents supplied by the UN. There were no shops, cars, electricity, running water or telephones. There were also no clinics or doctors except for the medical help provided by the UN forces.

The Rangers provided as much medical aid as they could to the local people. In Atoon the troops were warmly welcomed by the locals. An elderly woman smiled and waved to them from the door of her mud hut. She had a tumorous lump the size of a melon under her chin. The woman would not seek medical help which the Rangers offered to arrange for her in an Australian hospital.

In summer the people cleared an area of the jungle to grow crops and rice to sustain them for the rest of the year. Any little surplus they had they brought to sell in a market on foot almost 50 kilometres away. When the first Rangers had arrived the children asked them not for sweets or toys but paper, pencils and chalk for their schools which were also torched in the militia's rampage. The secretive soldiers were happy to oblige. One of the Rangers told me:

> One young lad in one of the villages was lifting wood and broke part of his little flip flop which are his only shoes. It broke the poor kid's heart. His world was shattered by it... imagine that happening to one of the kids back home? After that we ordered in a consignment of flip flops during a resupply to make sure we had them for other such emergencies.

When they first arrived the villages in their area were empty. But as they and the other special forces detachments began to secure the region and drive out the militias the people slowly began to return. In Atoon the population had been restored to almost 250 and was still growing.

One of the Rangers recalled: 'These people have suffered unthinkable horrors and hardships. They had very little to start with but then to have been so savagely attacked is beyond comprehension.' The first problem the Irish forces had was gaining the trust of the returning locals. The Irish commando continued:

> After looking at brutal men in uniforms for over twenty years they were understandably suspicious of us. When our patrols came across women and children out foraging for food they would freeze with fear. They were so used to the Indonesians and the militia men casually attacking them and just taking some of them away and raping them. Then they would stand and bow to us as we walked by on the road because it was beaten into them to do so before. But gradually they began to trust us and understood that they do not have to bow or be subservient.
>
> Now they go out of their way to show their gratitude that we are there to protect them. To see these little kids smiling and

> being happy again is job satisfaction for us. Most of us are family men and have kids of our own. While we are here we will do everything to prevent them ever going through this horror again.

Patrolling the jungle with the Rangers was one of the most fascinating and memorable experiences of my entire life. Journalism has always been a learning curve but what we witnessed in East Timor was in a completely different league. Apart from Lebanon it was the only other place where I came close to seeing the results of the pure savagery of war. It was heartbreaking to see firsthand how much those gentle impoverished people had endured. Man's capacity for inhumanity defies comprehension and understanding. We only have to look at the unbelievable genocide being waged against the people of Gaza by Israel, a supposedly civilized society that knows more than any other the meaning of the word 'holocaust'.

Remembering the experiences in East Timor reminds me that there is more good than evil in the world. It was heartwarming and inspiring to see how a small group of brave young Irish soldiers were happy to endure hardship and danger to restore peace and hope to a downtrodden people.

For over sixty years Ireland's troops have earned a reputation for their humanitarian work on peacekeeping missions. The line goes that not all heroes wear capes. In this case they wore combat fatigues and carried guns. It exemplifies why I have always had an unshakeable pride in our Defence Forces.

EPILOGUE

FULL CIRCLE

Poetic justice. Karma. What goes around comes around. Just deserts.

Those words and phrases swirled around my head as I read with a degree of relish that my once arch criminal nemesis John Gilligan is spending his twilight years in desperate financial straits and crying for help. The once powerful multi-millionaire godfather, who helped usher in the era of the narcos in Ireland, is living in penury. He has been reduced to begging for money from other villains in his orbit at the bottom of the drug-trafficking food chain. How the mighty have fallen.

In August 2025 it was revealed that the brutal psychopath responsible for the execution of Veronica Guerin had been circulating a begging message to a number of WhatsApp groups. The arrogant, diminutive mobster who spent his life bullying, terrorizing and killing people who crossed his path had been in a Spanish jail since December 2024. He was busted by Spanish cops as part of an investigation into the sale of the synthetic drug pink cocaine. Gilligan's arrest revealed how he had been reduced to the rank of a lowly street level drug peddler; the kind of individual he once would have treated with utter disdain.

At the age of seventy-three the grandfather of organized crime didn't even have the money to raise his bail. Reports suggested that without the money to post bail he could remain in prison for a number of years as he awaits the decision of a Spanish magistrate on whether or not to charge him.

Gilligan's difficulty stemmed from the fact that he didn't have the cash to pay his lawyer from the previous occasion in 2020 when he was arrested by the Spanish on a separate drugs charge. The elderly mobster had been involved in a low-level mail-order drug racket. Eventually he got off with a slap on the wrist and a fine.

During the summer of 2025 one of Gilligan's few remaining friends sent around the begging text message on his behalf. It read:

> My name is **** I am a good friend of John Gilligan, he is 73, and in prison in Spain broke. John helped loads in his life and now he needs help money wise, no amount too small. Please share this WhatsApp wth you friend an how John's friends get to see it. To sent to lawyers bank account [Details given]. RE: John Gilligan. Money gram, western union or bank transfers.

However it was then revealed that Gilligan finally scraped together the €10,000 for his bail at the beginning of September after nine months trying. But the text provides gratifying evidence of the ignominious downfall of a narcissistic thug who was once the most feared gangster in Ireland. The fact that the grandfather of organized crime is financially destitute comes as a bitter irony for the little man. It illustrates that there is a chronological symmetry to life. In the same month thirty years earlier Gilligan was building the biggest drug empire yet seen in Ireland.

In September 1995 he savagely beat up Veronica Guerin because she wanted to know about the source of his wealth. The motive he had for ordering her murder was to protect his money. Gilligan's greed forced the Government to finally take on organized crime by going after and seizing the money that is at the heart of all criminal enterprises. The CAB, which is part of his legacy, eventually took possession of his property, after he fought them for decades. Now he has nothing to kill or intimidate anyone over. In gangland terms he is a nobody.

Gilligan's current predicament demonstrates how even in his twilight years he learned nothing from his unsuccessful life of crime. He had no intention of going straight when he was released from prison in 2014, after serving seventeen years for drug trafficking. Instead he reckoned he could resume his position as a major godfather and began putting the squeeze on other drug dealers for 'welcome home' money. But the gangland landscape had changed drastically while he was away. There was a new power dynamic which had the ruthless Kinahan cartel at its head. He realized that fact when they sent assassins to kill him. Gilligan was critically injured in the attempt but managed to survive.

After lying low in the UK for two years hiding out with a clan of criminal travellers he returned to Ireland. In a highly symbolic gesture his return in 2016 coincided with the twentieth anniversary of Veronica Guerin's murder. Gilligan again showed he had learned nothing from life and went straight back to crime.

In a recent interview in 2024 before his arrest in Spain Gilligan went to great lengths to dismiss rumours that he was dying from cancer. He told journalist Jason O'Toole:

> I just couldn't stop laughing when I read that. No, I don't have prostate cancer. On my mother's grave, I don't have cancer. I will

not die of cancer one thousand million per cent because, from my head to toe, there's no cancer in my body.

In many ways cancer would be too good for Gilligan. The prospect of him having to live out his final years as an impoverished and imprisoned gangland has-been is a much more fitting epitaph.

Personally, I wish him a long and unhappy life ahead.

ACKNOWLEDGEMENTS

I thought, when I sat down to write *Crooks* and now *Crooks 2*, that it would be an easy task: all the information is in my head and my extensive files, accumulated over forty years. Dredging up the past to tell the story of my journey in journalism was a lot more difficult than I thought it would be. It has, to paraphrase the old *Godfather* line, been much more personal business than any of my previous books. It has afforded me the opportunity to acknowledge the roles played by some of the finest people in the media business who guided and supported me over the years. Among them are Michael Brophy, Colm MacGinty, John 'Dot' Donlon, Sean Boyne, Liam O'Connor, Gerry Lennon, Derek Cobbe, Stephen Rae, John Burns and so many others that I don't have the space to mention here. You will find them all between the covers of this book. I also want to give a shout-out to some of my other loyal friends who have been a major part of my life: people like Joe Duffy, Dave Monaghan, Damian Boyle, Gary Nielson, Sean O'Brien, Kevin 'Bridie' Dolan, Pat Tobin, Seamus O'Brien and Gay Prior to name but a few. This also gives me an opportunity to remember the legendary lawyer Gerry Fanning who sadly passed away in 2004 – his picture over my desk keeps his memory alive.

I want to thank from the bottom of my heart the real stars of this book, the extraordinary, inspirational people who trusted me to tell their incredible stories of tragedy, adversity and bravery. It was an absolute honour to be given the chance to make their voices heard – it's what this job is all about. Many of them have become friends: people like Steve Collins, Ruth Dunne and John Hennessy. And I want to thank the many members of An Garda Síochána who protected me and my family and also trusted me enough to share the information I needed to expose so many bad people over the years.

My gratitude to my colleagues at Mediahuis Ireland (formerly Independent News and Media) for giving me the space to write this book, and their support – Editor-in-chief Cormac Bourke, Group Head of News and Executive Editor Kevin Doyle and *Irish Independent* news editor Gareth Morgan, who are responsible for making Mediahuis the top media group in Ireland. I want to especially thank the multi-award-winning photographer – and friend – Mark Condren who provided the cover photographs for the *Crooks* series. Mark has won so many accolades for his work that he will need an extension to his home to accommodate them all and I am not exaggerating. And to Robbie 'Red Breast' Farrell, my long-time pal, who put together the picture section and tried to make me look presentable.

As always my deepest thanks to my incredibly talented, and patient, editor Aoife Barrett, of Barrett Editing, who has worked on most of my books – and makes the manuscript both legible and understandable. I would not have been able to write this book were it not for Aoife. After almost twenty-five years working with me, she knows me better than anyone. So much so that I call her my publishing wife!

And of course there is Ireland's top libel lawyer and my dear friend Kieran Kelly – the Consigliore – of Flynn O'Driscoll Lawyers. I hope that *Crooks* and now *Crooks 2* reflect just how important Kieran has been in my professional and private life. Kieran has always had my back and has helped me navigate some of the toughest times in my life.

I would also like to sincerely thank my publishers, Atlantic Books, who have released my last four books, and especially group associate publisher, Clare Drysdale, who has been gifted with the patience of a saint when dealing with me. Thank you, Clare, you are an absolute joy to work with. I also want to say a big thank you to publishing agent Simon Hess of Gill Hess Associates and his staff especially Declan Heeney. I don't think anyone knows as much about Irish publishing as Simon. In fact, he is the first port of call for me when I am considering what to write about next. He is better than any literary agent.

Finally I express my love and gratitude to the most important people in my life: Anne, Jake, Irena and my best pal in the world, Archie. Writing these last two books reminded me that I have to live with the regret that my work often placed Anne and my kids in potential danger over the years. For that I have to say on the record that I am deeply sorry. Our kids have turned out to be the best people that they could become thanks to their mom, who always maintained sanity in the Williams household. Thank God – and the gardai – that we came safely out the other end.

And to you, my loyal readers, who have stayed with me for thirty years and made my books best sellers – thank you.